TWINLESS

A Ride Exceeded Its Destination:

The Story of Rusty and Randy Perrone

By

Russell Perrone

with Jay Hoecker, M.D.

The authors and publisher of this memoir have worked to ensure that the information in this book is accurate to the extent possible from memories of events and conversations that actually occurred. Names have been changed to protect the privacy of individuals. The authors have also worked to respect any copyright responsibilities regarding material in the book.

Copyright © 2017 Russell Perrone

All rights reserved: In accordance with the U.S. Copyright Act of 1976, scanning, uploading, and electronic sharing of any part of this book without the permission of the publisher constitute unlawful piracy and theft of the author's intellectual property. If you would like to use material from the book, please contact the publisher at www.RRPerronePublishing.com

R and R Perrone Publishing Company
1801 L and A Road
Metairie, LA 70001
Web: www.RRPerronePublishing.com

ISBN: 978-0-9988648-0-8	Paperback
ISBN: 978-0-9988648-1-5	Hardback
ISBN: 978-0-9988648-2-2	E-book EPUB
ISBN: 978-0-9988648-3-9	E-book MOBI

Printed in the United States of America

TWINLESS

A Ride Exceeded Its Destination:

The Story of Rusty and Randy Perrone

Dedicated to
My loving twin brother, Randy, who continues to guide me.

Painted by Randy Perrone when he was 18 years old, 2001

PREFACE

This book is dedicated to the memory of my loving identical twin brother, Randy. I always feared life without him, and that is exactly what I came to face. The purpose of this book is to provide a look inside the lives of identical twins and to show how the adventures between twins can mold the future behaviors of each. Life with an identical twin is unique with each reliant on the other.

The eventual separation of twins through death forces the survivor to adjust to life without not just his closest companion, but indeed without a portion of himself. To understand what it is like to be a twin or to lose a twin would be difficult; therefore, this is my attempt to shed light for singletons and other twins to appreciate what joys, sorrows, and grief twins experience in their shared lives. The events in this book are actual events, not exaggerated joys, fears, sorrows, and angers. Characters' names, people with whom we shared our lives who are sometimes called our "partners in crime" have been changed to protect their privacy and honor their feelings. As I share these imperfect memories with you (all memories being imperfect), I wish upon myself this Irish blessing:

"May you never forget what is worth remembering
Nor ever remember what is best forgotten."

Now come with me on a journey that is still in progress, and beware: as is so often the case, the ride will likely exceed the thrill of arriving at any particular destination. There was a consistent steadiness in the bond between Randy and me. Friends would come and go, the bond with them tenuous, but Randy's presence was always with me. The episodes of our story present themselves as expectations altered by encountering surprises, as storms interrupting plans or changing lives, and as uninvited lessons taught to unwilling or unsuspecting students. The pairing of souls is not limited to twins, but also includes writers and their readers.

Before he gave up the office, President John Adams told his son, John Quincy, regarding writing a memoir,

> *"It is a delicate thing to write from memory. To me the undertaking would be too painful. I cannot but reflect upon the scenes I have beheld."*

Indeed, writing this book to share my story with others, as difficult as it was to recall events, words, and actions that were painful for me and for my family, has been worth the effort, or as Mr. (Fred) Rogers put it,

> *"How great it is when we come to know that times of disappointment can be followed by times of fulfillment; that sorrow can be followed by joy; that guilt over falling short of our ideals can be replaced by pride in doing all that we can; and that anger can be channeled into creative achievements...and into dreams that we can make come true!"*

Table of Contents

Chapter 1: Serendipity	9
Chapter 2: Italian Immigrants: The Perrone Family	11
Chapter 3: Twin Shenanigans	15
Chapter 4: Adolescence and Young Adulthood	26
Chapter 5: All Grown Up and No Place to Go	40
Chapter 6: On Our Own	45
Chapter 7: College: Something To Rave About	48
Chapter 8: Tipping and Flipping, Out	52
Chapter 9: Saved by a Storm	56
Chapter 10: Rock Bottom	59
Chapter 11: The Prodigal Sons Face the Music	63
Chapter 12: Mistakes Can Be Teachers, or Not	66
Chapter 13: Spring Break	71
Chapter 14: Time Out: From Primitive Camping to the Ritz	74
Chapter 15: A Funeral in New Orleans	78
Chapter 16: A Memorable Christmas	80
Chapter 17: Hurricane Katrina	85
Chapter 18: Trees Down, College on Hold	101
Chapter 19: Recovering	110
Chapter 20: When the Saints Go Marching In....Back to the Superdome	117
Chapter 21: Post-Katrina Trauma	123
Chapter 22: Discovering Sweden, Germany, and Holland	127
Chapter 23: Love: A Different Kind of Music	134
Chapter 24: Aloha: Miles to Go and Promises to Make	144
Chapter 25: Significant Others and Significant Changes	148
Chapter 26: Wedding Bells and an Italian Honeymoon	153
Chapter 27: Your Eyes May Look Like Mine: Randy's song to Julien	159
Chapter 28: A New Home Sweet Home	167
Chapter 29: Isaac Pays a Visit	174
Chapter 30: An Excuse to Party: Hurricanes	177
Chapter 31: Oh Baby!	183
Chapter 32: Close to Being Far Away	191
Chapter 33: Breaking News and a Breaking Heart	196
Chapter 34: Surgery	214
Chapter 35: Edge of the World	235
Chapter 36: After Good-bye	241
Chapter 37: Willful Intentions and a Will Full of Tension	246

Chapter 38: Trouble Following Grief	261
Chapter 39: From Legal Recordings to Musical Ones	265
Chapter 40: Decency and Deportment in the Digital Age, or Not	271
Chapter 41: Desperate for Order	274
Chapter 42: Finding Peace	290
Chapter 43: A Meeting of the Minds	295
Chapter 44: A Special Hike Near Knoxville, Tennessee	298
Chapter 45: Differences of Opinion	301
Chapter 46: Where You End, I Begin Absent the Second Opinion	304
Epilogue	312
Postscript: A Message to Randy	316
A Tribute to the Author	320
Acknowledgements	322
Links to Randy's Music	323

Chapter 1

Serendipity

Two strangers whose paths logically never should have crossed found themselves at dawn one April morning in the same place at the same time. These two strangers were myself, Rusty Perrone of New Orleans, LA, a millennial working in my family's fourth-generation Italian food business, and Jay Hoecker, a retired baby-boomer whose career as a pediatrician occurred in a variety of venues including Mayo Clinic in Rochester, MN, the institution from which he had retired seven years earlier.

I was attending a food show in Minneapolis, the first food show in my life that I attended alone. There was one seat remaining on the plane, and it was the dreaded middle seat. That is where Jay sat down next to me.

Right before takeoff, the flight attendant announced it was time to put away electronics. I turned to Jay and said, "I guess you have the advantage with that pre-electronic print compared with my computer." That started a conversation after the usual questions about destinations and reasons for being on a pre-dawn flight. We two travelers coming from two different generations, ages 32 and 69, and coming from different locales, found we had enough in common to form a link that could not be explained. For whatever reason I was compelled to share my life story with Jay, and found that during our conversation we had a few things in common. I have spent my life in New Orleans, and Jay had been a graduate student at Louisiana State University in Baton Rouge, so he was familiar with New Orleans. I am of Italian heritage, and he had close friends who were Italian. I had, as you will learn, life changing experiences in Houston, TX, involving M.D. Anderson Cancer Center, where Jay had spent time as an infectious disease fellow after his pediatric residency;

so we both knew the institution well. As I explained my story I soon found out about his knowledge of medicine as he helped me understand some anatomy of the brain. As our conversation progressed, he interrupted me and said, "You should write your story down." I told him that I thought about it but just didn't have the time. I said that I wish I had a ghost writer. He offered to help.

As the airplane emptied and we were about to leave the plane, Jay tapped me on my leg and said, "I have to tell you that my only two cousins are named Rusty and Randy." Of course whenever I tell people this it sends chills down their spines, because these are my and my twin brother's names. Sharing these coincidences created a curiosity if not an immediate bond between us. Be mindful of commonalities as you hear my story, because you are quite likely to find yourself sharing many of them, both the good and the bad, the happy and the sad, and the journeys that leave us changed.

I proceeded to meet via Skype with Jay every Monday to discuss my story, and he has related to the experience as a spiritual sojourn, because life itself is a spiritual journey. Randy wrote in a song called "Cemetery Trees":

"If you walk the cemetery trees, you would think this place was full of death, but in between the numbers are existences and dashes spelling out someone's life."

The first number is our birth and the last number is our death; the space that lies between them shouts more questions than it whispers answers. That is the nature of most truthful spiritual quests. Indeed our journeys are magnificent, complex, sometimes complicated, always uncertain, and often even exceed the expectations we hold for our destinations.

Chapter 2

Italian Immigrants: The Perrone Family

To understand the present requires knowing the past, and Randy and I would not exist if it weren't for our family's classically American immigrant past. Everyone can say that without their parents their life wouldn't be possible.

My family emigrated from Sicily, Italy, around 1905. My great-grandfather, Bartholomew Perrone, was a poor Italian who came by boat to New Orleans like many other Italians. He had some experience in the food business in Sicily, so naturally that was what he knew and that is what he did when he landed in America. He started working for a small Italian grocery store until he became partners with two Italian gentlemen, Gaetano De Majo and Salvadore Lupo, and the three opened a small store called Progress Grocery on Decatur Street across from Café Du Monde in the French Quarter in 1906.

My great grandfather is the second from the left in the picture above, circa 1906.

The stores in those days were small, 800 square feet, packed with imported goods from Italy. The aromas from the cheeses, olives, dried salted cod, and other Italian signature ingredients were very unique. Several years after they opened, Bartholomew Perrone bought out Mr. De Majo, split with Salvadore, and ventured into the business on his own. It was around this time that our family and several other Italian delicatessens helped create the Muffuletta sandwich. Its creation catered to the Italian farmers' and dockworkers' requests for sliced Italian meats, cheeses, and muffuletta loaves (a large 8 inch round heavy bread bun with sesame seeds on top), complemented by each Sicilian having his or her own version of pickled vegetables and olives in hand. Eventually the Sicilian customer, being in a rush, requested the meats, cheeses, and olive salad be put on the sliced Italian muffuletta loaf for a more portable lunch. We began offering prepared versions of the Italian sandwich. At the time, the Muffuletta was measured on a scale, and the customer was charged by weight.

My great-grandfather had five children: first two girls, then two boys, followed by another girl. The older of the two boys was my grandfather, John, Sr., who was interested in the business at a young age. At this time in America children were expected to work, and my great-grandfather utilized as much of his kids' help as he could. When my grandfather was fifteen, his mother passed away, leaving the burden to raise five children to my great-grandfather alone.

At this time, all of the Italians who had come to New Orleans lived in the French Quarter, and my great-grandfather lived right around the corner from the store. He worked from six in the morning to ten at night, doing as much as he could on his own. His oldest child, Inez, would take care of the family while he was at work, and she would take care of him. His perseverance and dedication to his family was unquestioned. Here is one of my favorite stories about him that reminds me of my own drive and determination to continue the business to the next generation:

During the Great Depression, one of many storms the Perrones and New Orleans would endure, business was terrible, prompting his bookkeeper to say to him,
"Mr. Perrone, at this rate you will have to close your doors in a couple of months. I suggest that you close now to save some money."

In his rich Italian accent he said to the bookkeeper, "Sir, do you see thata door over there (pointing to the front door)? I want you to go outa thata door and never come backa."

He said that he wasn't going to let anyone tell him all of his hard work was for nothing. This was the foundation for me to weather many of my own storms. I put myself in his shoes and just imagined how hard it was for him to keep his head above water. Without my great-grandfather's perseverance there wouldn't have been a family business for my grandfather to take over, and without my grandfather's determination to keep the business alive for the next generation, my father wouldn't have had the opportunity to continue building the family business.

My grandfather, John Sr., was a tough man, as most men of his generation were. He fought in the Second World War, being part of Patton's 3rd infantry. He witnessed many of the famous battles as they marched to Berlin. He and his wife raised a girl, a boy (my father), and another girl. My dad was the only sibling to go into the business. I love hearing the stories of their business encounters and their relationship. I compare it to mine with my father. Through my father's words I have come to the realization that my grandfather was a hard worker and always had his mind set to plan on the next big disaster, war, or great depression, which hardened his generation more than those that would follow them. He pushed with all his might to have a business to leave for my father.

My father was able to build the family business to surpass what his forefathers had done. Consequently, he was able to afford as many children as he and my mom wanted, even though Randy and I weren't exactly planned, in more ways than one. Considering that Randy and I were the last to join the family, if it were not for my great-grandfather's, grandfather's, and father's work ethic and drive to better the family's situation, neither Randy nor I would have had the opportunity to experience the world as we did. We've experienced the classic American dream with each generation being left better than the previous one. I

am aware of the privilege I have enjoyed, and I am aware that privilege does not spare one from heartache and loss.

My parents, John and Debbie Perrone, had three children before Randy and I were born. Andrea is the oldest of us and a mother figure for Randy and me. Two years later, Dayna was born. Two years later, John III was born. He was the first boy to carry the Perrone name from the preceding generation from my father who also carried the same name of my dad and grandfather. My parents wanted to try and have one more boy. But what they soon found out was they would not have four children but five. My mother nearly fainted when she heard that she was having identical twins.

But life isn't certain, and what life gives, life can take away just as easily. There was a situation in which Randy almost drowned at age two years, which would have left me without my partner in crime, or as many twins call their twin, my *womb mate*. Thankfully he was young enough that he swallowed the water instead of breathing it into his lungs. If that were to have happened, my life wouldn't have been the same. I would have missed out on one of nature's most generous gifts, living life as a twin.

I naturally have no memory of that incident, even though I was there in the hot tub as well. But where my memory starts isn't chance: it is at the family business store in the French Quarter of New Orleans. I have a mental snapshot of the swinging doors, old and abused, with a silver round hand push plate that spanned both doors. There was a window allowing us to see from the back portion of the store, which was the warehouse, to the front portion of the store. One of my earliest memories is being in a stroller of some type that rolled backwards away from those doors. Memory is a powerful thing. Sometimes memories are triggered by smells, or sight, or sometimes by sound. Naturally it was no wonder that when I would walk in the store and smell the rich aroma of pecorino Romano, olive salad, and spices all mixed together that I would be reminded of those first memories. It is memories like these that mold us into the men and women we become as adults. It is these memories that create this story.

Chapter 3

Twin Shenanigans

Ideas bounced back and forth, and oftentimes bounced among three of us, our brother John included. Fortunately, we had parents who wanted to video document our lives extensively growing up. Seeing some of the things that Randy and I did when we were tiny shows how ingrained our partnership was. As toddlers, we would on occasion make our way to the bathroom and unroll the toilet paper all over the floor and all over our heads. Then we would turn the lights off by a string when any suspecting guardian or sibling would come by. Once we were caught, we scrammed like roaches do when the lights get turned on. Naturally John was left holding the unrolled toilet paper rolls trying to convince our dad that the "babies" did it. Even at our young age we were trying to pin our shenanigans on him.

When Randy and I were about five years old, our mom often took us twins and our other siblings to a grocery store called Schwegman's. As a child going to the grocery store was an adventure. We could sometimes convince my mom to put some special treats like cereal, snacks, and even the occasional chocolate candy into the basket. After several separate instances when my mom would deny our requests for candy, it was time for me to take things into my own hands, literally. I realized that at the checkout counter there was a self-service candy rack inviting me to put some items into my pocket without being noticed. Such candy-laden checkout counters must have been masterfully invented by a childless person who thrilled at tempting the weak and vulnerable among us. I, being weak and vulnerable, had several successful trips when no one in my family noticed my visits to the candy rack. I would keep the candy under my pillow and sneak away from playing with toys in the family room with my siblings to get a quick snack. One time I came back with some evidence on my face, which prompted Randy to stalk me the next time I sneaked off.

"Russ, what are you doing?" Randy said to me as I was lifting up my pillow.

"What?" I turned around, surprised by my visitor. "This is my secret candy stash."

"Where did you get that?" Randy asked.

"I got it from the grocery store. If you don't say anything to anyone else, I will show you how to get it next time we go."

It was a deal, and now I had a partner in crime that could double the take. At this point Randy hadn't become my Jiminy Cricket conscience as he did later in life. The next time we were in the grocery store, I showed Randy that after you put some items in your pocket, you have to put your hands in your pockets so that you don't get noticed. We had our first successful grab together which we enjoyed that night after everyone went to sleep. Randy, very motivated, decided that on the next trip to the store we would get more than what I was used to bringing back. Greed and self-confidence feed on small successes, and we were ready to be fed. We got up to the checkout line, and we started to load up our pockets. I thought I was finished with my grab, but Randy told me that I could fit more and showed me his pockets. They were overloaded, so much so that he couldn't fit his hands in his pockets, but rather had to hold them right outside his pockets.

My mom looked our way and said, "Randy? What do you have in your pockets?"

"Nothing!" Randy shot back quickly. "I don't have anything in my pockets, just my hands."

My mom didn't buy it and said to him, "Pull your hands out of your pockets right now! Why are your pockets filled? Start pulling out what you have!"

He started to pull out the candy bars and other snacks one by one. Then she looked over at me.

"Rusty, what do you have in your pockets?"

"I have candy too."

She made us empty out our pockets and told the lady at the checkout counter what we were doing. She said to her, "Do you have a police officer around?" Well as soon as we heard that, we were terrified.

"You're lucky there isn't a policeman here in the store," she said, pointing her finger at us. "You shouldn't be putting candy in your pockets. That is called stealing, and it's against the law." There went my mom, being the detective she always was when it came to my brother and me. This was a foreshadowing for her of what life would be like raising twins.

We were both ashamed, less for what we had done and more that we got caught. I guess there is just no right way to do the wrong thing. On our way home we passed a police car and my mom threatened that she would tell the officer what we did and we could go to jail. We both shrugged and told her that we were very sorry, which fortunately she accepted but said that next time she would stop the policeman and we would be taken away. Our mom would also have made a great Broadway dramatic actress, because we certainly believed her. This was my first lesson about life: taking things without paying was not only illegal, it was wrong. Experience is the most difficult of teachers, bringing lessons we seldom invite nor soon forget.

Not all of our happenings were the illegal kind at our young age. We thought it would be a great idea to pretend that we were the Easter Bunny for

our family. We went throughout the house gathering trinkets and toys and collecting them under our beds until we had enough to give to the whole family. We planned on waking up in the middle of the night while everyone was asleep in the house. We made baskets out of paper and filled them with the goodies. Randy and I made a basket for ourselves so that it looked as though we had also received goodies from the Easter Bunny.

Finally it was time for us to enact operation Easter Bunny. We had the baskets made in the closet for everyone, including ourselves, so all we had to do was wake up in the middle of the night. After four nights of failing to wake up, we had to reformulate our plan. One of us would stay awake for a couple of hours while the other slept, and then we would rotate until everyone in the house was sleeping. Success! The next day my mom asked us if we had received a present from the Easter Bunny, and we played it as best we could without giving away our secret. We assumed, of course, that we had fooled her, but looking back, the mother of five children was not likely to be fooled by the Easter Bunny, and a dead giveaway was that it wasn't on a Sunday nor Easter!

The summertime was a great time for us. We started year-round swimming at the age of six, and in the summer our practices would begin at 6:00 a.m., allowing us all day to get into mischief. We made it clear to my mom that we didn't want to do summer camp at such an early age, so we had free range around the house to do what we wanted to do. We made clumsy attempts at building tree houses in an empty lot every summer, but we had to take them down toward the end of the summer because the families on either side of the lot didn't want a hurricane to blow the wood into their houses. Hurricanes are a fact of life in New Orleans. This was okay because it really made us proficient with building things on the job training for future ventures.

Our true entrepreneurial spirit blossomed with a lemonade stand. Many children have had lemonade stands; so I realize that did not necessarily qualify us as being entrepreneurs. However, each year we took it to the next level.

Toward the last years of doing our summer business, we turned the lemonade stand into a full blown concession stand with chips, candy bars, hot dogs, and drinks, plus we even set up a delivery service for all the construction workers building houses in our neighborhood. We would hook up wagons to our bikes and load them with drinks and goodies, then ride through the neighborhood. Forget about waiting for the customer to come to you, we used the family business principles of delivering the goods to the customer and put them forth for our business venture. We started to become so successful that one summer we staged a fireworks show for which we charged the neighbors admission. We had our concession stand in the front yard ahead of the show to make additional sales and even included "The Meal Deal" which was a hot dog, drink, and chips for a dollar. We had chairs set up so that everyone could enjoy the fireworks. We closed the concession while we did fireworks and then reopened it after the show to feast our bellies made hungry from our most amazing fireworks show. It was our most successful summer yet. When the summer was over, and we had snacks left over, we would put them in our room to be able to ration them to ourselves over time. It didn't hurt that we were always involved with the family business, and the concession stand was the planting of the seeds for entering the multigenerational family business.

We were always adventurous, and not solely with things that our parents would have accepted! We also excelled at things they did not accept. One particular thing we loved doing every year was helping our dad decorate our house for Christmas. Every year we would add to what we were decorating until one year we were completely on our own decorating the entire house. We had just finished watching the movie *Christmas Vacation* and wanted to make our house as close to the one in the movie as possible, you know, the one with the over-the-top Christmas lights. We didn't have enough lights to line the roof completely like in the movie, so we opted for the next best thing: we were going to write Merry Christmas in lights on the roof. We sat on the roof trying to figure out how we were going to do this. We just couldn't think of any way to secure the lights up there until I had the clever idea of hammering nails into the roof to outline our design. The task needed to be done so we threw out reason in an effort to achieve our goal. As we were doing this our neighbor just so happened to come by and inquire what we were doing on the roof:

"Hey guys," he said to Randy and me. "What are y'all doing up there?"

"Hi, Mr. Rick," Randy replied quickly and jovially back. "We are making an outline to hang Christmas lights so they spell Merry Christmas."

"Oh that's great guys," he answered with some suspicion. "Are y'all hammering nails into the roof to do that?"

I blurted out all proudly, "We sure are. It was the best way we could think of to make it big and bright."

When he walked off, we thought we were the coolest kids in the neighborhood. We could see his house from the rooftop of ours and noticed he had minuscule decorations. We felt we had shown him up. Little did we know, he was going to alert our dad that we were actually hammering nails through the shingles and into the roof. I suppose you can say our dad wasn't all that upset because we were doing something we thought was harmless, but after a consultation with a contractor, he warned us "Leave, them in!" We left them in, and every time it rained thereafter we had to go into the attic to inspect the roofline to make sure there were no water leaks. Not too many years afterwards, we had a hail storm that damaged the roof enough that it had to be replaced, and thank goodness we had that storm, because we were finally off the hook if there were to be any water leakage. Some storms cause pain and suffering, but that one relieved ours.

Sometimes we did something that we weren't supposed to be doing, but we were able to pass it off as though we were innocently in the midst of a terrible situation that was completely out of our control. One day we were down at the store in the French Quarter wandering around that 18th century three story building when we found an old BB gun. We were both excited to stumble upon such a great find. It was old looking and we instantly started dreaming up situations and scenarios that this gun may have possibly encountered. We ran down the stairs to show our dad, proud of our discovery and eager to show him something he wasn't aware was up there, only to find out that it was his from his childhood. He told us some stories about the gun and naturally we fired out the question that any boy would ask, "Can we have it?" We knew it was a long shot but we asked anyway, and boy were we surprised and happy by the answer.

"You can keep it, but please don't tell your mom," he said to us.

As twins often do we said at the same time, "No problem." We sounded like the Little Rascals we had seen on TV.

That afternoon we got to go home early because my parents were going out to dinner with some friends. When we got home we noticed that my mom was in the shower, so we hurried to the back yard to play with the BB gun. We started out shooting at the fence and engaging in some target practice with Coke cans when we noticed that if we pumped it over three times it would fire by itself. Both of us were mindful of this and continued on our search for higher quality things to shoot. Then along came an innocent squirrel running on a power line, and Randy decided he would use it for target practice, elevating our gun experience to the next level a living thing. He aimed at the squirrel and fired. He missed. We reloaded and tried again as the squirrel retreated farther from us. Missed again. John came running out saying that mom was out of the shower so we finished up a couple more shots and started to head into the house. That's when we noticed that a man was talking to John at the front gate. We dropped the gun so he wouldn't spot us and walked to the gate. We could hear the man speaking with a rich Mississippi accent.

"You boys shot my wife with a BB." He said to John, "I could hear a gun pumpin' back here and then it stopped after you shot my wife in the arm."

"Sir, I think you have us mistaken; we don't have a BB gun," John said to the man.

Worried that my parents would come out, we answered quickly to him, "We weren't aiming at your wife. I think something must have just fallen to the ground and hit her."

He walked off, and we thought we had just gotten away with this one. Oh, would we be in some trouble if my mom were outside to hear that. Just then our parents came out and jumped into the car. We waved them off like three good little altar boys. We were so good at making people think we were angels. They were gone, so we ran to the back and grabbed the gun and put it under my bed. At this point we had forgotten all about it and watched TV the whole time they were away and then went to bed. The next day we were getting ready to go to church when from upstairs we heard the doorbell ring.

"Boys!" we heard my mom yell up to us. "Come down here now!" Even at this point we weren't sure what was going on, completely forgetting about the incident the evening before.

"Yes, Mom," I said to her.

"These people are our neighbors and they said that you shot them with a BB gun," she said to us, puzzled. She looked at our neighbors and said, "We don't even have a BB gun."

My dad walked up right when she said that and he interjected, "Well I gave them my old BB gun that they found at the store yesterday." He looked over to us with a face of irritation, "Guys, did you try to shoot this nice lady?"

"No, Dad, it must have misfired." Randy said really quickly, even catching me off guard. My twin-sense picked up where he was going, and I hopped aboard instantly.

"Yeah, Dad, when we pump it four times it shoots off on its own," I said.

Now he was suspicious about this excuse and prompted us to get the gun. We grabbed the gun and gave it to him. He pumped once, twice, three times, and fire! Thankfully it went off on its own. We were free from this one.

"I guess they are telling the truth, it must have fired on its own and hit you," my mom said to the lady and man. "Plus, knowing my boys, if they were trying to hit you, they would have aimed for your butt." We thought, hearing her say that, our mom would have made a great stand up comedienne, another of many professions she could have chosen. I couldn't believe what I was hearing. We had sold our parents on this and they were even backing us up. We had pulled some wool over their eyes before, but this, I had to say, was the best yet. We turned to start walking upstairs with haste when the man spoke again.

"Well, I believe that they tried to shoot my wife and we are not okay with it," the man said angrily to my parents.

"Well, I know just how to solve this," our mom said quickly and confidently. "I will send the boys over to your house to do some garden work, or whatever work you need done."

"Garden work will be just fine," the man said. "How about next week?"

"That will be just fine," our mom said to him. "Once they are done you will know that they are good boys."

We couldn't believe how quickly that just turned against us. But we weren't afraid of hard work, because we were used to it. The next week we started working, and they were not too friendly to us. After they saw how much work we had done, and how we hadn't complained one bit about planting their trees and flowers, weeding the garden, and cleaning up the yard, we had sold them on who we really were: good boys who were just out for fun and adventure. When we were finished working, they told us to come over anytime for a Coke and to talk. They appreciated our hard work and knew we weren't trying to shoot them.

It really felt good to prove ourselves to them and to show that we weren't entirely the mischievous twins our wounded neighbor had made us out to be. It was also rewarding to have created yet another opportunity for our parents to hone their parenting skills! We gave them a lot of practice in that regard.

Being a twin was a set-up for an untraditional childhood in several respects. First I always had a partner in crime. We would always bounce ideas off of one another and carry them out with the mind of two working toward one goal. Again not all of our endeavors were politically correct. There were even times when one idea had to be better than the other, like shooting fireworks out of the upstairs den window. We had already made the mistake of setting off a smoke bomb in a closet in our room, so this time we had the intentions of leaving no traces behind of our adventure. That didn't work out well because just as Randy was saying, "We could totally get in trouble for this," my sister Andrea walked up behind us and said, "Oh yes, and you will." Needless to say our dad did not share our fascination with domestic fireworks.

The village certainly played a role in making sure Randy and I were not getting into trouble. Our family and teachers were a big part of taming our mischievousness. One teacher in particular would literally punish us with lipstick kisses on our cheeks when we would do wrong. This was supposed to embarrass us because we would have to go around school all day sporting big ruby red lips on our faces; however, Randy and I used it as a trophy of our bold behaviors.

A lot of our foolishness involved our bicycles, riding the neighborhood and finding anything to keep us entertained. We had regularly been warned not to leave our neighborhood nor cross the main road that fed the neighborhood. On several instances we tested those limits. Once we wound up getting caught by police while trespassing in the parking garage of a nearby hotel; and on another outing we got caught riding our bikes to the mall, which entailed crossing several major roads. To add some drama to these occasions Randy and I would mess with each other when we went to places we weren't permitted by saying, "I think I see Mom," or something along those lines. It would always get my heart jumping when he would do that, and I knew it always scared the crap out of him as well. The one time, though, that I didn't believe him, he was telling the truth, and there she was making a beeline right for us. She was so mad that she made us leave our bikes at the mall unlocked, hoping that someone would steal them. She drove us back later that evening to see if they were still there. Thankfully they were, but I have to wonder what life would have been like had we become bike-less. Unfortunately, it wouldn't take us long at all to have our bikes taken away by my parents. We just so happened to ride beyond our limits yet again to a parking garage, in which we were trespassing. Randy also thought it would be fun to throw a Coke bottle off the top of the parking garage, which landed in some nice lady's pool. She called the cops, and as we made our way down the parking ramp, those nice police officers were in our path to the exit. As the officer called our mom, I could just imagine the face she was making on the other side. Needless to say we lost our bike privileges for some time. Our mom would have made a great security guard or law enforcement officer. She had so many talents!

On one occasion that involved a bike, I had tried for the first time to use my twin ESP powers to talk to Randy. There was a boy in the neighborhood who owned a brand new bike. Randy and I were riding the neighborhood and noticed him on it. We stopped and talked to him, then rode off. Randy came up with a plan that he would steal the bike from him. We didn't think we needed a good reason for theft if the plot were satisfactorily exciting enough. When we rode back and started to talk with this biker, I decided I didn't want to have any part of Randy's plan. I told Randy I had to go to the bathroom and rode off. I didn't look back. The whole way home I tried my hardest to tell him not to do it, using ESP of course. I would strain my brain as I said, "Randy don't do it." I went home as fast as I could, and when I got home Randy was right behind me, not on the boy's bike but on his own. I was so relieved that he didn't do it. I asked him if he heard me telling him not to steal that bike, but he just said that he couldn't do it. I always wondered after that if he in fact had received my thoughts through extrasensory perception. Difficult to prove one way or the other, I'll admit, but I suspected it had worked.

One thing we certainly shared was our bed wetting problem. It was so bad that we would have to wear pull-ups at night. We thought it was more fun to kick off a full and heavy pull-up across the room and under the beds than throwing them away. Needless to say our room smelled like an unattended locker room. We wet the bed until we were twelve years old, so you can imagine the stories that resulted just around bed wetting, including being picked on by my cousins, making excuses to friends as to why we couldn't do sleep-overs, and putting blame on others when we had the chance. One time in particular I was successful in putting the blame on my cousin, William, when we were around seven years old. He came to sleep over that night. I went to sleep without a pull-up. I woke to his crying because he was wet. I quickly told him that he wet my bed. My mom came in and brought us to the bathroom to get cleaned up. I will never forget his face when he kept repeating to himself, "I never wet the bed. I can't believe I wet the bed." I used his vulnerability to my advantage and made him feel worse. It was a payback for some of the mean things he had done to me at that age. Rationalizing was a skill I was continually perfecting. During another instance, Randy tried to blame it on me when we slept at a friend's house. I already knew this scheme so I quickly told him he was aiming at the wrong person in this blame game, and he knew he couldn't convince me and cleaned up the bed and himself.

Our humor didn't stop in the bathroom. One afternoon when my parents were out, we had a friend come over for a bit. As that friend was leaving, Randy and I thought it would be fun to moon (show our hiney's) to them as they pulled off. A couple of days later, my great detective mom called us down and asked us about our full moon trick. We were puzzled as to how she could have known that. Come to find out, our grandmother, who lived seven houses away, just so happened to be driving by with some friends when we pulled down our pants and drawers. When our dad found out that five older ladies saw two white behinds, he was horrified. Come to find out, those five older ladies thought it was the funniest thing they had seen in years. Bad luck finds those that push the limits, and we certainly found our luck in this instance to be just that, bad.

Chapter 4

Adolescence and Young Adulthood

"When the game is over, both the king and the pawn go back in the same box"
(an Italian proverb)

When we turned eight years old, we moved out of our childhood home and moved into a rental unit while our new house was being built. The temporary home was a three-story house, and the boys' room was all the way up on the third floor. For two eight-year-olds and a ten-year-old, it was exciting to say we lived on the third floor. I have some good memories of living in that townhouse. Especially on Halloween, because the house was on an oak-tree-lined boulevard that at night was creepy, so it played well into the Halloween holiday. We lived there for two years until the new house was finished. John, Randy, and I were very excited to move into our new house because we'd finally have a room that was large enough for us to avoid being on top of one another. Our bathroom was luxurious: three sinks, one for each of us, two showers, and a urinal. That was the coolest feature we loved showing our friends when they would come over. Randy and I shared a shower and John got his own. Another feature the house had was a motion detector that was connected to a buzzer in my parents' closet. It would buzz when we would walk in the hallway. The buzzer would alert my parents that there was likely some type of questionable activity going on. Well we found a solution to that! We put a baseball cap over it to prevent it from picking us up.

We weren't in the house but a couple of weeks when we started our natural boyhood inclinations toward destruction of the place. Occasionally after we finished swim practice, we would throw wet paper towels against the wall to see who could get theirs to stay up the longest. Well, Randy and I decided it would be fun to try with wet toilet paper. We threw two wads into John's shower, and it stuck right above his head. When it would hit the wall it would make a thump and squish sound. He yelled at us and instantly threw them back. We weren't just going to keep playing with the original two wads, so we made over two dozen and threw them back and forth at each other for over 45 minutes. We were in there so long that my dad started to get concerned that something may have gone wrong. As soon as he entered he saw the wads flying back and forth and heard them squish and thump against the wall. He was furious. He yelled at us and commanded we get out of the shower. He took us all downstairs in our towels, and we sat on the sofa waiting for our mom to come home so that we could explain to her what we had done. Needless to say neither was amused by the escapade and we each got a whipping, and then were sent to the room to clean up the mess and go to bed.

We seemed to find trouble even though we weren't looking for it. I remember one evening, while we were sitting at the dinner table eating as a family, our dad asked me to open the window to let in some nice cool fall air. When I opened the window, I didn't hear the chirp sound from the alarm. I didn't let anyone know my findings, but I noted it mentally to bring it up to Randy after dinner. After dinner I went up to Randy and asked him if he heard the chirp from the alarm system go off when I opened the window, and he knew exactly where I was going with this. The Perrone Family house, a.k.a. Fort Knox, had a flaw. We had always talked about sneaking out but never could because of the alarm system. Now we realized we could. We planned that night to go out by way of the window. We really felt anxious getting ready to crack open the window. We looked at each other and closed our eyes, held our breath, and turned the knob to open it. We opened our eyes and looked at each other and looked at an open window. Freedom lay beyond that window. We climbed out. It was so quiet on the other side of that window. We walked through the backyard and jumped the fence to go into the empty lot next door. We weren't out long, but now we knew we could sneak out anytime. We would sneak out almost every weekend, not really going anywhere, staying near the house. It was the feeling of freedom that we were after, one that later in life would wind up getting us into trouble. As Janis Joplin said, "Freedom's just another word for nothin' left to lose."

One of those times we would get into trouble was the night of our eighth grade Homecoming dance. Randy and I were going to sleep over at a friend's house several miles away from our house and meet up with some girls in our neighborhood. When it came time to go home from the dance, Randy thought it was stupid going so far away to our friend's house when we would be risking getting caught by cops while heading back to our neighborhood. He wound up going home. Back then there were no cell phones, just beepers, so we developed a coding system to let each other know when we were leaving and when we got there. I paged Randy but didn't get a response from him. I tried again with no response. So my friend and I decided we weren't going to wait any longer and jumped on our bikes and rode on the lake side of the levee to conceal ourselves from police. In retrospect, it probably wasn't really against the law to meet girls in the eighth grade. As we came up to one of the pumping stations that drains the city of rain water, we noticed the bridge over the canal was lit up like a Christmas tree. This was our most vulnerable moment for getting caught by police. It was like the moment when Chris, Gordie, Vern and Teddy started to cross the train bridge in the movie *Stand By Me*. We slowly and cautiously started across the bridge. We were halfway across when we saw headlights from the levee police, and we immediately hit the ground. We lay there like sitting ducks in the middle of the bridge as a police car stopped on top of the levee.

"Did he see us? Why is he sitting there for so long?" I thought to myself. It felt like forever but was probably closer to five minutes before the police took off in the opposite direction from us. We waited a little while and then continued our journey to the girls' house. As we got closer I decided that we would sneak into my house to make sure Randy was awake, since we didn't get a page back from him. As we were turning onto our street I saw a car zooming down the street screech to a stop, back up, and speed up to us. It was either some crazy person wanting to kidnap some kids on bikes, or it was my mom, at that moment in time I wasn't sure which one would be worse. As soon as the car came closer I realized it was my mom. "Oh crap!" I said to myself, and I am positive my face said the same thing. She pulled up next to us and said, "Rusty? What are you doing out? Go home now! Randy sneaked out of the house." My heart sank to the pits of my gut. We were busted. I got home, and Mom came storming into the den where I was sheepishly waiting with my two other accomplices. She was so mad, but was more concerned with finding Randy. She called my friend's house where we were supposed to be sleeping and his brother was convinced that we were still sleeping. I wasn't sure if it was the stuffed beds making it look like we were sleeping or if he didn't even check on us. She then had my friends call their parents to pick them up at our house. I will never forget the phone call to one of my friend's parents, who were older in age than most of our other friend's parents.

"Dad, this is Joey, I need you to come pick me up."

"Joey is upstairs, sleeping," his dad said back.

"Dad, this is Joey," he said really slowly and firmly. "We are at the Perrone's and I need you to come pick me up. We snuck out."

It seemed like it took him a couple more minutes to figure it out. For my other friend, it didn't take long at all for his parents to figure it out. I could tell by his face that his parents were much like mine, to be feared when we were in trouble. He looked like he was indeed fearful of the impending encounter.

We didn't stay long enough to see my friends get picked up because we were off in the car looking for Randy. First stop was the girls' house as I hinted that's where he could be. I knocked on the door and they opened with a big greeting which I countered under my voice that we were busted sneaking out. I asked if Randy was there and she whispered to me that he was. I told her to tell him to go home now because we were busted.

As soon as she told him, he jumped out of the second floor window and traversed the streets in the cloak of darkness to try and make his way back into the house. We went home then, and I told our mom that I was going to look for him. As soon as I got to the room I could hear knocking on our bedroom window, which had been our escape hatch for some time now. He said to let him in but noticed that Mom had screwed shut the window and I couldn't open it. I went back downstairs not sure how I was supposed to cover for him and told our mom that I couldn't find him. Well this just made it worse because now she started to worry that he was kidnapped while trying to sneak out. She called the cops and we were back in the car searching the neighborhood for him. We went to a questionable part of town looking for him. I kept saying, "I just don't think he would be over here, Mom, he must be closer to home." Each time I said that she would question if I knew where he was.

We finally went back home because the police would be arriving soon. When we got home she asked me one more time if I knew where he was. I told her I would have to go to the roof to try to find him because I thought I knew where he was. I climbed out of another window, crawled over the roof to our bedroom window, and saw Randy sleeping on the overhang outside of our room's window. I called out to him once, and he didn't wake up. I called out a second time and he was startled out of his sleep. "Randy, we're busted! Come inside!" I pleaded with him, "Man, the freaking cops are coming." I convinced him to follow me. When we came down the stairs our mom went ballistic on him, screaming and shoving him. Up to this point in life, I had never seen Mom that upset at us. As we sat on the couch waiting for the police to come, she whispered a piece of information that we were worried about and anticipating: "You two will never, never, ever be allowed to sleep out again!" The only subsequent time she did let us sleep out, about three years after this, we wound up getting busted by the police for underage drinking, and then we were really never able to sleep out again. Our mom was a very savvy lady, not to be fooled, having learned well through some similar instances in her own childhood.

Even though we were not able to sleep out, we certainly were able to get ourselves into trouble. We always found a way to have fun at the house. We would have friends sleep over and would tell my mom that we were going to get some food to get out of the house to get beers. Before we would leave, we would drop an extension cord out of our window so that when we came back with the beer we could hoist it up by the extension cord. We wouldn't even make a fuss about getting upstairs to get the beer, instead we would sit at the table, eat our food and then slowly and calmly go upstairs to pull up the beers. It took her a while to catch on, and it was by accident that she did. One morning we were cleaning up all the beer cans and putting them in a trash bag. As Randy was picking up the trash bag, my mom walked in and heard all the clinks and clanks the beer cans made in the bag. Busted again! She wasn't too mad about it, and gave us a small talk about alcohol and the dangers of alcohol, but by this point we already knew many of her teaching points because Randy and I had saved several people from choking on vomit. Enough people drank at our house and got sick that we had started a wall of shame, and we had written about ten people's names on that wall.

A classic fun twins' prank was to switch classes, and as our luck would have it we were probably the only twins that got busted for switching classes. Growing up everyone always asked us if we had ever switched girlfriends or classes. Well, for whatever reason, girls were always able to tell us apart, so the only other twin game we could try was switching classes. We switched desks in fourth grade with success, so we thought we had this one in the bag. We might have if my friends had not known how to tell us apart so easily. I made my way to Randy's class and sat down in his seat; I knew which seat was his because one of my friends was helping me. Well as soon as I sat down, someone looked over at me and said, "Rusty, what are you doing in here?" I looked over at him and made a face that hinted to keep quiet. I looked at the teacher and he didn't seem to hear it. Well a couple of days later, which happened to be the last day before Christmas break, we heard our names being called yet again over the PA system by the disciplinarian. "Randy and Rusty Perrone to Mr. Skinner's office." We were always being called down there, so neither Randy nor I had any idea why we were being called. We sat down in his office, and he accused us of switching classes and didn't give us an opportunity to refute the claim, nor were we about to do so because I could tell he had some compelling evidence. He told us to come back after Christmas break to discuss what our punishment would be, placing us in an uncomfortable discipline purgatory.

That Christmas break was the worst holiday of our lives. The looming fear of punishment hung over our heads the entire time. As each day passed, it got worse. The first day back at school we avoided Mr. Skinner like the plague. He didn't give us a particular time to meet at his office, and with every page over the PA not being a call for us to come down, we thought that maybe he had forgotten about the punishment. We had one period left before we were dismissed from school for the day, and Randy and I just so happened to be walking together to our next class when we spotted Mr. Skinner. We instantly turned around to walk away but he saw us and called us out.

"Perrone boys! Come here," he yelled across the hallway.

"Well good afternoon, sir. Did you have a good holiday?" said Randy trying to make small talk.

"I hope that it was good," I continued to try and get him off the topic of punishment. "Did you get what you---?"

"Shut up, Perrone," he cut me off. "You can't talk your way out of this one." I shrugged and waited for the judgment to come down and he said, "I have thought long and hard about what you two did."

"Well sir, I want you—" Randy started to say before Mr. Skinner cut him off again.

"Perrone, I told you that you can't talk your way out of this one," he continued. "So I have given this a lot of thought and because we don't have anything like this in the handbook, I don't know how to punish you. Therefore, I won't, but I do have a warning for you: if you do this again, I will suspend both of you. Now move along to class."

We both looked at each other, made big eyes, and let out a sigh of relief. We got away with this one, except for the ruined holiday, but it wouldn't be long before we found ourselves, or more accurately, Randy found himself, facing a more serious issue. This instance happened to be the first time that Randy and I telepathically shared an emotion. I was sitting in my class one day and suddenly I felt a surge of disappointment and fear of going home. I couldn't pinpoint why I was feeling that way. I knew that I hadn't done anything, or at least had not gotten caught doing something for which I would have to fear my parents, so I just couldn't pinpoint why my feelings were the way they were. I went through the rest of the class feeling this way, coming in waves, stronger and stronger. Once the class let out, I saw a friend in the hallway.

"Hey, Rusty, did you hear what happened to Randy?" he said to me.

"Randy? No. What happened to Randy?"

"He got busted with pills. He is in Mr. Skinner's office right now."

I instantly knew that my feelings in the classroom were Randy's feelings. It was one of the worst feelings I had ever felt, especially because I knew that being caught with pills most certainly meant expulsion from school. I couldn't believe that Randy and I could potentially be going to different schools. My parents took him home so I didn't get a chance to talk to him until I got home. I didn't want to make him feel worse than he already did, so I didn't inquire much about it other than to ask what we could do to get out of this one. Well Randy had already started to think about it. He made up a story that the pills he had, which were Ritalin, happened to be from someone who left them at our house and that Randy was trying to find out who's they were and that is why he had them and was showing them to someone at lunch. I thought that there was no way Mr. Skinner would believe that. We thought some adults were naïve but there was no way he would convince Mr. Skinner that this story was true.

After several meetings with my parents and Randy with Mr. Skinner, there was a verdict as to what Randy's outcome would be. I couldn't believe it; I was so thrilled because Randy wouldn't be kicked out of school. He bought the story. Randy would be suspended for his stupidity and that would be it. Later in life as adults when Randy and I once ran into Mr. Skinner, Randy told the truth about the pills and apologized for lying to him about it. He told Randy, "I knew they were your pills, but I also knew that you were good kids and my decision to expel you would have been more harmful to your future than the lesson you would learn from being really close to getting expelled." We had benefitted from a much wiser and kinder "criminal justice system" than the country as a whole uses.

Most of our stunts after this one were funny and innocent stunts. One that I particularly love is when we borrowed a friend's crutches which would instantly get Randy and me access to the front of the lunch line. At our school if someone were in need of help because of injury or disability, the rules would allow a helper to come to the front of the line and get lunch for both of them. Well it worked and we made it back to the table with smiles of success in front of our friends. A couple of days later at home eating dinner, our mom asked us how Randy's leg felt. We looked at each other puzzled as to what she was talking about. Well, come to find out, the head lunch lady talked to our mom all the time.

She said to our mom, "Debbie, those twins are so sweet to each other. I just love how Rusty helped Randy get lunch while his leg was injured."

"Leg injury?" my mom inquisitively asked, "What do you mean leg injury?"

"Yeah, Randy was on crutches, and Rusty was helping him get food. They were so sweet with each other."

"Oh, I think they may have pulled a fast one on you. Randy doesn't have an injured leg. They must have found someone's crutches and used them to get to the front of the line."

They weren't mad at us; in fact they thought it was quite funny. My mom told that story to all of her friends, just like she would do with all of our shenanigans. It must have reminded her of her childhood, which sometimes led me to wonder how much trouble we would have found if we had been triplets.

We used to push the limits with authority, and at the same time try to make them laugh. We used to sit in the Resource Center at school when we had off periods. The Resource Center was a place where you could talk quietly but couldn't get loud as it was outside of all the class rooms. There were tables of six lined down the hall and we would all sit there to pass time. One day as we were sitting there, I saw Mr. Skinner coming down the hall and wanted to mess with him. I told everyone at the table, including Randy, to start to say the Our Father prayer as he was walking by, you know, to make him think that we were being good instead of supporting his natural suspicion that we were being bad. We started to say the prayer as he was walking by when he looked right at Randy and me and said, "Perrone, I know better than to believe that you were actually praying. Get some school work done for Pete's sake!"

There were many good memories from high school. Indeed, it was an instrumental part of our upbringing, especially for Randy because that is where he honed his artistic talents. We had the opportunity throughout high school to share the same classes. One of them was art class. This is where Randy started to excel in his expression of life. He made some paintings that represented the Creation and his viewpoint of the hereafter. I would look at what he was doing and would try to mimic some of his ideas, but it was clear that I couldn't keep up with his creativity. He wound up creating about 50 paintings throughout his life. The ones that were the most moving came from his early years of painting in high school. This was also about the same time that he started to learn how to play guitar. His songs were written as though they were explanations of his paintings and insight into his mind. Creative minds see things the rest of us can't see, but their creations can be our eyes.

Not everything we did was mischievous; in fact, we were good-hearted people, Randy and I. Getting into trouble was what we were known for, but helping others was also how people would remember us. One night Randy and I were heading out to meet friends at a bar. We were nearing Napoleon Avenue on St. Charles Avenue when we caught a yellow light and began to stop. As we stopped I saw out of the corner of my eye a lot of sparks and looked to see what was happening. When I turned my head I could see a motorcycle flipping around and two people falling off, a man and woman. The man rolled into another car and the woman landed on the ground and made several bounces with her head. Randy and I knew this wasn't good. We pulled over and rushed over to the scene.

We were the first people there and started to recall our CPR training that we had taken earlier in the year. First thing was to identify the person hurt the most. The guy was moving his hands around his head, but the lady wasn't moving at all and was lying face down on the pavement. I went right up to her and did the "look, listen, feel" method we were taught in CPR class. She wasn't breathing from what I could see, I couldn't hear her breathing, but I could feel there was a pulse. I knew since she had hit her head that it was imperative that we didn't move her without the proper neck support. I remembered the way they taught us, but I wasn't 100% confident that I would do it right, but we needed to do something because she wasn't breathing. As Randy and I were getting ready to turn her on her back I could see her chest start to move up and down. "Phew," I said to Randy, "she's breathing. We have to make sure she stays put until the ambulance arrives."

Just then some people came out of the bar, one saying, "I am a doctor, I am a doctor." I looked at him and gave him a report of what happened and said that the victim had started breathing. As I was talking to the doctor, the man driving the motorcycle started to come toward us saying, "Get away from my girl. Don't you f**cking touch her." The doctor right away got in his face saying that we were trying to help her and that he should not touch or move her. He kept trying to get close to her to move her and we tried our best to restrain him. Thankfully the police arrived and helped us out with this dazed and confused man. I was so mad because it took almost 30 minutes to get an ambulance to this poor woman who wasn't moving her body at all. They finally came and put her on a restraining stretcher and took her to the hospital. The police officer took my name and asked me if I would testify, and I quickly said that I would. It was a lesson for both Randy and me on the dangers of riding a motorcycle, and also a lesson that sometimes people need you. Of course, first responders are usually the ones that save lives. I won't say we saved a life, but years later I found out that the lady was a friend's mom and she had suffered brain damage and wanted to thank whoever it was that helped out when the accident happened. We may downplay the importance of events in our early lives, but they all play a role in creating the people we grow up to be.

One of our biggest learning events of adolescence had nothing to do with our shenanigans. It had everything to do with standing up for what was right, and suffering the consequences. During our sophomore year of high school, Randy and I met two of our closest friends through the swim team. Bo and Samson would become really close to us for the remainder of high school and throughout our adult life. It wasn't long after we met, maybe two months or so, when we also started hanging out with another group of friends, all of whom seemed much closer, with a longer history than what Bo and Samson had with Randy and me. Naturally, girls were the main focus at this age for us, and it just so happened that several of the group members including myself, Bo, and another friend named Adam had a crush on the same girl. It was obvious to me that she liked Bo, so I didn't want to get in the way of them starting to talk. Unfortunately, Adam didn't feel the same way, and one evening he pulled Randy and me aside and told us that if she were to go for Bo, he would fight Bo. Then he asked us what side we were going to be on. It was easy for us to recognize what the moral and proper action was, but it was not as easy as it seemed. We naturally chose to side with Bo, and sure enough the girl wound up liking him. Well from that moment on, high school life would change for all of us. Soon every single one of our friends from the other group had turned against all four of us. This was *Westside Story* in the heart of New Orleans, and we were center stage.

It started out that we would go to parties and the other group would threaten to jump us if they saw us there. We weren't about to be bullied or forced not to go to a party, and fortunately for the first several parties we attended they were either not there or they wound up leaving before we got there. At one party, however, we wound up being there at the same time and they tried to pick a fight with us. We didn't want to fight, so we stayed away from them at the party and didn't stay long. It got to the point where we didn't want to go to parties any longer so we started to hang out with Bo's sister, Elizabeth, who was several years older than us and in college. She knew some bouncers at a popular bar and was able to get us in. From that point we started hanging out at bars with college kids instead of people our own age. It was a relief not to worry about "the other group" being at the same place as us and trying to jump us. I joked with Randy about this change of venue and lifestyle, "Don't drink too much, that is my extra kidney inside of you. Oh, and I may need some of your liver too."

We still had to face some of our adversaries at school and deal with the occasional vandalizing of our cars or houses on the weekends. We even set up video cameras to catch them in the act and did one time. Instead of going to the principal, we made copies of the tape and handed it to all our school adversaries who were riding together in one car this particular time. We warned them that if they did it again we would report them to the police and the school. It worked, but we also found out later that they had just watched the video over and over laughing about what they had done; such was not really our intention, but we got the same results.

This avoidance continued for over a year until we all had had enough of avoiding parties in fear of the other group's being there. So we picked a party at which we knew they would be present to stand up for ourselves. When they confronted us we did indeed stand up for ourselves, and it felt great. They backed down, and we quickly realized that hanging out with people our own age was not as fun as hanging out with the older college kids. We left the party and went back to Bo's house and continued to drink. The more we drank, the more Bo wanted to go back and settle the issue once and for all. So we went back, and when we arrived, they were jumping into a car to leave, and we all saluted them with our middle fingers. Well they stopped the car, got out, and rushed toward Bo. Adam and a boy named Edward began fighting Bo, and Bo was holding his own against both of them. He had them wrestled to the floor and they were hitting each other as we all stood in a circle to watch. Then all of a sudden a boy named Perry was about to sneak up on Bo and hit him in the face while he was fighting with Adam and Edward. I looked around and didn't see any of my friends trying to stop this approaching disaster, most likely because Perry was a much bigger person than any of us. As he was getting ready to hit Bo, I jumped in the way. Pow! I was seeing white out of my left eye. When I came to, I was parallel to the ground. I had been knocked down. As I was getting back up, I saw a beer bottle right next to me. I was so tempted to grab the bottle and swing at his head. Logic took hold and I just got up without the bottle. I kept my hands to my side as he kept telling me to put up my hands to fight him. I said that I didn't want to fight him. Pow! My right eye lit up with a bright white light. He hit me again, and this time I stepped back a bit. This was it. I had enough. I turned toward him and just then he ran off because the police were coming. My chance was over to defend myself, but at the same time, I lived to see another day.

"The better part of valor is discretion, in the which better part I have sav'd my life" ...Shakespeare

This wasn't the height of our conflict with them, however. It would be several months later that we would run into the final conflict. We continued to go to bars with our new college friends, which meant we weren't going to be dealing with our peer group bullies. Well one day, one of the members of that group came to the bar where we were. He noticed us and we noticed he was alone. Randy finally felt that he was on our turf and we had a right to give him some hell. Randy and a college friend of ours named Rocky chased him back to his car and started banging on the windows while he was trying to escape the parking lot. Well this would not go without revenge and several nights later, after Randy dropped me off at the bar so he could go get something to eat, I heard someone yell at me, "Hey you pussy." I turned around and saw nine of them walking toward me. I knew this was going to be bad if it were to be just me against all of them, so I walked into the bar and alerted some of my friends.

"Hey Bo, get everyone together," I yelled at him with haste. "There may be a fight outside with Perry and the group."

I walked back outside and saw all of them right by the door. They surrounded me.

"Where is your gay brother," Perry said to me. "We are going to kick his ass."

"He isn't coming out tonight," I said. "Y'all are just going to have to settle this with me."

In my face Perry said, "Okay, if he isn't here then we're going to kick your ass."

Just then I heard the door of the bar open and it stayed open. Then I noticed that every person in the bar came outside and encircled Perry's circle around me. The looks on their faces were priceless. Just then my friend, Rocky, who was proficient at fighting, jumped right next to me and was starting to really get revved up. He was in each one of their faces just waiting for one of them to make a move. I finally felt that we were going to get some justice, but then I realized something very important so I spoke up:

"Now, we have you completely outnumbered. We could all kick your ass right now if we wanted, but we aren't. See if we kick your ass, then you will just want revenge. This shit stops tonight. No more harassment. Leave us alone, and we will let you go tonight."

"What the fuck is your problem?" Rocky said to Perry, "Why do you want to fight them so bad."

Perry came up with the answer of the century, "Because they are gay." (Years later I realized this answer was nothing but a sad commentary on bigotry and came from prejudice and the intolerances and ignorance of the time.)

"Really, because you think I am gay, Perry!?" I said back to him. "Really you need to turn around and leave from here. Don't ever mess with us again. You have no reason to try; it is time this is over."

They turned around and walked away, and that was the last confrontation we had with them. We walked back in and enjoyed the rest of the night the way we had set out to do. Some may say that my actions were because I was afraid to fight, but in reality, what does fighting solve? In fact, one of my main reasons I didn't want to fight is that it would be my luck that I would hit someone hard enough in the right place to kill them and then my life would be ruined. It was just not worth it. In fact once we were out of high school and their group had dispersed, I saw Perry at a college fraternity rush event I attended. I couldn't believe that he was there. I thought I had really left all of that behind. Just then I felt a hand on my shoulder and it was Perry, extending his hand to shake mine and apologize for everything they did. Since then we had made amends with the entire group except for one, Edward, who didn't feel like he was big enough to apologize and move on, but nonetheless Randy and I forgave him and moved on with our own lives.

Chapter 5

All Grown Up and No Place to Go

Senior year of high school was the longest year of our lives. I was so ready to be out of the grip of adults and be on my own. One day Randy and I decided that we wanted to get a job on the weekends. We decided to work in a restaurant being waiters or hosts, so we put in applications at a couple of chain restaurants. Unfortunately we never got a call back from either, so we utilized our connections with Chad, our brother-in-law, who was managing a restaurant called Feast's. We knew that he would be able to get us jobs, and all we needed was to prove to people outside our family business that we had great work ethics and could run circles around other workers.

It wasn't long before we got a call back from the restaurant to come in and fill out some paperwork. When we got there, they interviewed Randy and me separately, and shortly thereafter we were hired. We were to start a two-week-long in-depth training program over the Christmas holidays. This experience helped me a lot later in life by giving me examples of how to run a family business. A useful idea was that the team took care of the entire restaurant's guests as opposed to the servers taking care of just their own guests. After the training program was done, we were on the schedule working almost every weekend. We were, for once in our lives, making decent money on a consistent basis on our own, not just within our family business. This was something Randy and I wanted to prove to our dad: we were capable of learning another business and excelling there. We were gaining more confidence in ourselves with our ability to do a good job and save some money.

Before long we met a guy named George, who was working at Feast's as a waiter. We became really good friends with him. His family was a little different from ours. He grew up in a broken household where his mom raised him by herself. She was a good person, but she was always with her boyfriend, so she wouldn't really pay attention to George. We took to him, and with our natural caring personalities we tried to show him what a family should look like. He was invited to our house all the time, eating dinner with us, and experiencing a family who cared about him. We were intent on introducing him to good things, but trouble kept finding him, which wasn't necessarily his fault. Nonetheless, he was always on the radar of the police or getting involved with friends who introduced him to activities that could get him arrested. Naturally as we would hang out with him more and more, we too were introduced to situations and scenarios that were not in our best interests.

There were several times he ran into trouble when we were with him. One instance in particular was when he was driving, and a police officer pulled him over because his windows were tinted. Once the police officer ran his license, he learned that there was a warrant for George's arrest for missing a court date previously. He got hauled into jail, and Randy and I went to the Orleans Parish Prison and sat for hours waiting for him to be released. I wouldn't say that we were always a good influence on him, either, but we certainly tried not to call attention to ourselves when we were doing things that may not have been admirable.

We certainly became close friends and were hanging out a lot more with George as high school was coming to an end. We were so ready to be out of high school that we didn't make an effort to attend our senior prom; however, we decided after all to go to the prom and had dates with friends from Feast's Restaurant. It was funny because Randy brought a co-worker who was about ten years older, and could fill out a dress that would certainly draw attention to herself. With 273 young seniors, she certainly did catch many eyes, including some teachers. The girl I took was Penelope, who was married to Tom, both of whom were good friends of ours. Tom was happy for her to go with me because she had never experienced prom. She was my only choice, but it also was an opportunity for her to experience something she had been unable to do. We rented a stretch Hummer limousine and George and several other friends came with us. We went inside the school to take pictures and literally walked right back out to the limo and started the partying. George was of legal drinking age, so we had him get us plenty of alcohol for the party. We grew up in New

Orleans, so if it were not George getting alcohol, there would have been twenty other ways that we could find it. We had a good time at the party that evening without any major issues due to the fact we had returned to my parents' house, and they were home.

Graduation was finally here, and we wanted to play tricks on the principal as we walked across the stage. Some of them were really innocent and some weren't so innocent. One of the pranks that circulated around school was to get condoms, and as we would shake the principal's hand we would each put one in his hand. Naturally he would be embarrassed on stage and have to put it in his pocket, and eventually not having room in his pockets they would overflow to the ground. Fortunately, the school really made it clear that if there were any pranks, we would not be allowed to graduate. For two young adults who so desperately wanted to get out of high school, that punishment was certainly a deterrent to any stupidity from us. It was great to finally be free from a time of our lives in which freedom to roam and do as we pleased were inhibited by the tight grips of teachers and principals, otherwise known as "high school." Whether a fence meant to protect is perceived as a prison is in the eyes of the beholder.

With this newfound freedom we really started to go down a path of excessive partying. As a close family would, my oldest sister, Andrea, started to get concerned about what type of partying we may have been doing. She convinced my mom that she should do a drug test on us early one morning. She chose early in the morning because in the past we were given enough notice ahead of other drug tests that we could manipulate the results by drinking cleansing solutions. This time, however, there was no warning.

"Randy and Rusty! Hurry, get out of bed. Come see this. We want to show you something," my mom said. "Hurry to the den, we have a surprise for you."

"Come on, it's early! Let us sleep," Randy moaned back.

"No, you have to see this. Come on get up," Andrea said back.

We reluctantly got up and followed both of them to the den. As soon as we got there we knew there wasn't a pleasant surprise waiting for us, but a surprise that we really weren't expecting and wouldn't like.

"Okay Randy, you stay with Andrea and pee in this container," my mom said. "Rusty, you're coming with me to the other room to pee in that container."

I knew we were busted and I tried my hardest to avoid having to pee in the container, "But I don't have to pee! I just woke up and don't need to go to the bathroom. I don't have to pee!"

"Well, try hard to get something in this cup," she said back to me.

When this angry and forceful Italian lady demanded, we both complied fearing the consequences if we didn't. I went into the bathroom and made sure not to put too much urine in the cup and to dilute it with some water thinking maybe that would help. Well this trick didn't work, and Randy clearly had no way to dilute his. Our mom had home test kits she used to get results right away. Clearly the kits worked pretty well, because both Randy and I came up positive for marijuana. Naturally our mom and Andrea were not happy about this and told us that they were going to let our dad know after our work shift that day. Throughout the whole day Randy and I had contemplated what we would do once our dad found out. In situations like these, it was always comforting to know that I wasn't alone being in trouble. We were both used to each other's company when in trouble. Misery always loves company, and what better company than my twin.

That evening we got off our shift to find that our dad was sleeping. "Phew," I said to Randy. "At least we have dodged a bullet with him tonight." We crept upstairs and went to sleep. In a way we felt our mom had been very concerned about the situation. The next night our path took a turn for the worse. We were about to experience a watershed event in which we could have drowned. We got dressed to go out and went to give her a kiss goodbye. We were testing the warden if she would let us walk out, not knowing what jailing plans she had in our future.

"Where do you think you're going?" she said to us. "You're not going anywhere. You're being punished."

Randy came back right away and said, "Punished?! Punished for what?"

"You failed a drug test, that's why you're punished," she told him.

I wasn't about to let Randy go at this alone so I chimed in, "Mom, we are adults. You cannot punish us. It isn't going to teach us anything by punishing us." I thought this would work but she was adamant.

"No, you are punished. Go back upstairs because you are not going anywhere."

"Well, we are adults, and if you are going to try to punish us, we will just move out," Randy said. When I heard this I knew we had come to the proverbial point of no return.

"You are not going anywhere, especially in the car that we bought you," she said.

As soon as she said that, Randy pulled out his keys and I pulled out mine and said, "Well here you go, here are our keys. We are leaving." Then we walked out the door. I thought it was going to be a bluff but I could tell by the way things were going this was going to be the real thing.

"Johnny! Johnny! They are leaving," she yelled to our dad.

"Let them go," my dad said to her in an aggravated and confident voice.

That was the last thing we heard as we walked out the door. We started walking to the levee which was two blocks down the street. The whole way my heart was racing and I could tell Randy's was too by the way he was talking to me. We had done it: we had walked out of the house. Our whole lives we would fantasize about running away when in trouble, and this time we finally did it. We felt totally free and all we could do was give each other comfort knowing we would be all right as long as we were together. We called our friend Bo to come pick us up at the levee. The levee was built to keep us safe from storms; however, in this case, we were walking directly into a storm, a storm that no levee would be able to hold back. Our storm had begun, and there was no turning it back from this point.

I looked at Randy and said, "Are you sure you want to do this?"

He replied confidently and calmly, "Yes Russ. We can do this on our own. We have each other and that is all we need to make it in this world." He spoke confidently if not accurately.

Chapter 6

On Our Own

Our friend Bo and his sister, Elizabeth, came to rescue us from the levee, and we all went to their parents' house, where they also were living. My parents had a great relationship with Bo's dad, who called my parents to let them know that we were safe. It was comforting to me to know that at least my mom knew we were in good hands, and the more they talked the more it seemed that my parents were accepting our moving out. Bo was not too excited that we had moved out, but he had supported our decision. We stayed at his house a night or two and then we found our way to our friend Andy's apartment. He was staying in a one-bedroom apartment, and he was willing to let us stay with him until we could all find an apartment together. My mom had come over to drop off clothes to us and pleaded with us to come home. Our mom was really a saint just short a couple of required miracles.

"Mom, this is something we have to do," I told her. "Don't worry about us, we will be fine. How is Dad doing?"

"Your dad is extremely upset right now. He doesn't understand what you two think you are doing. This is just a bad way to move out of the house."

At this point, I discovered later in life, my dad had started changing the business succession in his will, keeping Randy and me out of it. I can't say that I blame him, because in his mind we were out of control.

"Yeah, but Mom, we are adults and we can take care of ourselves," Randy said.

"Mom, we will be fine. Don't worry about us," I said ending the conversation. After all, we were almost somewhere; we just had no idea where we were going.

We were on the hunt for apartments but didn't really see anything that we could afford. All I knew is that I wanted to get into a bigger place quickly because living in that small apartment with three of us was becoming hard. Andy wasn't the cleanest person, and his apartment had flies because he kept a pile of trash and dishes in the kitchen. One night Randy and I were on the two sofas he had in his apartment, Andy was in his room already, and I looked at Randy and said, "Randy, I am not so sure I want to move in with someone else. I just think we can do it on our own."

"Russ, I just don't think we have any other options. We need him to help pay rent. There is no way that we can afford an apartment on our own."

"Don't worry, it's me and you and that's all that we have to worry about."

Since we didn't have a car, we relied heavily on Andy to take both Randy and me to work at Feast's. One day after work, I happened to pick up the paper and noticed a four bedroom house not too far from work. I called the owner and arranged to see the house that day. It was in a good neighborhood, and it had plenty of space. Plus, with four roommates it would be very affordable. The only problem was that we didn't have a fourth person. Once Andy picked us up, we went back to his apartment and tried to figure out who else could live with us. Suddenly I remembered that toward the end of our senior year our good friend Tim had always talked about getting an apartment with Randy and me. I quickly called him and told him that we had an apartment ready for four people and he could be the fourth person. It didn't take him long to convince his mom that it would be okay to move in with us, people he knew.

The next day we called the landlord and told him we wanted the apartment for a little less than what he was offering, and he agreed. We finally had a place that we were going to be able to call home. The apartment was available right away but Andy still had a couple of weeks left on his lease, so Randy and I moved in right away even though neither one of us had a bed. The first thing we did the next day was go to the mattress store and buy mattresses. Before you can stand on your own you need to be able to lie down. I had saved a little more money than Randy so I bought a queen mattress and he bought a full. I remember feeling bad that he had to buy a smaller mattress and offered to give him some money for it, but he declined and said that a full-sized bed was big enough.

The next step was to stock up on the things that brought some normalcy and comfort to our lives, such as toiletries, food, and room decorations. Randy and I had fun shopping for all of these things. There was a pharmacy right by the house, so we walked there for some essentials. We were just amazed at how easy it was to start to feel comfortable in our new apartment. When you start at zero, anything is a lot. I was starting to feel like we had made a good choice to move out and was getting confident in our ability to survive independently of parents. This was our time to prove ourselves, and so far we were handling things on our own.

We started going back to my parents to eat every now and again, and they were becoming more comfortable with our departure, at least on the outside. My sisters and brother would tell us how they were upset but guarded their emotions. The conversation came up one evening at their house about school. We told them that we didn't have any way to get to school so we were not going to go. Well, this did not fly with our mom, and she convinced our dad to give us some money to buy my brother-in-law Chad's Honda. He sold it to us for three thousand dollars, and, finally, Randy and I had a car again. This meant, however, that we had to sign up for college at UNO, the University of New Orleans. We signed up, but we were not really enthusiastic about school. We were making money at Feast's and enjoying our perceived complete freedom from teachers and from parents. Perceptions are sometimes delusions seen through rose-colored glasses.

Chapter 7

College: Something to Rave About

The first days of college I really felt that I wasn't ready to be back in school. One day I was asked by a friend to skip class to go to the racetrack.

Out of habit I told him, "I can't skip class, I could get in trouble."

"Rusty, you're in college; you don't have to go to class if you don't want to." In other words, you don't have to actually use everything you buy.

"I guess you are right." I said to him, "Let's go see some horses."

We went to the fairgrounds and spent the whole day there drinking beer and betting on horses. I was really starting to enjoy this adult life. I could skip class if I wanted, and there would be no one there to tell me that I was doing wrong. That evening I told Randy that I skipped class and went to the racetrack, and he surprisingly wasn't happy about it. Randy didn't approve, and for him not to approve really made me think twice about doing it again. So I let some weeks go by before I skipped class again, but no matter how many classes I attended, I was just not focused on school. There was no way that I was going to go home after working a shift and do homework. My grades were obviously suffering from this, and it didn't take me long before I started dropping classes. At school I didn't have a horse in the race, and at the track I was betting on the wrong ones. Now, years later, as I write this book John Steinbeck's words seem fitting: *"The profession of book writing makes horse racing seem like a solid, stable business."*

We were enjoying our freedoms and had the ability to do whatever we wanted to since our "strict" parents were not able to keep tabs on us. It was a learning experience. Naturally one's first taste of freedom can be pretty exciting, but this freedom can get out of hand. Excitement can be exhausting. Bob Dylan said, *"A hero is someone who understands the responsibility that comes with his freedom."* We were not yet heroes, and we were not yet free.

One night there was an event called a rave downtown that Andy, George, and I were going to attend. Randy had to stay behind because he had to work the next morning. This was the first time I had ever been to a rave; I had always heard about them, but never had the opportunity to go to one considering we were never able to sleep out during our last two years of high school. Waiting in the line I was excited to go inside to see what a rave was all about. When I got into the venue the music was thumping through the walls. As soon as I looked through one of the doors that led to the dance floor, I could see what appeared to be a sea of people dancing and having a good time. The lights were flashing and dancing all over the heads of the ravers. I was amazed at how many people came to these things.

We had all made a point to stick together. Before I knew it I was getting a call from George. I looked at my phone and was puzzled because I didn't even notice he was not next to me. I answered the phone and a freaked-out voice spoke:

"Rusty! Rusty! I am outside," he nervously said to me. "I bought a pill that I thought was ecstasy from someone but I don't think it is. I ran into someone who is an enemy of mine from high school so I got out of there. I am freaking out badly; I need you to come out."

"George, what are you talking about? Come back in. We are having a good time, man. What are you doing outside?"

Then our phones disconnected and being caught up in the noise and excitement of the rave I somehow forgot that we had talked on the phone. I was in the moment, just not George's moment. We started dancing again and having a good time until I got another phone call from him about twenty minutes later.

"George, did you make it back in," I screamed into the phone so he could hear me.

"Dude, I am so freaking out right now," he cried on the phone, "I need you to come and help me. Please help me."

At this point I knew that he wasn't playing around. "Where are you, George? Call Randy; he is home and sober. Call Tom and Penelope as well, they are home and sober." Before I knew it Penelope was calling me and she was very serious on the phone.

"Rusty, you and Andy need to get out of there and go help George," she said. "He is freaking out on some type of drug, and he thinks that everyone is trying to kill him. This is serious; you need to get back to your house immediately!"

By this time they had picked him up from wherever he was and made it to the apartment. They were waiting for me to get there, and when we pulled up, I could tell that he was not right in the head. He was pacing back and forth out front wanting badly to get inside the apartment. As soon as we got inside he closed all the blinds and locked all the doors. We woke up Randy, to talk some sense into George. Randy was always able to calm people down with his cool demeanor.

Randy, George, and I were in Randy's room. As soon as we entered, George closed the door and locked it. Randy looked at me and said, "What the hell is he on? What did he take?" I shrugged my shoulders and told him we lost him and he called me and said he was outside. George was looking under the bed, looking out of the window, and was pleading with Randy and me not to let him die. He kept telling us to call his mom and tell her that he loves her. Every time we tried to tell him that no one was after him and that he wasn't going to die, he would just go back into his paranoid ranting.

I knew that he needed to get some water to help his body flush the drugs out of his system. I convinced him to go to the kitchen so that he could get some water. He reluctantly did, and when I poured him some water and gave it to him, he looked down at it with suspicion and looked back at me and said, "You drink it first."

Penelope slapped him across the face and said, "How dare you say that to one of your good friends. He is trying to help you."

He looked at me and it was like a switch flipped in his brain. He cried and apologized and looked confused. I thought to myself that finally he was coming back to reality. It took him several more hours to come back to normal, and when he finally did, he had absolutely no recollection of what transpired!

This was a lesson for all of us in so many ways. First, I did not at all want to go to another rave again, and second I never wanted to be around people that were doing hard drugs ever again. The thought to this day of that type of lifestyle gives me the chills. This was a real turning point in our expression of freedom which led to our starting to mellow out a bit and just enjoy being home with the safety and comfort of sober friends. But too soon we found ourselves in another learning situation. Life is a persistent teacher, and youth is a school that refuses no one.

Chapter 8

Tipping and Flipping, Out

Every Monday night the House of Blues would have a SIN night, which is short for "service industry night." We went just about every Monday night with people from work. SIN nights can be mood and judgment altering events. One particular Monday after leaving the House of Blues, some of our friends thought it would be a good idea to go to the West Bank to go "cow tipping," or trying to push sleeping cows over. We had gone before to this particular field, which was near our uncle's house, so we were very comfortable with the idea. It was about three in the morning and we were on our way to the West Bank crossing the Crescent City Connection Bridge. The funny thing about New Orleans is that nothing seems to make sense. Going to the West Bank anywhere else in the world you go west, but in New Orleans you go east. Another thing that didn't make sense was why we wanted to go cow tipping in the first place, but there we were on our way. Randy, Tom, Penelope, and I were riding in the car. We had our flashlights ready and decided that Tom and I would go into the field while Randy and Penelope would drive back and forth waiting for us to finish.

The night was perfect for tipping. There was a full moon so we could see the grounds without flashlights. The temperature was pleasant and the conditions were ripe for tipping. We negotiated a bend on the two-lane road, and the bridge over the canal was just in sight. We had to make two passes as there were cars near that could spot us stopping. On the third pass there was no one around. We stopped the car on the bridge; Tom and I jumped out, hopped the fence, and ran for the trees while Randy and Penelope took off. Now the only sounds we could hear were the distant sound of the car and the chirps of crickets and moos of cows. Cows are a critical piece of this adventure. We made it to the clearing of the field and started searching for cows. This was like an *Ocean's Eleven* field trip, and we were determined to come away with some memorable tips. Unfortunately, the cows weren't near the tree line, so we were forced to go farther into the open field.

We found ourselves next to one of seven phone towers in the field and could hear muffled conversations emitted by the giant boxes that received the lines on the towers. We had spotted some cows and started slowly toward them when all of a sudden I got a call from Randy.

"Are y'all visible from the street?" he frantically asked me.

"We aren't flashing our lights if that's what you are asking," I said back to him. "Why? What's going on?"

He nervously replied, "We are being pulled over by the cops, get down and don't move. I'll call you back."

Just then I grabbed Tom by his shirt and pulled him to the ground with me. I am sure we were lying in cow patties, but at this point it didn't matter. Either way we were in a crappy situation.

"Dude, what the hell are you doing?" Tom asked me.

"Randy and Penelope are getting pulled over. I think the police know we are out here."

We were frozen there lying on the ground face down amidst cow patties. That was not my chief concern at that moment: it was whether or not we were going to get busted in the field for trespassing. It is possible to do one's best thinking when lying in the dark face down in cow patties, so we put our minds to work. We were as close to the ground as we could be for what seemed like forever but which was probably only fifteen minutes or so. All of a sudden the cell tower started bursting out the "off the hook" sound which we instantly assumed was some type of alarm. We were pretty sure we were about to be "on the hook" for trespassing. We were freaking out, looking around for any sign of police, and then it stopped. We looked at each other and decided that sitting in the field made us an easy target and that we had to make a run for it to the tree line. We weren't outstanding in our field work, but we were standing out in that field. The distance from us to the tree line had to be somewhere around a football field's length. We whispered our countdown:

"5,4,3,2…1, go go go," I whispered to Tom.

We got up and ran as fast as we could back to the tree line. As soon as we made it back there I dragged him back to the ground and started observing our surroundings.

"I don't think I see anybody. Do you?" he said to me.

"I can't see shit; actually that's all I can see. No, I don't see anyone. Let's make it back to the canal and walk toward my uncle's house. We can try to call Randy and Penelope then. If not, I can call my cousin and I am sure he will let us in the house," I whispered.

We got up and ran to the canal and started in the opposite direction from the road. The canal made a 90-degree turn behind the field. We were making good progress, all the while trying our hardest to be quiet and also trying our hardest to see where we were going without the use of flashlights. My uncle's house was probably a mile or two down the road. Not too far away were some subdivisions so we would be away from the cow field and out of immediate danger of being caught. The only problem once we reached the subdivision was that the lights from the houses made our escape a little more visible.

We stumbled upon a boat tied up on the canal bank near one of the houses. I had the clever idea of taking the boat down the canal which would be lower and out of the line of sight, plus it would be quieter than walking on twigs and leaves. The only problem was that we could only find one paddle. Now we were literally up a creek without a (second) paddle. We got into the boat and I started paddling down the canal. At one point I thought that I had hit an alligator with the paddle because there was a splash and my paddle moved violently. I thought to myself, "Great! I picked what seemed to be the safest mode of travel, and we are going to be eaten alive by alligators." To run that kind of risk we should have been searching for diamonds, not cow tipping. Finally after all this time my phone started ringing. It was Randy! They obviously weren't arrested, and we explained that we were making our way down the canal to my uncle's house where they could meet us.

We were relieved that they weren't arrested, but we still had the task of paddling down another mile or so to my uncle's street. On the way we found another paddle on the bank and commandeered the extra paddle so were moving faster now. (Believe it or not, we were not even thinking of Huckleberry Finn's nighttime canoe escape from his pa's shack on the Mississippi, but we were following Huck's logistics rather closely.) We reached my uncle's street and got out of the boat and started toward the house. Randy and Penelope were driving toward us after I called them. We met up with them and jumped into the car.

"Holy shit!" yelled out Penelope

"Man that was close," said Randy. "How the hell did you end up all the way down here?"

"You wouldn't believe what we had to do to get down here." I started bragging to them about the journey, "We hit the deck, ran to the tree line, followed the canal, commandeered a boat, and paddled our way to freedom. What the hell happened to y'all?"

Randy started, "We were parking behind the window supply building waiting for y'all when all of a sudden the alarm starting going off. We tried to get out of there but when we were turning onto the highway a police car was coming around the turn and spotted us coming out. That's when I called y'all and told y'all that we were being pulled over. We threw the pot out of the window before we got pulled over so there was nothing on us for the police to find interesting."

"What did the cop say?" I asked.

"Well, he said that a week before they found a dead body there and the building we parked behind had installed a motion alarm. He must have thought we were trying to get busy with each other and let us go after a thorough search of the car."

"Whoa man!" I said back, "All I know is that I want to get as far from here as possible. We certainly got lucky that we didn't get busted." At this point we were unsuccessful after a vigorous crawl in cow manure, a brush with an alligator, and an encounter with a cop on the prowl for dead bodies. Our high risk, low yield adventure had been exhausting.

By this time the sun was starting to come up and we all decided to go for breakfast. While we were at breakfast all we could do was laugh and boast about the adventure we had just had and how we got lucky. It has been said that luck is what happens when preparation meets opportunity; however, in our case there had been no preparation for a questionable opportunity. After this adventure we vowed to tame ourselves a bit.

Chapter 9

Saved by a Storm, Briefly

Fortunately not too many days after this episode we had some "relief" coming in the form of a hurricane with its sights on the Mississippi and the Louisiana Gulf Coast. School was canceled for the week so that students could evacuate. Storms had always been a form of a vacation and a brain cleanse for us, and this time around it couldn't have come at a more beneficial time. I needed a break from worrying about how poorly I was doing at school and a much needed break from the rave and tipping episodes still haunting my memory. It wasn't hard for our mom to convince us to stay at my parents' house for the duration of the threatening hurricane.

Still, however, trouble seemed to find us, or did we find it? While we were hunkered down my mom had asked me to get sandbags for my grandmother's house. So I borrowed my brother-in-law Brian's SUV. I took his car because it was the first out of the driveway, and also because he was deployed to help with the storm since he was in the Army National Guard. Well, on the way back from the store I took a street that had plenty of standing water. I was used to driving in water, but this time the water was too high. I wound up stalling the car, and Randy and I had to push it to a driveway that was higher than the street to get it started.

That evening Brian came home and I had to tell him that I stalled his car. Well he was so angry with what we had put my parents through, plus stalling his car, that he hit me upside of the head. Looking back I don't blame him, because we were not doing well by the family, and now we had messed up his property. Nonetheless I was so mad at him that I went to my sister to tell her. She, however, wasn't too upset about it. I was ready to go back to the apartment.

It wasn't long afterwards that Randy and I left my parents and went back to our perceived freedom. Not long after the storm we were back in our regular routines, and things were starting to look good for us. I was starting to save some money because all we were doing was going to work and then hanging out at the house.

That all changed when our own car's engine started to give out on us. Both Randy and I knew it was coming, because slowly it was getting worse until one day it wouldn't start. A wise old man once said, "Never own an internal combustion engine, because all it will do is cause you internal combustion." It was back to having to walk to and from work and catch rides whenever we could. The last thing we were going to do, though, was ask our dad for any more money. We were going to handle this on our own. We had the car towed to a mechanic and he gave us the bad news: three thousand dollars to fix it. I looked at Randy and told him that I only had two thousand saved but that I needed some of it for rent. He didn't have much saved at the time because he was still a restaurant host making much less than me. We tried to think of whatever we could to get our car back up and running but were not successful.

We were going to pick up more shifts to help save money for the car but unfortunately another storm was heading our way, a hurricane in the Gulf called Lilli. This time it was going to come to the west of us which is the direction of storms that usually bring the most water and wind. We chose to stay at the apartment instead of going to my parents' house. Why I am not sure, except that it was more fun to stay with friends at our house and have a hurricane party, which in New Orleans consists of drinking, music, gathering with friends, and just having a good time while some rain and wind whip up the city. We got a frantic call from George that he was being stuck at his house for so long.

Wanting to get out in the storm we excitedly said to him, "We are on our way to meet you. We can have a good hurricane party tonight." We asked Andy to take us to get him.

We were all thrilled that we at least had some friends to hang out with which seemed to be a light at the end of our hardship tunnel, or so we thought; hence, we set off in a hurry not thinking about all the rain that had fallen. As we made our way to George's house, about four miles away, we were met with several obstacles including flooded streets and downed trees. It was as if the storm was trying to prevent us from reaching a greater storm and even deeper water. All of a sudden we got a call from George:

"Man, I am stuck. My car stalled and I am flooded out. I have marijuana with me and I am freaking out. If the police come to help me and they get suspicious, I am screwed."

"Hang in there, man, we are on our way. Where exactly are you. We're trying to find roads that aren't flooded to make our way toward your house." We were first responders to friends in trouble always at the ready.

"I am in front of some apartments near the Interstate, but you have to come up from the south side because the street is completely flooded and the water is deep. Cars are stalling all over the place," he nervously told me before getting off the phone.

We traversed the flood waters and saw him sitting in his flooded car in the parking lot. He must have had enough momentum to pull into the lot, which was better than being in the middle of the road like a sitting duck. We immediately waded to his car and he showed us how much marijuana he had on him.

"Wow!" I blurted out. "What are you doing with all of that?"

We left George's car there and started making our way back to the apartment, trying to remember the exact path we had taken so we wouldn't become stranded as well. By this point the storm was passing so it wouldn't be long before the flood waters would recede, but I was nervous driving with marijuana. We got home and started making plans to go out. The storm had passed. Oh, but were we wrong about being clear of storms ahead, and little did we know how deep the water would get.

Chapter 10

Rock Bottom

    A party was in order and we certainly made good on that by going out to get drinks with friends. Andy thought it a good idea to look for some girls to hang out with us. After a while Randy and I noticed that a girl was hanging all over Andy, and it was getting late, so we wanted to bring the party back to the house. Arriving home, we began a lot of partying in the form of drinking and some smoking. Andy had retired to his room with the girl he met at the bar, and the rest of the people at the house went to sleep.

    The next morning the party continued with alcohol. The entire day was a blur with more drinking. We got a call with news that a friend with pot was going to come by in the evening. I wanted to make sure that I had some money ready, so I needed to go to my room for it, but I needed to do so in such a way that I would not be giving anyone a suspicion that I had a good bit of cash in there. When I went to get the money, I noticed some money missing. This was a common theme while I was living there; consequently, I had previously started marking my money with a unique mark so that, if I were to see it, I would know who had taken it. I knew it wasn't Randy and I also knew it wasn't Tim, our other roommate, because he was hardly ever home. I heard the shower turn on and both Andy and the girl went into the bathroom. This was my chance to see if he was stealing my money. I searched the room a bit and didn't find anything. The girl's purse was slightly open, and as I was walking out of the room I could see a couple of twenty dollar bills in there, so I took them out and saw my markings on them.

    Once they got out of the bathroom and came out of the room I confronted the girl about my money being in her purse. She insisted that she didn't take it, but I didn't believe her because the markings on the bills were clearly my markings. I wound up telling her to leave the house and she left wearing some of Andy's clothes.

Shortly after she left there was a knock on the door and I went to answer it because I thought it would be her. It was the guy delivering the pot so we let him in. We all went to the kitchen table where he showed us what he brought. Then all of a sudden I heard a hard knock on the door. That was a knock that would be heard around my world.

"It's the police," said Randy as he opened the door.

"Everyone freeze!" said one police officer. "Don't move!"

I had already removed myself from the table when I heard Randy say it was the police. Apparently they had barged in without being invited and stormed our den area, which was hidden from the front door. The guy with the pot was still sitting at the table and they rushed him right away and put him in handcuffs. I was so relieved that I wasn't holding any of the marijuana and that the police were appearing to leave us alone. They had told everyone in the house to sit against the wall and started asking who lived in the house. Andy, Randy, and I all raised our hands and they approached us all.

The officer came up to the three of us and said, "We have some paperwork for you to sign that says that the marijuana we found was not yours and then we will be out of your hair."

Right away I was eager to sign it so that they would leave the house and we would not be associated with the guy being arrested. They pulled out the paperwork and gave a pen to Andy. He signed the document and then it was handed to me. I signed the document and handed it to Randy to sign. Randy gave the document back to the police officer, and I felt a wave of relief.

"Well guys, thank you for signing this document, which is a search warrant for the rest of the house," the police officer said. "Just sit tight while we search through the house. Is there anything you think we should know about before we start making our way to the rooms?" The devil was in the details, and the details were in the unread fine print.

My heart sank into my stomach and I knew that the police had just tricked us. I was dumbfounded as to what just happened so much that I couldn't answer the officer. I think that everyone else couldn't answer either as they felt the same way. All I could do was hope that they didn't plant anything in our rooms to try and get us in trouble. As we were sitting there I could hear that they were in Andy's room. He had a marijuana plant that he was trying to grow in there which was news to both Randy and me. They called out, "Who lives in this room?" Andy got up and went in there. Shortly after he entered he was led out in handcuffs.

Just then I heard the landlord at the front door. He must have been called by the neighbors that there were some police officers at the house. He instantly spotted Randy and me and said that we were going to be evicted. He also said that he called my parents to let them know that we had to move out the next day. I couldn't believe my ears. Evicted! Where had that precious freedom gone? What sort of storm was this going to be?

As Andy was being handcuffed and led to the cars outside, I heard, "Those are my sons in there, Officer." This was our dad, and I knew right then and there that we had failed, and failed so miserably that our lives would never be the same.

I looked at the officer standing next to me and said, "Officer, that is my dad right there, so please take me to jail instead." I was more scared of having to face my parents than going to jail, but facing my parents with failure was going to be our prison.

I got up slowly and walked toward my parents. The impending doom of facing my parents was before me and there was no turning back. It's the same feeling when you reach the top of the roller coaster and you know that there is no turning back and there is only one way to go from there, and for us it was down, down a road of shame and guilt, down a hill of defeat and failure. We got in the car, and surprisingly not much was said.

"Not in my entire life did I think I would be picking you two up because you had been evicted," said my mom. "You really have screwed up now."

"I am extremely disappointed in you two. You have been evicted from the apartment, so you have no choice but to move back in with us. You will follow our rules. If we say jump, you better come back with an answer that inquires as to how high you should jump," our dad said. "You two are lucky that you didn't get arrested for just being around illegal stuff. Tomorrow we will go to the apartment and get your belongings. You really have disappointed your mom and me beyond belief."

To me, I would rather be whipped or yelled at, but to be spoken to in such defeated voices and tones of disappointment from our parents really made me realize how much we had let them down. The feeling of letting down my parents was worse than physical pain.

I sheepishly replied to their comments to us, "We will do whatever you want us to do. I know that we really messed up, and we will do whatever we can to regain your trust and fix this."

That night we went back to our room. Opening the door and walking into that room I could smell defeat and hear the words of failure bouncing off the walls. I had never in my life been so low and ashamed of my actions as I was at this point. I kept replaying the scene over and over in my head, wishing I would have done things differently. The more I played it back, the more I realized how foolish we were for walking out of our parents' house. All I knew is that we had some big time work to do in order to regain our parents' trust. That night my mom slept in our room and I could hear her crying. I too cried myself to sleep, not because of my own situation, but because of the predicament we had placed on our parents. As Alexander Pope said so eloquently,

> "A man should never be ashamed to own he has been in the wrong, which is but saying...that he is wiser today than he was yesterday."

There was no doubt that we were in the wrong, and wiser today than we were yesterday, but tomorrow would decide how wise our mistake had made us.

Chapter 11

The Prodigal Sons Face the Music

The next day we got one of the business' trucks and drove to the apartment. There were still some friends there from the prior evening. We didn't say much to them as Randy, our mom and dad, and I packed our things and loaded them into the truck. I could sense the mounting disappointment and disgust from our parents as they helped us. It was obvious from the sighs and held back tears that they couldn't believe the situation just as Randy and I couldn't believe it. It certainly made for an awkward and depressing task, but we all pushed through our emotions and disgust as we completely packed up our lives, loaded the truck and headed back to their house. The long road home was only a few blocks, ending in an emotional sinkhole.

Once we finished unpacking and settling in, the feelings of shame and failure started to wane a bit, and I became a little excited to be back home. I had nothing to worry about such as missing a certain party, or having to entertain friends, because there was going to be none of that. I knew where I would be and what I would be doing day and night, and the thought of that was somewhat calming and relieving. This was our opportunity to prove ourselves again without having to pay rent and utilities. It felt like we had been given our second chance which felt good. However, the bad feelings would come though when I would replay recent events, and that stress would return to hit me in the center of my chest knowing how much we let our parents down.

Being home and not going out with friends gave Randy and me a lot of time together to entertain ourselves. It wasn't hard for Randy to find something to do as he had his guitar to play in his free time, and indeed he would play the guitar to drown away his fears and sorrows. He was writing some really good songs at this point, and I would sit in the room as he played and just think about life.

One such song is called "Time Moves On" written November 5th, 2002, and it brings me to tears reading the lyrics.

> *I look about and all I see is pain,*
> *From a time in my life that my heart was stained.*
> *So many bad decisions were all around,*
> *My soul was lost nowhere to be found.*
> *And in the midst of memories*
> *I hear the whistle of a steady breeze*
> *To tell me to learn to live with what I have done.*
> *'Cause eventually time will move on.*
> *Ain't it funny how time just passes you by when nothing's wrong.*
> *But when you're in a struggle time seems to double and you look back and then it's gone.*
> *Did you ever want to hold time by its hands, take a breath, and move on with your life.*
> *Saw a picture of me when I was three.*
> *I seemed so happy; my heart was free.*
> *Every time I look at the smile on my face*
> *It brings me back to that special place*
> *When I had no worries on my mind.*
> *It took a second for my thoughts to unwind*
> *Just to think how long.*
> *Time had really moved on.*
> *I know, I know, I've done some things in my life that I would love to take back,*
> *But all I have to do is look forward to what the future brings with no regrets.*
> *Tomorrow the sun will rise, a new day comes for me to move on with time.*
>
> *"Time Moves On" by Randy Perrone*

With a lot of time on our hands being back at home, we started getting into our own hobbies. I would play some video games on the computer and Randy was playing more and more guitar. One day my Uncle Billy and Aunt Jane came to the house to visit my parents, and somehow we got on the subject of my uncle's closed recording studio. We had asked him what he did with the equipment, which he said was in storage. We asked him to let us borrow one of his sound boards and he quickly obliged. Now Randy and I had a project to do that included building, so we were happy to have something to keep our minds focused and off of our screw-up. After all, we had all that early carpentry experience we could put to good use now.

My brother John had moved out of our room which left his walk-in closet empty. We had a plan to convert my walk-in closet to a soundproof recording room so that we could start recording Randy's music. We removed all of my clothes and transferred them to John's closet and removed all the wire hanging racks in the closet. We had Leland, one of my dad's employees whose wife was in the flooring business, bring us some rolls of carpet padding. We stapled a layer of the carpet padding over the sheetrock. Then we bought some medium density fiberboard from the hardware store, which is used to build speaker boxes with the proper acoustic properties, and put those boards over the carpet padding. Next we went to my uncle's old recording studio and salvaged all of his soundproofing foam to staple over the fiberboard. We drilled a hole in the wall and put a PVC pipe through it so we could fish through the cables. I had a desk in the cubby of one of our dormer windows, and that is where we put the sound equipment. It took us a week or two, but it was great to have a purpose and a project to complete. We were ready to create some music.

Days turned into weeks and time had certainly moved on since our eviction. Life was starting to feel more like normal being at the house. We were recording a lot of Randy's songs and having fun in the process. We recorded "Time Moves On," and I would listen to it over and over. Every time Randy would play it I would cry by myself on the outside of the closet studio. Randy always found a way to express my feelings through his songs. This song certainly said the things that were in my mind, things that had no other outlet. I kept the feelings inside for the most part with no way to express my sorrow and guilt, but thankfully my right brain, Randy, was able to draw out those feelings in the form of a song. Even now when I listen to it, I feel the same guilt and sorrow for what we had put our parents through.

Time flew and before we knew it six months had passed. My parents had planned a trip to Europe for the family and we were excited to leave our problems back home. It felt like we were young again, and we felt like our parents were starting to trust us again.

Chapter 12

Mistakes Can Be Teachers, or Not

The weeks turned into months, and the months into a year since our eviction. We were in school but barely getting by. I had totally screwed up my first semester and part of the second semester of college both while we were living in the apartment and also shortly after returning home. I really had no desire to be there. The school was entirely too large for my comfort, and I wasn't being properly guided with my class selections. Before long I dropped some classes and only finished the semester with one passing grade out of four classes. My parents weren't too happy about those results especially because I lost my scholarship in the process. On top of doing badly in school, I was starting to stay out late with friends at bars around New Orleans. Feast's Restaurant was a big factor in our not being focused on school and being exposed again to illegal substances. One morning I was sleeping late and the door of my room burst open with my dad rushing in.

"Get up. Get up now." He screamed at me. "I am tired of this lifestyle. You cannot continue to go out all hours of the night and just waste away your money that you make."

I was falling again and my sister had found out and told my dad. I couldn't believe that again I was feeling guilty nor could I believe what I was doing.

"You're getting dressed right now and going to quit working at Feast's," he demanded.

"I can't just go in and quit, I have to give my two weeks' notice to them!" I yelled back.

"There will be no notice to them." He yelled louder, "I am bringing you there now, and you will let them know that you cannot work there anymore. There is no other way around it. You can tell him that Randy will not be working there either."

I got dressed and was rushed to his car. We raced to the restaurant and I went in to the general manager and could barely get a word out, I was crying so hard.

"My dad…my dad wants…he wants me to quit," I was sputtering to him between crying. "I can't put in….my two…weeks."

He cut me off, "Rusty, I understand what you're trying to tell me. You have a good father who cares about you. Go, don't worry about your two week notice or your shift today. You need to follow his guidance."

He knew my past and he felt that being out of the restaurant industry and away from the influence of people that tend to favor doing drugs and alcohol would be the best path to a bright future. I said my goodbyes to my friends at the restaurant and walked out not to return again for over a year. I got in the car and didn't say anything to my dad.

"You told them?" he asked.

"Yes, I told them." I tried to explain the situation but he wouldn't hear any of it.

"You and Randy are going to start working for the family business starting next week. You will be stocking supermarkets with our products." He continued, "We are also going to take you out of UNO and look for a smaller school that we think will work better for you."

He was surprisingly calm now that we had quit working at Feast's. Looking back on that event, I realized that he had truly saved us. Speaking to him later in life about that event, he said that he was tired of just letting us figure out what we wanted to do. He knew that the restaurant industry had taught us some good lessons, but also that it was giving us the wrong impression of what life is about. Apparently the restaurant industry in New Orleans is surrounded by drugs and alcohol, and he wasn't going to sit back any longer and let us soak in that environment. I found out that sometimes doing the things that are hard and uncomfortable, like forcing your adult sons to quit working in a bad environment, can pay off once the smoke has cleared. It is the persistence and the care shown that creates the building blocks for a strong life ahead. If they come at all, second chances are scarce and third chances are even rarer. Another viewpoint is that of Andrew Greeley who said,

> *"We're given second chances every day of our life. We don't usually take them, but they're there for the taking."*

I certainly wanted to take advantage of my second chance, and my opportunity to do so was when we started at a new college, Our Lady of Holy Cross College. This college was a smaller Catholic private school, classrooms sizes averaging twelve students, and was not known for its extra-curricular activities. In fact, there were none. I started the summer taking nine credits. This joined with the three credits I barely attained from my whole first year of college would only put me a semester behind. I was surprised at how much better I was doing with a smaller classroom size environment. I was getting back into the groove of being in school and wanting to achieve good grades. I did so well that summer semester that I wound up getting the highest grade point average I had ever attained in my life, a 4.0. I was back on top of the world, and this time not only was I proud of myself, but my parents would be proud and accepting of me also.

I was so confident in myself after that semester that I had a dream to follow in my sister's footsteps and become a doctor. The second semester I did very well again, except for one course, biology. For whatever reason I couldn't get into biology enough to make the required grade of a C, and so after that semester I chose to change my goals to ones that would be more attainable and more suitable for me. I chose to major in business and minor in sociology. I figured the two together would be good for my future in the family business, for which my dad required a degree.

We were working good hours as well while in school. Randy and I were really starting to get the hang of what we were doing, and we were learning a lot about the grocery business. As the weeks would pass, we could tell that our dad was really starting to see our full potential. We knew we had it the whole time, but our dad needed to see results in the form of good grades, good behavior, and also business savvy that one only gains from experience. The business savvy came from countless evenings sitting at the dinner table and talking with my dad about the work day and what we were doing. It was becoming clear to me that what we were doing in the supermarkets was foreign to what our dad was doing, which was dealing with restaurants. I could tell that the more we learned about that part of the food business, the more he began to admire our interest and drive to learn and succeed. The feeling I got from his continued approval and admiration reminded me of my adolescent days when I would get his praise for being his helper and being sincerely interested in the business. In a way it made me feel like a kid again, but with the respect of an adult.

The next semester we met a friend named Ben Nolds. He had transferred to Our Lady of Holy Cross College from Ole Miss, the University of Mississippi, where he hadn't done so well in his first year either. We started to become really good friends and he brought us to his apartment where we met his dad, Mark T. Nolds. He called him Pere, a French word for father; naturally, we had to adopt that name for him as well. It wasn't long after we met that we turned twenty-one. My whole life I had always thought the drinking age should be lower, but once I had made it to twenty-one, I had a viewpoint that was much more mature than when I was eighteen, so I was a believer then in the rationale behind the age limit. We partied together responsibly, unlike my high school years. Ben had introduced us to his whole network of friends and to his family, and we were happy to become part of his group. It felt good to have adult friends with like mindsets, and another good part of all of this was that our dad and Ben's dad started to become friends as well.

I also had become a great friend of Ben's dad such that when Ben would be out of town, I would still go over to their apartment to hang out with Pere. The man had such a great way to talk to people and give advice. One look at him and you knew that he had experienced a lot in life, and what lessons he had learned he was eager to pass on to our generation in order to help prevent us from making the same mistakes. When we were all together it was like we were all young. We taught him how to play video games, and he got such a kick out of it. He was always home because he had Hepatitis C and had received a liver transplant. The medicine he was taking qualified him as technically disabled. This meant that whenever we got off of school, we could go to the apartment to play video games or watch TV with him because he was always available.

My dad bought a camp, or summer home, in Buras, Louisiana, which is almost to the mouth of the Mississippi River. He bought it because it was close to good fishing, but also because it included some extra land. We spent a lot of time there; Ben and his dad were included. There were times that our dad wanted Pere to go down there to help him pick out a tractor or help with maintenance, and he was always willing to go. They became pretty close while Ben became really close with Randy and me. In our lives friends had always come and gone, but it seemed that this time Ben would be in our life much longer than our previous best friends had been.

Chapter 13

Spring Break

Ben came up with the idea to make a road trip during spring break, something Randy and I had never been allowed to do, nor would my parents be too keen on us going even then, though we considered ourselves adults. We came up with a story that we were going to Mississippi to go tubing down the Tchefuncta River, but instead went to Destin, Florida. We didn't even have a room booked, but we planned on sleeping in the car if necessary. We got there pretty late in the evening, after a long five-hour drive, and luckily found a hotel that had vacancies. We booked a room for the night and were excited that we had a place to stay and that we had made it to our destination our first spring break. In the morning we heard some girls' voices outside our door, so naturally we sprang up to see what all the chatter was about and saw three girls trying to fix a light bulb in their hotel room right next door. (How many girls on spring break does it take to change a light bulb? Answer: however many it takes to pair up with the number of boys surrounding the light bulb.) I offered to help the damsels in distress and changed the light bulb for them. This led to conversation and an eventual invite to hang out with them at the beach.

We managed to keep talking to the girls the whole time we were in town, and then afterwards kept in touch with them. Randy had liked one girl and I had liked another. Jailin, the girl Randy liked, was dating someone else, but Isabella, the girl I liked, was not, so right away we started long-distance relationships. About a month after talking frequently on the phone with Isabella, Randy, Ben, and I made a road trip to Atlanta. We were always excited about road trips, so naturally we were all happy just to go somewhere outside of New Orleans. Once in Atlanta, I spent most of my time with Isabella and her family while Ben and Randy went to a music festival. We made it a point to meet up with Jailin and some of her friends so that Randy had an opportunity to hang out.

In high school Randy and I didn't date all that much, so this was the first time in our lives that we both had serious relationships to fit into our schedules, requiring some juggling. Fortunately, being a long-distance relationship, I didn't have to choose too often between being with Randy and being with Isabella, other than when she was in town. Randy and Isabella were really starting to become good friends, which pleased me, but that didn't last long after Jailin started coming to New Orleans to see Randy, with Isabella along.

Jailin hadn't broken up with her boyfriend, but was showing a lot of interest in Randy. Isabella and I pressured her to break up with her boyfriend and be with Randy, but it just seemed that she wasn't making a move, even though she had expressed interest in breaking off her other relationship. One evening Randy and Jailin really started to flirt a lot and that was the beginning of Isabella intervening in Randy and Jailin's relationship. It was the start of a friendship gone sour, and I was stuck in the middle between Randy and Isabella's fighting.

Isabella would go on and on to me about Jailin and Randy being wrong for flirting as much as they did while Jailin was dating someone else. I felt the same way; Randy shouldn't be getting too comfortable with Jailin until she had in fact broken up with her boyfriend. I sometimes would say something to Randy agreeing with Isabella, but mainly I let them figure it out. However, when Jailin finally did break up with her boyfriend and made it official with Randy, Isabella continued to intervene in their relationship. A good gumbo requires the right number of cooks and the right amount of spice, and our romantic soup had a little too much of both.

Isabella and I had been dating a year when Randy and Jailin started dating, and Isabella became very jealous of their relationship being in the honeymoon stage while ours was maturing out of the honeymoon stage. She would create conflict between them which would cause a fight involving Isabella with Randy, Jailin with Isabella, and Isabella with me. Unexpected and unwanted stormy weather had invaded the scene like a hurricane over the Gulf. I couldn't understand why Isabella was so insistent on having an issue with my brother's relationship. The only logical conclusion that I had was that she was falling victim to the intricate dynamics of the life of twins. Randy and I had grown up learning how to share and respect each other, being close as twins. It seemed Isabella was almost trying to put herself in twins' shoes but did not have any experience in how to act like a twin.

Eventually the turmoil affected my relationship with Randy, and Randy didn't want to have anything to do with Isabella. He made it apparent that if she were around, he didn't want to be there. It was extremely hard for me because for the first time I had to make a tough decision: who would get my time. I just couldn't get why there had to be so much conflict with these relationships, but I guess time keeps its secrets about one's destiny.

At about the same time that Isabella was starting college at the University of Alabama, Randy chose to go back to UNO to pursue a music degree. Ben and I started to match up our school schedules so that we had the same classes at Our Lady of Holy Cross. I started to figure out the scheduling process and made sure that we had Monday and Friday off, which gave us good long weekends. During weekends when Isabella would come to town, we would hang out at Ben's apartment, and during other weekends I would go visit Isabella. We occasionally would all go to Tuscaloosa, including Randy. Ben had a girlfriend in Tuscaloosa, so it all worked out that we had female interests to see. This helped the situation with Randy and Isabella because we all had something to do, whether it was all together or with our significant others.

We were hanging out in Tuscaloosa when the topic of music festivals came up. At this point in our lives, we tried to hit as many concerts as possible, but hadn't attended a good music festival other than Jazz Fest, an annual festival of Jazz music and other great music held at the Fairgrounds in New Orleans. We chose to do Bonnaroo, which is a three-day music fest in the middle of Tennessee. The accommodations were primitive camping, which was right up our alley. Isabella and Jailin didn't go to the festival, which was good because it gave Randy and me some time to enjoy each other's company and the company of friends without having our guards up around Isabella and Jailin. It turned out to be one of the best trips we took in the pursuit of music. The sweetest music is made when discord is not part of the melody.

Chapter 14

Time Out from Primitive Camping for the Ritz

We were always trying to fit as much into life in as short a time as possible, so a month later we had planned a trip with Ben and his family to Jamaica. Ben's brother, Max R. Nodes, a lawyer, explained to us that a resort he had found would provide us with our own villa with a private swimming pool, a butler, a chef, and a maid. Ben's mom was paying for the villa; all we had to do was buy plane tickets to the island. We were more than excited to be going, especially because my mom had no objections and was even paying for the plane tickets. The only tickets she could get with her rewards mileage had us arriving in Jamaica a day earlier than Ben and his family. Being that Jamaica is a third-world country, she was a little hesitant for us to go, so she paid the extra money for us to stay at the Ritz Carlton, knowing that brand of hotels would provide the best security. Obviously as young adults, we were totally fine with staying at the Ritz Carlton. Oh, the sacrifices one must make in the name of a respite from romance. We were certainly up for transitioning from primitive camping to the Ritz Carlton, no worries.

We took off from New Orleans for Jamaica by way of Miami. As soon as we landed we got a taxi to the Ritz Carlton. It wasn't a minute before we were offered marijuana by the cab driver. We had always heard that in Jamaica even the cab drivers will offer you marijuana. The temptation was there, and it was ours to resist, so we politely declined. As we pulled up to the hotel we were greeted by views that you normally see on postcards, tall palm trees swaying in the wind and beautifully groomed gardens full of color. The smell of salt mixed in the breeze, similar to back home but different. We were in paradise.

We woke up to a beautiful picture-perfect view of the beach. We had to hurry and pack so we could make it to the villa to check in. When we got there it was apparent that we were in paradise. This was truly something out of the movies: our own private pool that was near the beach, two golf carts to drive around the sprawling resort, a dining room with French doors on both sides that opened to allow a refreshing salty ocean breeze, a courtyard that led to all of our private rooms, and of course our personal butler, chef, and maid. Ah, the sacrifices we were willing to make!

We were so excited to have everyone else arrive so that we could all enjoy these luxurious accommodations. Randy and I wanted to surprise them on their arrival with a feast of food prepared by our chef. Our chef had given us a grocery list of items to buy at the local store so she could prepare a traditional Jamaican dinner of jerk chicken, beans and rice, and other local fare that was colorful and delicious. Our friends were supposed to arrive at 2:00 p.m., so Randy and I took the golf carts to the main building where they would be arriving. We found that they hadn't arrived yet, so we hung out there for about a half-hour and then chose to drive back to the house to check on the food.

Unfortunately our phones didn't work so we couldn't get in touch with our friends to find out how much longer they would be. Randy and I drove back and forth several times asking the nice ladies at the front desk if they had arrived or if they had received any calls from them. This went on for a while until Randy and I started to get anxious and silly. On one of our trips to the front desk, we started a game of bumper cars and wound up running one cart into some bushes and then into a wall. It was great to get to play again with Randy and not have to entertain girlfriends. We giggled the whole time we were racing, playing bumper cars, or just exploring along the path between our villa and front desk, which provided plenty to see and do. There were sections of beaches with barely anyone there so we were able to explore like we were pirates exploring foreign Caribbean lands.

Evening arrived and the sun was setting. Dinner was almost finished, so we made one more trip to the front to see if they had arrived. This time the lady at the front desk informed us that our friends left a message saying that they were stuck in Miami due to computer glitches with the airline. At this point we reminded each other that we were going to give Ben crap for not wanting to come with us a day earlier in favor of flying over with his family. We raced back to the villa and chowed down on the feast that was beautifully crafted for seven people. Randy and I invited all three of our house keepers, who seemed reluctant to join but did, and we all ate like kings, with bellies bulging and no room for another bite. We made the best of the situation and were able to share it with local people who usually don't get to enjoy themselves with their guests.

We woke up the next day and had a small breakfast cooked for us. When our friends arrived, we told them about the dinner we had planned for them and how we kept trying to find out information. It felt good to have them finally there, especially since Ben and Max's mom was paying for the villa.

We ragged on Ben a bit about waiting to fly. We had some laughs about it and quickly started enjoying our vacation.

Several days later we had a phone call from the front desk. The butler came by the pool and said that the phone was for Randy and me. I answered the phone.

"Hello," I answered.

"Rusty, I hate to call you with this news but Pawpaw, (our grandfather), just passed away." My mom continued, "We have you and Randy scheduled to be on a flight out first thing in the morning for the funeral."

"Oh, wow!" I replied. "How is Dad doing?"

"He is doing okay I guess, but he really wants to see you and Randy."

I told her to let Dad know how sad we were to hear the bad news. He wasn't in the mood to talk on the phone so we said our I-love-you's and hung up. I told Randy and emotion flooded his face. We told Ben, Max, and their family what happened and told them we were booked to fly out the next morning. They were trying to convince us to stay, which was pretty compelling, especially when they said we could heal better in paradise than back home. We thought about it and even mentioned it to our mom, but she quickly squashed the idea and said that we needed to come home for Dad. We didn't put up a fight and made it a point to hang out as late into the evening as we could. We made sure that evening to go out with a bang and had a great time playing games, going to the beach at night, and staying up until it was time for us to pack our bags and head to the airport. We said our goodbyes and it was back to being just Randy and myself on our journey home, except this time we were flying into a storm of sadness and pain compared with the happiness and excitement we were leaving in Jamaica. Storms come, plans change, and the river of life keeps flowing.

Chapter 15

A Funeral in New Orleans

As soon as we got back we went to see our dad at work. He was not in good shape, but he hid his emotions. The wake was that evening and the funeral was the following day. It was really weird for Randy and me to have come from a place of happiness and celebration into a place of sadness and emotional pain. It didn't take long at all for the reality to hit us that Pawpaw had died, and we too were experiencing the pain and sadness.

Our dad was to give his father's eulogy and I wanted to listen to him closely. He wasn't always open with his emotions, especially sadness, and I knew that with his father's passing away, and his writing my grandfather's eulogy, that I would get a sense of how he really felt. As he spoke, some of his words that became embedded in my memory included, "…I can remember the day my grandfather died and I looked at my dad. He was the saddest I had ever seen him and I knew right then and there that I didn't know how he felt or what he was going through. Well, now I know what he felt, because I feel it now." He cried a little bit but held it together for the most part. I looked at him and wondered the same thing he wondered at his grandfather's funeral. I certainly didn't want to think about the day our father would depart. I was never good dealing with the thought of someone close to me dying, especially Dad, and even more so Randy. Those thoughts of the day I would lose my brother always brought tears to my eyes, so I could only imagine what Dad was going through. Just in that instance a generation of the family business was no longer here. So many stories that I would never get to hear from his mouth. There would be so much history about my heritage that I would have to rely on hearing from my father and grandmother.

Shortly after my grandfather passed, the school semester started. Ben and I had started to figure out our schedule so that we would only go two days a week but still be able to register for fifteen hours a semester. We were doing great in school, even though we would go out a lot on the weekends and stay up long hours of the night playing video games. We would play a round of a game and then do some studying, then start playing again and would study between rounds. This was one of the best semesters we had so far and we did it while having fun. Life was really starting to get better for all of us, until a friend presented Randy and me with a painful dilemma, and the surge of another storm began to brew. New Orleans is a town with many storms, some of which involve the weather and some of which don't.

Chapter 16

A Memorable Christmas

That Christmas we had snowfall, which hadn't happened on Christmas Day in New Orleans in over fifty years. I remember it clearly because that morning I got a call that came from Orleans Parish Prison. It was my friend Christopher.

"Rusty, I got arrested last night and I need you to come pick me up. I had memorized my mom's credit card number and called a bail bondsman and made bail. Don't tell my parents because they wanted me to stay in jail. I can't spend Christmas Day in prison."

"What did you do this time, Christopher?" I said to him, "I cannot keep bailing you out of your problems. You have to start shaping up or you will wind up either dead or in jail for a long time."

Christopher just couldn't fight his demons. I went to pick him up from jail and he explained, "I had taken twenty Zanbars," which is slang for Xanax, an anxiety reliever that could knock a person to the ground with just one. He said, "I fell asleep at a stop sign and when I heard a knock at my car window, I started taking off. I thought that I was playing a video game but I was running from the police and it wasn't a game after all."

"Christopher, I can't believe you would take that many," Randy told him. "You really need to watch out; that isn't healthy or safe. You could have killed someone else, which would have been on Christmas Eve."

"I am dropping you off somewhere and we are going back to my parents to spend Christmas with my family," I said in a harsh tone. "You really need to get better if you want Randy and me back in your life."

Christopher was such a great friend but this was one of those instances where tough love seemed necessary to supersede enabling his addictive behaviors. When Christopher was our brother John's friend as high school sophomores, he was doing what many teenagers at that age were doing: drinking and occasionally smoking marijuana. Then as Randy and I became friends with Christopher in his junior year, I started to notice that he was going a little overboard with his drinking and also his drug choices.

Occasionally he would pick us all up to go to school, considering we lived in the same neighborhood, and it wasn't uncommon to smell marijuana in his car. In fact, if I didn't roll down the windows on occasion, I could probably have gotten high just breathing in the car. I started to really notice some problems when he would show off how much alcohol and drugs he could consume. One evening while hanging out at our house, we were in the upstairs den away from my parents and he counted out twenty Valium pills in his hand. He opened two beers and popped all of the pills at once into his mouth chasing them with the beers. Within a half hour he was passed out on the couch. Being young we didn't think about how dangerously slow his heart was beating or anything like that. All of a sudden he popped out of his semi-coma and yelled out, "Trash can, trash can!" We threw him a trash can and he threw up all that he had consumed. We all laughed about it, including Christopher, and continued to drink for the remainder of the night. There are two types of indiscretion: those that we commit, and those that we enable. Very little light passes between them.

By the time he was twenty-one years old he was already an alcoholic. One evening we met at my house to go out, and he pulled out a flask of vodka from his pocket. He opened it and turned it upside down clearing the whole thing in a couple of gulps. "Now we are ready to go out," he said. When I saw that, it became clear to me that what we used to think was fun and awesome was really something else: it was a problem. No longer impressed with his ability to hold drink or pills, I was realizing that he had an illness. I wanted to test my suspicions and told Randy that the next time we went out I would ask Christopher to drive. This I called the designated driver test for alcoholism.

"Christopher, since I am always the designated driver, I would like tonight to be able to drink and not worry about someone drunk driving us home," I said to him. "I would like you to drive for us."

"Yeah dude, no problem," he said to me without hesitation. "I don't have any money anyway."

I thought his eagerness was strange and for a moment I was second-guessing my suspicion of his being an alcoholic, which would have been a welcomed time for me to be wrong. However that evening my doubts were put to rest. I noticed that as soon as we got to the bar, he was roaming around asking friends for money so he could buy a drink. I had a drink or two and realized that I would be the one driving home because he would not be able to stop drinking. Sure enough after several hours at the bar, I confronted him about his drinking. I could tell he was wasted and I just lost it. I started yelling at him and we got escorted outside by the bouncers. I was giving him the biggest guilt trip I could, thinking that tough love would help him. He wound up getting angry back at me and started walking away into the neighborhood, which wasn't a safe spot for someone as drunk as he was to roam. Bo, Randy, and Samson ran after him and convinced him that we needed to go home. The drive home was silent. Everyone was thinking what I had already concluded to myself, that Christopher had a real problem. Christopher was an alcoholic.

Not long after this episode I made it clear to Christopher that I couldn't be around him any longer if he was going to be drinking and doing drugs. I even went so far as to talk to one of his friends, who was providing him with drugs, pleading with him not to enable Christopher any longer. That didn't work, so I had to have the tough conversation with Christopher.

"Christopher, I can't be your friend anymore." I continued, "Your drinking and drug use has gotten out of hand and I want you to choose being a friend with me and Randy, or continue drinking and using drugs."

"R-r-r-Russ," he said to me in his nervous stutter, "d-d-dude, don't make me pick. I don't want to l-l-lose you as a friend. Yo-yo-you're my friend, Russ."

I interjected, "Christopher, I just cannot see you do this to yourself anymore. You have to pick being a friend with me or not. It is just that simple. I am going to walk away now and you can let me know later today what you choose by either calling me or not. If you call, I'll know you chose our friendship, if not then I'll know how much we don't mean to you." I looked at his face and he was about to cry, and I walked away. That was really hard for me to do because I could see in his eyes that his demons were either stronger than our friendship or were stronger than his will power.

Over the years we would on occasion get a call from him, from either Miami where his parents had paid for an apartment for him or back home when he would be in and out of New Orleans. One time Randy met up with him, and in true Randy fashion he was able to talk to Christopher about his problems. He admitted to Randy that he had problems, but Christopher was unable to cope with those problems and get better. When Randy told me that, it was clear what he was running from. He was the biggest guy on the football team, with the biggest heart, but as big and as good hearted as he was, he couldn't overthrow his demons. Every book has more to its story than the cover suggests; every present has a past.

On that Christmas Eve when he asked me to bail him out of jail, I was not in any position to want to enable his behavior and have him brag about what he did to get thrown in jail. We dropped him off at a friend's house, hopeful but concerned about him. I sensed that the snow falling was a foreshadowing of something big that was about to come. I wasn't sure what it would be. We all had guessed that maybe the big snow storm meant the Saints would go to the Super Bowl or that Christopher wouldn't make it much longer. A month or two afterwards he overdosed on Zanbars and alcohol.

At his funeral I wanted to say something to his parents but couldn't muster the courage to talk to parents who had just lost their only son. I just watched as they went about, saddened by this loss, talking to all their friends and family who had come to see this poor young soul lying in a coffin. One of life's sweetest creations, someone that couldn't find it in himself to hurt a fly, was lying there as the world's hopes and dreams for him came to an abrupt stop.

Randy always found a way to write about his feelings, and long after Christopher's funeral I listened to a song he had written and put two and two together and realized that the song was about Christopher. The last verse said it all:

> *"Today's pain is tomorrow's memory, I look around all around and all I see is faces, spaceless minds trying to go back in time... I have got to go where my thoughts can run free. And get away from all of these things deep inside, that are killing me. And there is no lower that he can go, all of his tears fall down like rain. With every drop that he drinks it*

seems to numb, to numb his pain. And there is no more low that he can go, and when I look he is there, but is he really, really there?"

What took Christopher's life? Did he overdose accidentally or purposely? Regardless of the answer, the truth is that Christopher couldn't overcome his demons, and all of us suffer now because of this. May the lessons he taught bring us into the light so he need not have died in vain. Little did we know that after the snow storm change would come to his family's life, and one of the biggest life-changing events in the city's history would come to New Orleans. New Orleans is a town of many storms, some of which do indeed involve the weather.

Chapter 17

Hurricane Katrina

A couple of weeks before my second year of college was to start, I got a phone call from a friend of mine named Henry, who had moved to San Francisco for the summer. He was going to be heading back to New Orleans in a week and wanted to know if I wanted to fly out there and drive back with him. I had started saving some money working for the family selling to supermarkets, so I figured it would be a great opportunity to visit California, which I hadn't seen yet. There was only one extra seat in Henry's car available and Randy didn't want to go, so I committed and bought my one way ticket. I was excited for numerous reasons, two of which were that I love to fly in airplanes, and that I was excited to see California. As we approached San Francisco flying over the bay the view was spectacular. We passed over several long bridges, and the size of the bay resembled Lake Pontchartrain. The landing was the best part because the approach was right over the water until the last minute. Suddenly there was land and my heart was able to settle down. Randy would have loved it. Another friend, Snow, who was living there as well, picked me up, and we met Henry and headed to Santa Rosa, which was on the other side of the Golden Gate Bridge. By this time it was dark and foggy. Fog is a common occurrence in the summer time there, so I was a little bummed that I couldn't see much. What I did see of the bridge was amazing. As we were driving, the main cables appeared right next to the roadway, and I was just amazed at how big they were before they sneaked back into the fog and disappeared, like huge arms reaching out of the sky to hold us up.

The next day we went to some wineries to sample some Napa Valley wine. By 10:00 a.m. we were feeling pretty good and decided to get an early lunch. As I was sitting outside, I just looked at the trees blowing in the wind, and knew right then and there why people flock to this place. The weather is amazing that time of year, especially compared to a New Orleans August which can be like living in a sauna. Going to the coast was a great experience. It was the first time that I had seen the Pacific Ocean. This was the point when I started my tradition of throwing a rock in whatever body of water I might visit. This way I could tell my future children that Daddy had been there and thrown a rock in the water. Kind of silly some may say, but for me it's a neat tradition, a way of making my mark on a new place without leaving a trace.

  That evening Henry decided that he wanted to leave a day early to head back to New Orleans. I was kind of bummed but just took the attitude that I always take: go with the flow, and make the best of what you have. So we packed the two-seater Ford Ranger with all of his belongings, my luggage, and a box of wine we purchased the previous day. We decided that we were going to leave at midnight, so we tried to get some sleep, and before I knew it, the alarm clock was going off and we were moving. We drove down Interstate 5 in the dark, so I couldn't see any of the countryside of California. It wasn't until we cut over into the Mojave Desert that the sun started to rise. I could see silhouettes of giant wind turbines. It was so amazing to see these giants just taking advantage of what seemed to be constant wind and turning it into electricity. At this time, wind turbines weren't as well known or popular, so to see these was awe inspiring. It seemed, as we made it over the mountain, we were going downhill forever.

  As the sun came out, I could see why it felt that way. We were headed to the center of the desert. This was the first time I had seen a desert, and my mind was just going a mile a minute. I had read about deserts and how they get really hot and are extremely dry. I put my hand on the window and it already was hot, and the sun hadn't been up but for thirty minutes. We drove and drove through the desert. We would switch out every 250 miles, which seemed like it was going by very fast. We were making good time when we hit New Mexico, where the sky began to get dark, and before we knew it we were in a torrential downpour. The entire interstate traffic pulled off the side of the road, and we just sat there with hazard lights blinking trying to wait out the weather.

  Henry asked me, "Isn't this a place where tornados are pretty common?"

I said to him, "I think so but as long as we don't get hail we should be okay."

As soon as I said that, it started to hail and we both looked at each other and blurted out some expletives. We put the car in gear and putted our way down the road. What was funny is that a few seconds after we started to move on the highway, the wall of rain just stopped. We both laughed that we were so close to the edge and we were just sitting there like ducks in a pond waiting to become targets.

The drive became a blur. Everything looked the same and before we knew it the sun crept back to its hiding place. As it was getting later and later, we were getting more and more tired. It was to the point that after twenty-seven hours of nonstop driving, we decided we needed to stop in Dallas, which so happened to be where my older brother, John, was attending a gaming convention. We spent a day there before heading back to New Orleans. By the time we got back, I wanted to be as far from that car as I possibly could. We ended the trip with a good evening of playing video games and having some drinks. It turned out to be an adventure, and one that I would appreciate to this day.

I wasn't too excited to be going back to school, but I got myself psyched for a good semester and was starting to get excited about returning to college life. The first couple of days were a little rough getting back into the swing of things. In a few days I was completely adjusted when people in the classroom started talking about a storm at the southernmost tip of Florida, which was supposed to cross Florida and head toward Mobile. I just thought to myself, "Well, it looks like we may get a couple of days off if the city decides to take precautions and shut down." This was a common thing growing up, an extra holiday. Usually at such times in my life we only had close calls, and we got off of school with nothing major happening to the city. Everyone my age loved these close calls because it gave us an opportunity to have a hurricane party.

The next morning I woke up and started to get ready for school when my mom blurted out on the intercom, "Randy and Rusty, you aren't going to school today, we need to start preparing for a hurricane." I remember looking at Randy with a smile because I knew that we were going to definitely get some days off.

The first thing we did was turn on The Weather Channel. Always when a hurricane was projected to come close, The Weather Channel was all that we watched. Over and over again, we would watch it, waiting for the most recent update on the coordinates of the storm, looking for the predicted change of wind-speed and direction. Just thinking of it now gets my blood pumping with adrenaline.

As we would take breaks from preparing the outside of the house for the storm, we would again turn on The Weather Channel. As each update would come, the situation turned more serious. Katrina was becoming a serious threat to New Orleans, and evacuations were fully underway. In fact it was the first time in my life that the city implemented a mandatory evacuation. Randy and I knew that this storm was not going to be like any of the storms we had encountered previously. This would be a big deal. This was going to be the real thing. The pressure was mounting to get windows boarded up, to fuel the cars, and to get supplies from the grocery store. We finished getting the house ready. The next day we were going to go to Ben's apartment to see him and Pere, to go hang out and give them a hand if they needed it. They were going to evacuate to the Northshore of Lake Pontchartrain, which is across the twenty-four mile bridge which we call the Causeway. Up north they would still get wind and rain, but they wouldn't have to contend with any storm surge.

I will never forget talking to Pere, Ben's father, about the storm. He was always a cautious person who would look at all the possibilities and then give advice. He was, in a true sense, a wise man, to whom we listened most of the time. This time, however, we didn't take his advice. His advice would prove to be prophetic.

He said to us, "It's not the rain you have to worry about. It's the flood walls that should concern you. If those walls break, and the city floods, we are going to be in a world of trouble. It will be miserable with no air conditioning, and no way to evacuate. If I were y'all, I would head up with us where we have a generator but will not have flooding." We shrugged him off and explained that our house was higher off the ground than the levees which were built with modern day technology...and couldn't fail. That opinion proved to be flawed.

My mom was frantic, and during storms she wanted us to be close to home. As it was starting to get dark, Randy and I gave hugs to Ben and Pere. As I was walking out I saw a waterproof waist-high jumpsuit that people usually use when they go duck hunting. I looked at it and said in a joking manner, "Maybe we should borrow these." Naturally they offered them and I said, "Nah, we won't be needing those," and we walked out. We should have just accepted the loan.

As we were driving back home, the interstate was not having its normally busy traffic, but rather a frantic evacuation. Cars were lining up to get on the contraflow, in which, during an evacuation, the city will change inbound lanes to be outbound, helping with the mass exodus. I took pictures of this and just thought how people in most parts of the country have no clue what this is like and felt I needed to document it and later share it.

That Friday evening Randy was going to play a show at the Howlin' Wolf, a popular music venue in the Warehouse District of New Orleans. We had practiced together earlier in the week with me on a bass guitar, my first ever birthday present from Randy. Growing up we wouldn't tell each other happy birthday, then we started to tell each other happy birthday as a joke, but would always omit gifts because we could buy our own.

I was a little nervous about playing, but it would be a great distraction to the city's impending doom. There were many people who came to see Randy play. When we came to my song, I reluctantly walked up to the stage. I had never played any music in front of anyone other than Randy, and now I was in front of 150 people, attempting to play a song on the bass. The song went off without a hitch, and at the end I got a taste of what Randy loved so much: applause and appreciation for a talent of producing sounds with instruments. Looking back on that evening, it was a great experience with few cares in the world, not only for me and Randy, but for everyone that came out to see him play. Little did any of us know what was in store less than thirty-six hours from that night, which turned out to be the start of a completely different way of life.

Sunday, August 28, 2005, was "the calm before the storm" with the majority of the population gone and all of our preparation done, so we turned to watching The Weather Channel and visiting the levee. During one walk to the levee I looked at the sky and it was crystal clear, not a cloud in sight. I thought to myself about what it must have been like in the days before current technology was available to warn of a storm, not knowing that in less than twenty-four hours this clear sky would look as though God was unleashing another flood like the one in the Bible. It's amazing, because at this point the animals were gone. We didn't see birds flying any longer, or squirrels jumping in trees. They had taken their cover; noticing the absence of animals in the earlier days would be the only way of knowing you had a short window of time in which to prepare for a storm.

As the afternoon crept closer, so did Katrina. The outer bands of clouds had arrived and we knew that it wouldn't be too much longer before we would start to get some rain and some light winds. After we ate, Randy and I went to a neighbor's house to check on them. They were the only other people we knew who were not evacuating. As we got there, another neighbor was trying frantically to start her Jeep. We tried to jump it with our car but it wouldn't start. She explained that her husband and kids had already evacuated and that she had stayed behind to finish her work before she left. Randy, our neighbor, and I convinced her that the point of evacuation had already passed. If she were to try and evacuate now, she would be riding out the storm in her car. We convinced her to stay, and our neighbor promised to keep checking on her. I felt terrible for her because she was all alone, wanting to get out but not able.

By the time the sun was starting to go down, we were getting the occasional wind burst that would move the trees in a way that warned of nature's upcoming wrath. The sound and the look that they give is just another sensory stimulant that gets one's adrenaline going. The sky begins to talk, at first as a whisper, but eventually as a roar. We decided that we would all sleep in the den that evening since it was the sturdiest part of the house, being reinforced with steel. As we were finishing with our showers I was watching TV in our bedroom. I remember seeing the storm, in all its grandeur and its textbook perfectly formed eye, heading right for us. It was at this point that I had a moment of uneasiness, wondering if we made the right decision to stay. I quickly thought to myself, "Well, we have passed the point of evacuation. To evacuate now would be more dangerous than staying in our house."

As we walked downstairs for the night, my mom was a nervous wreck. She even at one point said that we needed to evacuate. I quickly reminded her that if we were to leave now, we would be in more danger than staying. She understood that and accepted it, but she was still not happy about being in New Orleans for the largest storm to target the city since Betsy in 1965. I suppose our mom would have made a great meteorologist or fortune teller.

My mom, dad, brothers John and Randy, and I were all sleeping in the house when we were awakened by a loud boom followed by the loss of power. It was 4:30 in the morning on Monday, August 29, 2005, and we could all tell that Katrina was getting really close. Looking out the front window, one of the few that wasn't boarded up, we could see the wind and the rain illuminated by the lightning. We were starting to hear the wind make its way through any small crack or opening in the house, which made a distinctive whistling sound. Houses become woodwind instruments under these conditions. I thought to myself right away that it was a good thing my mom had the air conditioner set as cool as it could go before the power would likely go out. And it was a given with this type of storm that we would lose power. We had a wind-up radio which would last for a minute or two when cranked for about five minutes. At first we were like Tom Sawyer wanting to paint the fence, each of us excited to wind the radio and listen to what was happening. That didn't last long, though, and it became a chore that nobody wanted to do. This was our only link to the outside world, a way to know where the eye of Katrina was going to land, how fast the winds were, and whatever else was happening that we might have needed to know.

I will never forget how eerie it was when the radio would slow down, and we could hear the sound start to fade away. Each time it would start to fade away, it was like our safety net was being ripped apart. To hear the voices of the news commentators was somewhat a relief, a way to know that the entire city hadn't succumbed to the powerful forces of Mother Nature's way to cleanse the earth. Intermittently we checked the front door window to peek out and try to get a glimpse of what was going on around us. It wasn't long before we started noticing that the water was rising in the streets. As soon as I saw this, I knew that like our location, other parts of Metairie (the only suburb of New Orleans that shares the same below sea level issues) were in a serious situation. Our street notoriously wouldn't flood unless there was so much water throughout the city that it had nowhere to go but up the side of the "bowl" of the city. Metairie, similar to New Orleans, is like a bowl. On the outskirts of the city we have Lake Pontchartrain to the north and the Mississippi River to the south. Moving inland from either body of water, the land begins to sink far below sea level, below the banks of those two bodies of water. So when water was in the street where we lived, right by the lake, then we knew that in other parts of the city there had to be even more water. It was surely a concern because the sun hadn't even come out yet, and we still had about six or seven more hours of rainy weather.

As the sun started to rise, it seemed the sunlight fueled Katrina's winds. In the back of the house we have five sets of French doors that are connected to the den. The wind was so strong that it blew the rain and plant matter against them and virtually made them opaque. We could tell, however, looking through them, that the wind was continuing to pick up. This was certainly starting to be a situation making us all uncomfortable! We huddled in the den and just listened to the wind and its destruction. Bang! We would hear every so often. One of us would say, "I wonder what that was?" We would all try to guess what it could have been. "At least it wasn't a window yet," I said after some of the bangs. Some time passed and all of a sudden we heard glass break. We knew right away that it was our house. Instantly, John, Randy, Dad and I jumped up. I was the first to run to the stairs. "It came from upstairs," I yelled out. "Get the wood, hammer, and nails, Randy! Let's move!"

We ran upstairs and went to the family room first because there is a huge bay window there facing the direction of the wind. We opened the door and saw that the window was intact. We were puzzled in a way and then snapped to it and started checking all the rooms. We split up and all went to separate rooms. I had my oldest sister's room. As soon as I tried to open the door, I couldn't push it open. I screamed out, "It's Andrea's room! I can't open the door!" Randy came up behind me and we started to push the door open. All of a sudden I let it slam shut, remembering something I had seen on TV the evening before. The news anchor said that if a window breaks, you should come to it with a sheet or bed spread so that any glass that may be flying at you gets stopped by the sheet.

I yelled, "Get a bedspread off of my bed. We can't go in there until we have the bedspread in front of us." John or Dad went to get it and I just remember being impatient because I didn't want the wind to start uplifting the roof. If wind makes it into the house through a window or door, you have to act quickly before it whips in enough to create a vacuum that pulls the roof off.

Finally they came back with the bedspread. Randy and I pushed the door open with the bedspread in front of us. Dad and John had the piece of wood and as we bum-rushed the window, they put the piece of wood against the window frame. "Nails!" I screamed out and started hammering the piece of wood to the window frame. As soon as we were done, we all let out a huge sigh of relief. I was worried that in that short amount of time the wind may have been able to create some roof integrity issues, so I took the flashlight, and Randy and I went to the attic to check the rafters to see if we could spot any weakness or flexing. As we walked up there we could hear the wind whipping around the roof. The rafters were flexing and creaking like wooden floors in an old house. The roof didn't appear to be weakened any by the wind. We quickly made our way back downstairs, and as we passed Mom, I could tell by the look on her face that she was really nervous. I sat down and we all discussed what just happened, and how impressed we all were with the speed with which we had sprung into action.

I can remember looking at my watch, and comparing it to the weather predictions for the position of the storm. I wanted the storm to be over, and it just seemed like it wasn't letting up. Listening to the radio, we weren't sure of how much damage the city had sustained, because there wasn't really anyone out surveying the damage due to strong winds. As the winds were starting to die down, we were starting to hear reports of damage. At this point there were no reports of flooding; however, some of the levees had already failed, but due to communication towers being down, word spread slowly. The water in the street seemed like it was still rising. The wind was slow enough that we were able to open our doors and venture out onto our porch. The wind would whip up every so often, reminding us how powerful Mother Nature is. Looking down the street both ways we could see that several houses not as high as ours were flooded.

We took some pictures and video of the street. At this point the water was only six inches from reaching our front door. I remember Dad saying, "Why are they not turning on the pumps? This isn't good." I could hear the stress in his voice, and this was the first time that I fully realized why adults always feared getting a storm. We always thought they were fun and gave us time off. Well, now looking all around, I could see that hurricanes bring damage in the form of water and wind. We surveyed the backyard and noticed we were missing some storm gutters and began to look around. The neighbor's house was missing its chimney, and it clicked in my head what some of those loud bangs were. Randy and I wanted to get a view of the city from the roof. We were comfortable climbing on the roof from our escape episodes of earlier years. I will never forget the view I got from up there.

There was a tall building not too far from our house that we had been able to see from our bedroom windows. This building now looked like a honeycomb, because all the windows were blown out, and we could see debris flying out of some of the windows. As I looked toward downtown, we could see a slow and steady plume of smoke that blanketed the city. Symbolically, the dark plume was the beginning of our city's darkest and most horrible days, slowly drifting over the entire culture and flavor of the city I called home. The two of us just sat up there not saying much.

"This is really bad, Randy."

"Yeah, it's going to be a while before we recover from this."

We snapped some pictures of the surroundings. We could see the water surrounding all the houses. We couldn't tell where the canal was which runs by our house and helps drain the city. As young teenagers the roof was a place where we could escape our parent's grips and just experience the silence of the night. We would watch the stars making their dance across the sky and watch the cars making their trek across the Causeway. This time, as we sat on the roof, things were different. It wasn't the good feeling that we had known. Our viewpoint and our point of view had changed.

Suddenly we heard the portable generator kick on, so Randy and I climbed down from the roof and went inside to tell everyone how bad it looked. As we got down, my parents were listening to the radio and the mayor of New Orleans was speaking. He said that there were several flood walls that had failed, and most of New Orleans and Metairie were under water or would be soon. Suddenly Mom shouted, "Get the pictures and home movies and bring them upstairs now!" In an instant we started to grab pictures off the walls, grab our home movies, and grab some water and food to bring upstairs. Once we were finished we all went to the front porch and waited for the water to rise. We made a mark on the steps where the water line was so that we could detect changes in the water level. We waited and waited and the water didn't move a bit. Dad said, "By this point, if the levee broke on our side of the canal, we would have seen the water. The levee must have broken on the New Orleans side." New Orleans is separated from Metairie only by a thirty foot wide pump drainage canal, and we soon learned that the wall on the New Orleans side had a 200-yard gaping hole, but none on the Metairie side.

Shortly after the scramble to move pictures upstairs, Dad was starting to use food we had frozen in the freezer because as soon as we were able to leave, that would all go bad. That night we ate like kings. We had steaks and potatoes, and we ate as much as we could. At this point the house was still cool from the air conditioners being set so low the day before. The sun went down, and we all walked onto the front porch before going to bed. I remember looking up at the sky and seeing more stars in the sky than I had ever seen before. The sky was so clear that we all noticed it. I asked Dad why it was so clear, and if it were because the city was without lights. He mentioned to me that it was partially because of that but mainly because Katrina had pushed away all the dense air. It is truly amazing to think about that night while I write this, especially because I write this almost to the day of the tenth anniversary of Katrina.

That evening we were listening to the radio reporting happenings at the Superdome, and what we were hearing was frightening. The tiny jail cell down in the bowels of the Dome, kept for game-day security, was filling up. A man had been caught sexually assaulting a young girl. Reports of other rapes were widespread. Three people died in the Superdome; one apparently jumped off a fifty-foot-high walkway. It was becoming total chaos and my parents decided that as soon as we had the opportunity to evacuate, we were getting out of there. We figured, being on dry land, it wouldn't be long before the chaos made it our way.

The next morning we woke up to Dad cooking eggs, bacon, toast, and grits. I remember thinking to myself how lucky we were to be able to eat so well in the aftermath. We started to listen to the radio and heard report after report of New Orleans rescue efforts and also reports of the worsening situation at the Superdome. There were reports of rape, reports of shooting at the first responders, reports of massive death, and reports of widespread flooding. At this point they had announced that over eighty percent of New Orleans was under water. This was devastating to hear. Our city was in ruins, and there was nothing we could do about it.

At this point I remembered the waist-high waders with boots that we passed on at Ben and Pere's house and wished we had grabbed them. Randy and I were itching to get out, but our mom was so nervous about the standing water that she said we couldn't go unless we had boots or a boat. Randy and I went to our garage and found four five-gallon buckets. We grabbed four broomsticks and went to the porch. We stepped in the buckets and used the broom sticks to check the ground ahead of us. We were used to New Orleans' floods, and knew one common means of death from floods in New Orleans had been wading through deep water and falling into a sewer manhole after its cover had been forced off.

     Our mom was nervous about us venturing out, but as we always have done, we calmed her and did it anyway. She asked us to go check on her mom's house which was right around the corner. As we waded to that house with the buckets, we could see that she had about two feet of water in her house. We went to the backyard to make sure that there were no broken windows and noticed that her fence was down. The neighbor behind her had a canoe that he filled with water so it wouldn't float away. We looked at each other with excitement and let out a simultaneous, "Score!" We flipped the canoe over, drained the water and hopped in. We were so proud of ourselves and were excited to paddle back to our house to show John and our parents what we had found. As they saw us coming they had the same look on their faces that they always do when Randy and I would surprise them with something. Naturally they asked us where we stole the boat, and our smart and quick response was, "We didn't steal the boat, we appropriated the boat to check on Mr. Joey (our neighbor)." John wanted to get in and take a ride with us, so we let him sit in the middle and started off toward the canal and the main road.

     When we got to the canal the current was moving rapidly. The pumps must have been turned back on because we could see water moving through rather quickly. Suddenly the canoe started to move sideways, and we were being pushed over the canal. All of our lives each of us had been scared of the canals because our mom put fear in us about them. She would say, "Now y'all need to stay away from the canals because the pumps can suck you under and you could die." So it was engraved in our minds that being over the canal was not a good thing. As brothers do, we started to get heated with each other.

     "Rusty, what are you doing!" John screamed out to me.

     "I am paddling as best as I can. Randy, what are you doing! Paddle at the same time with me!"

     He screamed back, "I am paddling up here too, you need to paddle with me."

We all were getting tense until we finally managed to take control of the canoe and get it out of the main current. We finally made it down several blocks to our neighbor's street. We floated up to their house and got out on their lawn that was high enough to be dry. We shared some stories, ensured they were in good condition, and headed back to our house.

By this point the water was draining pretty quickly because there were some spots where we were hitting the bottom. We knew that by the next day the water would be down and we would be able to check on our family's warehouse. We pulled back up to the house, and as we were about to get out we could hear a helicopter flying near us. Suddenly from behind the houses, it flew right overhead. Later after dinner we were watching TV using the generator, and we saw the footage from that helicopter and saw ourselves getting out of the canoe. The newsman stated that there weren't too many who had stayed in Metairie, but some found ways to still get around, speaking of us. We felt like hometown celebrities.

The next day we got up to see that all the water was drained from the streets. It was starting to get hot in the house, so this was a relief to see that the water was gone and we could get off our house-island. We ate breakfast and then all jumped in Dad's car to make our way to the warehouse, which was about four miles away. With the radio on, we made our way out of our neighborhood. The damage was just indescribable. Trees were uprooted everywhere, power lines were draped across the roads, power poles were down on the ground, and buildings were missing parts of their sides. We had to travel on the wrong side of the road at times to make it past obstructions. You could see paths of cars before us, so we followed the tire paths through the mud-laden roads.

As we pulled up to the warehouse, everything appeared to be intact. We got out and made our way inside. The power was out and so we went to check the coolers and see how they were holding up. It was still pretty cold in there, but we knew that there was no way the power would be back on in time to save any of our product. Our dad said, "Well grab anything you may want to take with you, because this will all be bad when we come back." We all grabbed some cheeses and some specialty meats including prosciutto and salami. It was like we were looting our own warehouse, which seemed somewhat exciting. We threw as much as we could in our ice chests and made sure the rest of the building was secure before we left. Surprisingly the building didn't sustain much damage other than some vents that were missing and some bent siding.

We headed back to the house so that we could pack our bags and make our way out of the city. There were reports that two of three major routes out of the city were closed due to the lake swallowing the bridges and damaging them. There was only one way out, and we wanted to get our things and head for the city line as quickly as we could before the chaos of New Orleans made its way to Metairie.

We finished packing our clothes and headed for our cars. We were anxious to see our sister who lived in Charlotte, NC, at the time. Randy and I drove in my car, and John drove his car, and my parents drove their car. Randy and I turned on the radio to listen to what was being reported. What we were hearing was terrible. The Mayor of New Orleans was talking about the worsening situation at the Superdome and the Convention Center. As we reached the interstate we could see the line of cars and trucks with boats on trailers heading into the city. The canal that separates Metairie and New Orleans has a bridge over it on the interstate. On the Metairie side, it was dry, but the New Orleans side lay under eight to nine feet of water. That became a launching point for all the boats that were needed to rescue people from the tops of their houses. An interstate became a boat ramp, a city became a lake, and most of her inhabitants became urban refugees.

Driving away from the city was hard for us to do because Randy and I wanted to get in there and help people, but that wasn't in my parents' plans. It was amazing to see the number of first responders making their way into the city. Then the parish president of Jefferson Parish, the Metairie parish, came on the radio. (Just for clarity, what we call parishes are known in the rest of the country as counties.) The parish president was in absolute hysterics. At this point, two days after the storm, there was no federal help in the city. We were spiraling out of control, and the United States had forgotten about us. He said on the radio in a voice that still runs chills down my spine when I recall it, "This is Aaron Broussard, President of Jefferson Parish. We are hereby seceding from the United States Government. We are no longer part of the country; your (U.S.) aid should reach us faster, but it seems you hurry to help other countries in natural disasters before you help your own country. WE NEED HELP! Why are you not helping us! WE NEED HELP!" This was the hardest thing for either of us to hear. My city, where we grew up so proudly, one with so much character and essence, had been brought to its knees. We had to beg the country, to which we pay our taxes, to come down here with the resources with which our country has been blessed and help our city. We just sat there in silence, not able to say a thing. I held back the tears at this point because I didn't want to cry in front of Randy, and I am sure he was doing the same. Before long we were out of range for the radio, and it was not easy to change the channel to pick up another news station; indeed we felt we were abandoning our broken city.

Before long our cell phones started to get service, which was a good thing because we were almost out of gas. I called my parents in another car and let them know that we were running pretty low and needed to stop at the next exit. As each exit approached, the signs on the interstate said, "No Gas;" so we kept going. My tank was getting extremely low, and it seemed at every exit we passed there was no gas. I literally had three miles left to go on my tank before we ran out, and we found one gas station in the middle of nowhere that had gas. I went to use my credit card, and because our credit cards were tied to local banks in New Orleans, and there was no power to communicate with them: they were not working. Fortunately our dad had some cash, so we were able to fill up and continue our evacuation.

We made it to Tuscaloosa, AL, which was where Randy's and my girlfriends were living at the time, so, of course, Randy and I wanted to stop there for the night. It was hard hugging my parents and seeing them continue to the interstate toward Charlotte. We had just been through an event that changed our lives, and it was weird to be separating from them. At this point the emotions were spiraling out of control, and it took every ounce of restraint to prevent the tears from rolling down my face. By the time we arrived and went our separate ways I just lost control and cried. I just kept saying, "New Orleans is gone. My city is in ruins and it probably won't be coming back." It was the first time I was able to actually collect my thoughts about what happened and think about the devastation not only to me but to every single person who lived in the Greater New Orleans area. This thing wasn't just a small tornado affecting hundreds; this thing affected everyone from just west of New Orleans all the way to Mobile, Alabama.

Randy and I were eager to get back on the road the next day to be with our family in Charlotte. Dayna was the only sibling that wouldn't be there because she was with her in-laws in Picayune, Mississippi. Again, things during the drive to Charlotte were quiet between Randy and me. When we got there, my sister greeted us with hugs and was glad that we were safe and at her house. Fortunately she had some space for all of us there. My parents naturally got the second bedroom and John, Randy, and I had the bonus room over the garage. It was like we were camping out, and we started to feel a glimmer of hope that no matter where we were, as long as we had our family, we could create home anywhere. Not all New Orleans' families were as lucky, and we knew that.

Chapter 18

Trees Down, College on Hold

Storms indelibly inscribe in our consciousness the indisputability of impermanence.

While we were in Charlotte, our dad told us to take a semester off school and find something to do in the way of work, Katrina recovery work. John was going to work for the business to help Dad, who couldn't afford at the time to employ Randy and me. We called Ben and asked him what he was planning on doing. He said he and Henry were going to go into the tree cutting business and asked us if we wanted to join them. This was good news; we wouldn't have to look hard for a job, and we would get to hang out with our friends at the same time. A couple of hours later we got a call and learned that Henry didn't want to include us in the business. We were very surprised by this, and just said to Ben, "You don't have to do the tree business with us, but be careful working with others." Randy and I felt miffed, but we were tossing around other ideas. Our dad, along with the rest of the family, was helping us with ideas. We thought about draining pools of Katrina flood waters and refilling them. This job however came with a big risk of damaging the pool if not emptied properly. Since New Orleans is below sea level, the water table is rather high, a foot or two beneath the ground surface. Once the pool water is drained out, or almost drained out, the water underneath the pool wants to push the pool upward, which can crack the cement base, which would result in a big repair bill. The other job we were contemplating was gutting flooded houses. This came with its own health hazards due to mold and other contaminants from flood waters, so that job was quickly out. We also toyed with the idea of rebuilding fences, but we lacked the skill for building fences compared to already established professional fence builders. At this point we were still undecided what we would do, so we just tried not to be stressed about the situation in New Orleans. We had an appointment with the Red Cross and with the social services in Charlotte, so we all went as a family. Being so far away from New Orleans there were fewer refugees, so we didn't have to wait as long as some people we knew in other parts of the country. Since electricity was out and we banked locally, we had no access to our money; therefore, we needed assistance, and thankfully we were able to get help. The fact that there were services for Katrina victims was heartwarming, and so many people wanted to help however they could.

Every day we were in Charlotte we would call the house to see if the answering machine picked up, which would tell us whether power had been restored. My dad had a friend who went back to Metairie and was using a generator, and he would report back to us how things were progressing. Finally one afternoon we got a call from our dad's friend letting us know that the power had been restored at our house. "Finally," I belted out. We had been away for twenty days. All I wanted to do was get back home so that I didn't feel helpless not being able to help my city to recover. We were excited to be going home, but nervous at the same time because we didn't know what to expect. We knew that our everyday way of life before the storm was gone, but just how many conveniences would be available was not known.

Coming back, it was increasingly noticeable on the interstate that we were getting closer to the city by the look of the damaged trees. Getting back to the city brought back vivid memories of the storm. The outside of the house was much the same as we had left it. It was as if time stood still in our neighborhood. Debris was still everywhere, just the same as we left it. The main streets were clear, however, so that was noticeable progress, but we knew that for the first couple of days back we were going to be cleaning up and trying to restore the house and neighborhood back to normal. Ben and Max had asked Randy and me to check on their houses a few days later. I knew that New Orleans was still draining and that parts of the city would still be under water, but we were determined to check for them. As we tried to get off the interstate at the Metairie-New Orleans line, the state police stopped us and asked us what we were doing. I told him that we were trying to go check on a friend's house, to which he sternly said the area was closed to everyone other than recovery personnel.

Being that I knew my way around New Orleans as well as I did, I knew that I would be able to get back to the neighborhood through other exits. We continued on the interstate toward downtown which was not closed off to the general public and got off at Esplanade Avenue, then proceeded back toward the parish line. We were very nervous about this because we were going into a part of the city that was closed to the public, and debris was blocking the road in several spots. It was then that we noticed the "X" on all of the houses.

Each section of the X on a house meant something to the first responders. We weren't sure exactly what they meant, but we knew that one of the numbers on one of the sections meant the number of dead bodies that had been found there. We quickly realized that the hardships we experienced throughout the storm were nothing in comparison to that of the New Orleans residents. Dealing with flood water coming so quickly, and having no dry land for miles, all the while battling the storm's winds, must have been extremely difficult. This was a sobering realization. Among the destruction, disruption, disaster, and death, there were the lucky and the unlucky, and we were among the lucky. Luck, I've heard, is where preparation and opportunity meet, but for

many there was no way to prepare, and opportunity was too busy elsewhere to notice them.

We made it to Ben's house first, which was right by the Fair Ground's racetrack. We had the key to both houses, so we opened his house and went inside. It appeared in this part of town, which is near a natural ridge, that there was "only" two feet of water inside the houses. This was disturbing for Randy and me to see because we had spent so much time in that apartment. The chairs were moved around, mold was growing on the bottoms of everything, and the air was full of an unpleasant smell we came to know as the "Katrina Smell." His upstairs was fine, however. There was no damage to the roof or any visible leaks, so we gathered some things he needed and left his house.

As we were leaving, a truck from the Army National Guard came down his street and stopped us. They obviously saw that we were locking the house so they didn't question the legitimacy of our being in the house, but they were inquiring how we were doing and if we needed anything. They were very nice and approachable, so we asked them about the Cat Lady who lived next door. They said that she stayed for the storm and wouldn't open the door for them. They would leave MRE's (Meals Ready to Eat) which were eventually provided for all New Orleanians by the US Army. These meals were appreciated as they had everything one needed for a hot meal, and came in small waterproof packages. They said that they had been checking on her every day until, after several days of checking on her with no response, they went inside the house only to find her partially decomposed and eaten body on the floor. It was certainly something that spooked Randy and me to think that she had died in a partially flooded house that was only steps away from us. To think that her beloved cats may have actually been sustained by eating her dead body's flesh was revolting.

We left Ben's house and went to Max's house, but as we got close to Max's house, we were forced to turn back because there was still enough standing water to flood our car. Being stranded in the wasteland of the Lakeview neighborhood was too risky. We knew that by tomorrow the water would be down. The next day we made our long drive from downtown to Lakeview again, and this time we were able to drive on "the neutral ground" (a local name for a road's median) for a bit and make it to Max's house. I was going to keep watch while Randy went inside the house because Lakeview seemed creepier than Mid-City, where Ben lived. Max's house had nine feet of water inside it, so opening the door was next to impossible. I left the car to help Randy open the door and peeked inside. The hair on my back stood up as I looked at the destruction. The "Katrina smell" was pervasive. The walls were spotted with mold. The floor had about three inches of mud on it, and we saw footprints in the house. We were so freaked out by this that we jumped into the car to head out. Come to find out, another one of Max's friends had gone to his house to grab some of his important belongings, so our thoughts of someone squatting in his house were dismissed. As we left I told Randy that we should have tried to move some of Max's belongings on the first floor to the second floor as he had wanted. I remember when he asked us before the storm to do that, and both Randy and I assumed that his house was high enough off the street that he should not have any problems with flooding. Sometimes we're wrong.

It wasn't long before we were in the cone of danger for yet another hurricane, Rita. The storm moved east to west along the coast of Louisiana and made landfall at the Texas-Louisiana border on September 24, 2005, as the fourth-most intense Atlantic hurricane and the most intense tropical cyclone ever observed in the Gulf of Mexico. We received tropical storm force winds from that storm which brought back memories of Katrina occurring only a month earlier on August 29. This storm put the people who had come back on a stressful edge. It seemed like we were going to be under siege on a monthly basis by Mother Nature. Hurricanes were not the school breaks and party excuses they once had been. Hurricanes are teachers and disciplinarians of a very tough old school.

Several days later, Randy and I were sitting around when he sprang up and said, "Let's just go buy a chainsaw and see if we can spot people who may need a tree cut up and brought to the curb." I was willing to join Randy to pursue this idea, and we went to buy a chainsaw at the only place that we could find open. We picked up the chainsaw in a part of town called Harahan, part of Jefferson Parish which had not sustained the degree of flooding that most of the parish had. We made it back to my parents' neighborhood and drove around for hours trying to find signs of life. We saw plenty of trees that had been knocked down by Katrina's winds, but there wasn't anyone home to ask if we could saw up the wood.

After driving for several hours, we finally found a living breathing person in front of a house struggling to clean up around his fallen tree as best he could. We stopped and asked him if he needed us to cut up his tree so he could clean his yard. To our surprise he cheerfully said yes.

"How much will you charge me?" he asked. We had no clue how much to charge, when he blurted out, "How's four hundred dollars?"

Randy and I looked at each other and quickly said, "Yeah, that sounds good."

"When can you start?"

"We can start now," we said, which surprised him.

He nodded that it was okay, and we pulled out our brand new chainsaw, which just so happened to cost us four hundred dollars. We quickly realized that there is an art to cutting trees and also that cutting trees is hard work. When we collected our money, it seemed worth it and we would have no problem doing such work after that.

We finished our first job and rushed home to tell our parents that we had made some money. They were impressed with our hustle, and as we were talking to them about it, our phone rang. It was the guy whose tree we had just cut up, and he was giving us a lead on another job. This job just so happened to be for a popular chief meteorologist in New Orleans. This was exciting for us as we had never really been around local TV anchors. After we worked for him, when we spotted him in public, we would remind him that we were the twins who cut his trees; and he would always smile big and brag about us to anyone around.

He started recommending us to some more people. Before we knew it we were in a full-fledged tree cutting operation, calling ourselves R&R Tree Services. As we were saving more money, we started to buy equipment that would ensure our safety, which made us look more and more like a professional company. Randy came up with the idea to make postcards that we could use to give quotes for cutting up fallen trees. We would put as much information on the cards as possible, like describing the trees we wanted to cut, and how we would move the tree stumps to the curb without using yard damaging backhoes or tractors. We slid these cards under the doors so that our competition wouldn't remove the cards from the mailbox to replace it with their own. The calls were steadily coming. It seemed that our bookings were always about one week ahead, so it felt great to know that jobs were lined up. There was one shop open selling equipment which quickly came to know Randy and me as regulars. It felt great to be part of something that helped the city get back on its feet, and the beautiful part for us was more money than we had ever had. At the same time, we were charging less than half of some professional companies, which meant we were saving people money. We had moved on from our childhood lemonade stand, and we were now turning lemons into lemonade, and it felt good.

Cutting trees was good work, hard work, and dangerous work at times. There were several times we had close calls of either injuring ourselves or damaging property. We were great at taking trees that had already fallen, cutting them up, and bringing them to the road for pickup, but felling trees, or cutting down a tree that is still standing, was not so much our forte.

The first time we felled a tree that was leaning significantly from the storm, we had every intention to have it fall in a spot we had designated, but the tree and the wind had other plans. Fortunately the tree didn't fall on anything. With the second tree we cut down, we had a better plan, or so we thought. We bought a 100-foot steel cable, and our intentions were to pull the tree with Randy's car in the direction we wanted it to fall. This time it was imperative to get it right because there were fences on both sides that we didn't want to damage. We tied the tree at a good height, notched the tree in the proper spot, and made the final cut. Randy and I had signals that we rehearsed: stop, go, move out of the way, all the normal signals. I gave Randy the go signal to start pulling on the tree while I cut the rest of the way. I saw the tree start to pull in his direction, so I started cutting. The tree appeared to go in the direction we wanted when suddenly I noticed Randy stopped moving.

"Go, go, go!" I yelled out to him.

"I'm stuck in a hole, I can't get out of it," he yelled.

All of a sudden, the tree started to fall back toward me. "No!" I yelled out as the tree crashed into one of the fences. Randy got out of the car and ran back to me as we both gazed at the tree lying in a place it did not belong. We both looked around to see if anyone had seen it. Who were we kidding? This was post Katrina New Orleans, and there was no one around for several blocks. At least our pride wasn't compromised with onlookers, so we hustled to Lowes, bought some fence boards, and repaired the fence like it was new. However, this was indeed post Katrina New Orleans, and the fence we destroyed had been submerged in ten feet of water two months earlier. The new boards stuck out like a sore thumb, but at least the fence was whole again. The last tree we tried to fell went about the same except the fence on which it crashed was a wrought iron fence. The tree landed perfectly on one of the spires of the fence and embedded itself in the fence to the point where we were not getting that spire out of that tree. I am ashamed to say it, but we didn't mention this to the owner of the fence and figured that since some of the other spires were missing from storm damage, this wouldn't be noticed as something we caused.

There were two things that Randy and I remembered most about cutting trees. One was to make sure, when cutting a tree down without wearing a shirt, to check that poison ivy wasn't wrapped around the tree first. We had one job on the Northshore for one of our dad's employees, and the pine tree that we cut had poison ivy all over it we didn't notice. By the time we got home to Metairie, both Randy and I were starting to break out. It spread all over and we didn't even know it because the only parts of our body that didn't have a poison ivy rash were our privates and our faces. After three trips to the hospital, and one subsequent prescription for steroids later, we were back in business again. Those days and nights seemed like some of the worst few days that I could remember in my life, at least up until that point.

The second thing about cutting trees that we remembered most was the smell of Katrina. When cutting trees that were soaked in flood waters for two months, the smell was terrible. As we would cut the tree, the sawdust would blow up in the air and we could smell the toxic soup that Katrina left behind. When we were finished cutting trees two months later, and we encountered a house that was being renovated or gutted, the smell would always spark the memories of cutting trees. To this day, whenever I walk in a house, I know right away if the studs have been properly cleaned when gutting the house. In fact, years later I walked away from a house that I was going to buy because I noticed the smell. When we checked the studs in the air return closet, we found Chinese drywall (drywall that was toxic due to sulfur), and the studs were not properly remediated for the toxic mold soup.

Buras, LA, is where our family had a "camp," or house in the country. It was two months before we were allowed to go to Buras, about the time the tree business dried up. Also known as the spot where Katrina made landfall, it was clear when we finally make it down there just how destructive she had been. The difference between Buras and New Orleans with reference to Katrina was that instead of New Orleans, where houses were swept off the foundation and moved down the street, in Buras, the houses were completely gone. For the most part there were no signs of the houses anywhere, just the slabs or the cement steps leading to the house. Fortunately for us the camp didn't get swept away, but everything around it did. It was hard finding it because every landmark we were used to seeing was gone.

We ran into one of the neighbors who told us what happened to the neighbors in front of the camp. Those neighbors had decided to stay for the storm; consequently, a mom, a daughter, and the daughter's infant rode it out in a one story house. This area received nineteen feet of water, which forced them into the attic. When the eye of the storm was over their house, they thought the storm was over, so the mom swam to a boat tied up not far away. She paddled back to get her daughter and granddaughter and by the time they got in the boat, the eye of the storm passed and they were back into hurricane force winds. The winds pushed them all the way across our property to the Mississippi River. The only thing preventing them from going into the river was the top of a tree that they floated past and grabbed. Floating over the river would have been a death sentence for them, especially if they had capsized and had to fight the mighty currents of the river. They used an on-board radio and called the Coast Guard for help. They were the first people airlifted by helicopter out of danger while the storm was still raging. Hearing this story gave us chills knowing that people we knew had come so close to being killed. We did some cleanup and salvaged as much as we could, which wasn't a lot, and then returned to New Orleans, never to go back there again. Our dad sold the camp at Buras months later, closing that family chapter.

Chapter 19

Recovering

Post Katrina New Orleans and the surrounding areas were nothing close to being the same as before the storm. Everything was different. All of our friends had moved permanently to the Northshore, land on the north side of Lake Pontchartrain. All of the creature comforts that we had taken for granted were altered, and there was nothing to do for fun. We could still go to Bourbon Street if we wanted, but that is really for tourists, not the locals, so that was out. If you wanted food, you had to make sure you went to the grocery or restaurant before 8:00 p.m. or they would be closed. Finding workers was extremely hard to do, especially when there was plenty of recovery work that paid after the storm almost double what most places were paying before the storm. In fact, the recovery work was so tempting that some of our dad's employees threatened to go find work somewhere else unless he paid them more. Unfortunately that was the worst time to muscle the business for more money because there was really no business to be had due to the dramatic population decrease and tourism hiatus. Other than working around the house or helping with the business, we would spend a lot of time on the weekends going to the Northshore to hang out with our friends. This was getting old, however, because it required crossing the Causeway, the twenty-four mile bridge across Lake Pontchartrain to the Northshore, every time we wanted to enjoy ourselves. Over time our trips to the Northshore became less, so, we found a lot of time to work on Randy's music. We were able to record a lot of Randy's solo album in the converted walk-in closet studio. These are great memories because we both had a goal: mine was to get Randy's music recorded to the best of my ability, and Randy's was to get his music on a CD which he could use to search for band members. As Mardi Gras approached, we had finished a good portion of his first solo album. Randy had put an ad on Craigslist for band members, and the first to reply was a drummer named Andy. Both Randy and I met him in Lee Circle, which is downtown, and gave him the CD. Shortly after that he called Randy, and wanted to start playing drums with Randy.

Just as Randy was starting to build his band, my life with Isabella was moving in a new direction that would help us both know if we were a good match. Isabella was planning on moving to New Orleans for the next semester so that we could be a closer couple, not a long distance couple. We realized that we couldn't know for sure if we were right for each other while we lived in two different cities. This most certainly made it harder for Randy and me because I spent a lot of time with her at her apartment. We would get together with the group of friends; otherwise, Randy kept his distance from her to avoid any major blowups. She had gotten an apartment on Magazine Street and it felt good to be in the middle of the city and to be helping to spark its rebirth.

The First Mardi Gras after the storm was an important Mardi Gras for the city, and there was obviously no way that the city was not going to celebrate Mardi Gras. We used to ride in the parade organization called Sparta in high school. It had been a couple of years since we had ridden, but we felt compelled and obligated to the city to ride in the parade that year. It was one of the most rewarding rides we ever had. Mardi Gras rides before Katrina were fun and memorable, but the first Mardi Gras after Katrina was humbling. Instead of people holding up signs to get our attention over the other signs in the area in order to be thrown prized Mardi Gras beads, the people were holding up signs thanking us for supporting Mardi Gras and not giving up on our New Orleans' traditions. Never underestimate the resilience of New Orleanians; there would be no New Orleans without it. Even if we didn't throw a single bead, every person who came to see the parades would have been happy. This was one of the ways that we could see how the city was hurting for a sense of home and normalcy. In a way it was therapy for New Orleanians and for ourselves. For us, it was definitely a reality check, as well, that the city had been knocked down hard, evidenced by the low numbers of people who came out. Tourists were hard to spot. Those attending Mardi Gras parades were just the people of New Orleans making their way back to visit the city, or they were residents permanently moving back to the city. "Fat Tuesday" had lost weight and New Orleans had become half its size, but twice as determined.

This Mardi Gras Isabella's and Randy's fighting hit an apex. We were getting off the float when we met Jailin and Isabella; both of them had to use the bathroom so we let them on the float to use the bucket we had on there for the riders to use. About an hour later, Jailin became so drunk she was all over the place. Randy and Jailin wound up going home, and the next day Randy confronted me with a suspicion that Isabella had drugged Jailin. He had a theory as to how it took place and convinced me that she had done so. I then confronted Isabella and this created the fight to end all fights. The turmoil between us all was just unbearable. We never found out if in fact she did drug Jailin, and we left it as a mystery. This incident, however, just added to my doubts about the relationship working. I asked Randy to back off so that I could find out for myself if my relationship with Isabella could work without his opinions being the reason it didn't.

A new school year had started and so our visits to the Northshore to see Ben, Pere, and Max waned; however, it wasn't as quickly apparent that Pere was starting to become ill. During one visit Randy and I noticed that Pere didn't come out of his room. We asked Ben and Max what was going on, and they told us that he was starting to have issues with his liver. Pere had a liver transplant some five years or so prior to Katrina due to contracting Hepatitis C in his younger years. Apparently because the storm had interrupted his delivery of medicines through the mail, his body was starting to reject his liver, and the hepatitis C virus was making things worse. Pere was becoming yet another victim of Katrina. I went into his room and asked how he was doing. He was lying with the windows blacked out with blankets, and he didn't sound good at all. I was concerned with this and offered to help however and whenever I could. He naturally refused help as he was an independent and humble person who didn't want to inconvenience anyone on his account. Not long after, almost knowing that his time was short on Earth, he invited Randy and me to go to lunch. It was the last time we would see him traversing the land as he always had done. One weekday while at our parents' house, Randy and I got a call from Ben saying that Pere was on his way to University Hospital in downtown New Orleans, because he was in bad shape. Randy and I rushed to the hospital to see him.

He had developed a serious infection, was bleeding profusely internally, and his kidneys were not working well. They wouldn't let us into his room for hours while they tried to stabilize him. They finally came out and gave us news that he was stable enough to receive visitors. The doctor said that he was intubated and was on drugs to keep him asleep, but encouraged us to give him support to remain strong and fight for his life. Ben, Max, and their family went into his room to see him one by one. It was my turn to go in, and I was told by the doctors to make sure I sanitized my hands to prevent any further infection. When I saw him, he was very yellow-looking, and was asleep. I talked to him and gave him words of encouragement. I told him that I would make sure that Ben was looked after by me and by Randy. I could see that his vitals were relatively stable except when I would mention Ben. I could tell that he could hear me, and how much he really wanted to make sure Ben was going to be okay. After I finished talking to him for about twenty minutes, I went back into the hallway where the others were waiting, and the doctor came out and reassured us that he was stable enough for us to get some rest at home. We went to Max's father-in-law's apartment in the French Quarter because it was close to the hospital. We all gathered in the small apartment and just talked and hoped for some good progress. We crammed about ten of us into the small apartment. Randy and I slept on the floor, while others were on sofas and in the bedrooms.

We stayed in the French Quarter for about a week. Randy made plans to go to Bonnaroo, a music fest in Tennessee, because Pere seemed to be doing much better. The day after Randy left, things turned for the worse with Pere. We got the call while we were at the apartment that he was bleeding again, and this time it was really bad. By the time we got there, the doctors thought that he would pass soon, so he let all of us in the room to try to talk to him and see if our presence would help him to pull through it. When I walked into the room, he was shaking violently, and you could see blood bags linked to his IV and his stool bag was filled with blood. This was the first time I had seen someone so close to me in a condition like this. I was shocked and couldn't say anything, when suddenly I realized I needed to say something to him. I started talking to him begging him to hang on and fight for his family and for Ben. It seemed that after all of us had been talking to him and giving him encouragement that he started to stabilize again. The doctors asked us to go to the waiting room so that the nurses could resupply the room and get him cleaned up a bit.

After a while, the doctor came in and spoke to Max and Ben. He said that Pere was not going to make it with his current liver, and that a transplant at this point was out of the question because he wouldn't survive the surgery and because of his infection. He said that he was conscious, but not sure how long he would be and that if we wanted to say anything to him, now would be the time. I wanted to make sure that all who went before me were family, and when it was my turn, I wanted to assure him that I would watch after Ben. I told him how hard this was going to be for him, but that he didn't have to worry as long as I was living. He looked at me and I could tell in his eyes that he was tired of fighting. His eyebrows lifted when I would talk of Ben and mention to him how I would watch over him. I didn't want to leave him, so I made sure to tell him how much he meant to me and to Randy, and how lucky I felt that I had gotten the opportunity to have such a great friend. He squeezed my hand tight and I could see a tear coming down from his eyes. I hugged him and left the room so that someone else would have time to visit with him.

In the waiting room, Ben and Max said that he was unconscious now and the doctor said that it wouldn't be long. They told us that we could go in there and be with him. We played his favorite music, Van Morrison, while we all gathered in the room. The lights were out and we were all huddled together. Every so often we would talk about him and the funny things he would do. When all had finished saying something, we all started to cry. The nurses would come in and explain what they were doing, letting us know that the medicine they were giving him was just to make him comfortable. I remember looking the whole time at Ben and how he was hugging his dad so tight. It broke my heart to look at him and see how sad and terrified he was. While we were all telling stories about him, I started to notice that his vitals were starting to show he was about to pass. Just when I noticed that the CD was finished playing, I looked at his vital monitor and noticed that his heart rate was at zero.

The room erupted in sorrow and crying, and at that moment I received a call from Randy. I had been keeping him updated throughout all of this, but I didn't have enough time to let him know that Pere had passed away before he called me. He said, "Russ, I feel like something bad has happened. Is Pere okay?" I told him that he literally just passed away. Randy said to me that he could feel it as he was playing his guitar, and I reminded him that we were sharing these emotions. We didn't say much after that as we both were in a sad state. Shortly after I hung up with Randy, we all left the room. While we were in the waiting room trying to discuss what we were going to do next, Ben wanted to go back and see his dad. A moment later he came back and told me that he wished he hadn't seen his dad that way, and told me that he would recommend that I not do that for any of my loved ones because now he would see his dad that way forever. We all chose to go to Ben's grandmother's house Uptown for the remainder of the evening. It was a good closing to this horrible story because we got a chance to talk about Pere's life and laugh and cry together as a family. Parting was painfully sweet sorrow. Randy wrote a song about Pere and sang it at his funeral:

> *I found a place to run away*
> *I see you have found yours too*
> *All the stars came to get you*
> *As they took you by your hands*
> *Now your Journey has begun*
> *The pain and tears are left behind*
> *Don't go without ever knowing that you have moved all of us*
> *Now we go to do what you taught*
> *To love and make a change*
> *The sky has opened up*
> *Received you with your wings*
> *We celebrate all that has been*
> *Look forward to the coming of your wind*
> *Touch us in peace as far that we reach*
> *Forever rest in your dream*
> *Listen as my song is for you, you are my song*
> *A ceremony for your final leap.*
> "Farewell" by Randy Perrone June 20, 2006

In the days following Pere's death, Randy and I spent a lot of time on the Northshore with Ben, Max, and their family helping them and ourselves with the grief of our loss. At the time Randy didn't let me or anyone know that he was writing a song for Pere, which he began at the music fest he was attending when Pere passed away. When the funeral was scheduled, he let all of us know that he had a song and wanted to play it at the funeral. We were all so happy to hear it when he played that after the funeral we all asked him to play it again at Ben's mom's house where we gathered after the ceremony. We sat under a tree in her large backyard and listened to Randy play as I just sat there looking at Randy, so impressed and proud to be his brother.

Chapter 20

When the Saints Go Marching In...Back to the Superdome

Time marched on, and so did our everyday lives. Randy and I were getting back into our routines with school, and we started to work for the family business part-time. The remainder of the summer was sad and tough but things were starting to get back to normal. One of the normalcies was the Saints football team playing in the Superdome. They were about to start the second season since the storm and the Superdome was going to be ready for our first home game. The Saints and the Superdome were symbols of New Orleans, her trauma and her tremendous tenacity. They were important to us.

The New Orleans Saints are a special team for New Orleanians in spite of being a mediocre to poor performing team, and for some reason every New Orleanian stood by their team year after year. There is no doubt in my mind that we had the most loyal and participatory fans in the entire National Football League. The season directly following Hurricane Katrina was one of those poor performing years. It was also filled with controversy with the rumors of Tom Benson, the Saints owner, moving the football team permanently to San Antonio, where he already had business interests and houses. This would be a traumatic blow to the people of New Orleans, at least to the ones who remained, so Tom Benson was not welcome by the people. He was called a traitor, turncoat, and weak among many other names.

The season started with very little fanfare. I would imagine people getting their lives back in order was a major factor in the low key start, along with the threats of the team relocating to another city, and also because all of our home games took place in San Antonio and other cities, while the Superdome was in disrepair from the storm. The season ended with a losing record of 3-13, which was something I was used to my whole life. In the off-season, Tom Benson announced that the state of Louisiana had made a deal with him and the Saints, locking them into a 20-year contract to keep them in the Superdome. Some of the conditions included remodeling the Superdome, which needed it badly now more than ever considering its deplorable condition following the storm. The Superdome became a symbol of everything that went wrong during the storm. In the off-season, the team had released all of the personnel, including coaches and players. They picked up a quarterback who was just recovering from shoulder surgery, Drew Brees. The first thing I thought was, "The Saints are at it again, getting damaged goods at a high price." They had completely renewed the team with fresh coaches and new ideas.

This off-season was more energetic than the usual off-season, and surprisingly the whole city was paying more attention than usual to what was happening. The Superdome was on track to be finished for the second game of the season, and the Saints would be playing their arch rivals, the Atlanta Falcons. The pre-season was typical for the Saints, ending the four games with a losing record of 1-3, but the city still had faith, or at least hope, in the new regime and players. The first two games of the season were played on the road. We won those two games and were heading into the first home game of the season, and the first game back in the repaired Superdome since the storm, with some strong momentum. This game was very important to me and the entire city. It felt to me like a playoff game with all the national attention being paid to the city.

Any big game like this we would watch in our dad's theater room on the big screen. Every time the commentators would mention New Orleans, chills would flow down my spine. Adrenaline was flooding the room. We could hear through the TV the fans cheering in the Superdome, and it was the loudest it had ever been as the players walked onto the field for the coin toss. The Falcons won the coin toss and would elect to receive the ball first. They had no chance to drive the ball on this first possession; moreover, the Saints players were hyped up with the fans' energy. The Saints forced a fourth down punt, a "three and out," and the Falcons proceeded to set up for the punt. They lined up and the speakers from our TV were rattling with the fans' noise. The tension from the Falcons' players was felt not only by the fans in the Superdome but also in our seats at home as well. They snapped the ball; the kicker caught it, and then, wait! Steve Gleason was closing in on him! "The punt was blocked!!!"

I screamed out as the ball went backwards toward the Atlanta end zone. "Touchdown!!!" I yelled out as a Saint landed on the football and scored our first touchdown. The roof of the Superdome seemed to move more with the fans screaming than it did from Katrina. I ran out of the room yelling to my mom's friends downstairs who were playing Bunco, "Touchdown! Touchdown! We blocked a punt. Touchdown!" They all erupted in cheers. The knocked-down city was being raised up by every fan and non-fan of the Saints in the form of celebration and screaming. It felt great that it appeared we had a team worth mentioning. We went on to win that game 23-3. I don't think any other team would have had a chance to win in the Superdome that day. It was our day as a city to show the world that there was a reason to rebuild our below-sea-level city. Our crippled city had become a force to be reckoned with, on the field and off. That season the Saints marched on to have one of the best seasons on record. We were going into the post-season. Our first game in the post-season was won against the Philadelphia Eagles in the Superdome. Our next game was going to be the biggest test in the history of the Saints franchise, the NFC Championship, which we had never won. We were to play the Chicago Bears, and the temperature was a bone-chilling below freezing with snow in the forecast. We wound up losing that game, but our spirit was not lost. We had just had the run of a lifetime, and no matter what was said, it wasn't a fluke because of Katrina. This was the real thing. People who have suffered need a chance to celebrate something, and the Saints came marching in to help New Orleans do just that. Recovery comes in many forms, and those who continue to live below sea level in spite of hurricanes and continue to support the Saints do not give up.

That evening the Saints were to fly back home, and Randy and I wanted to go greet them at the airport. When we got there, there were barricades set up like a Mardi Gras parade with thousands of New Orleanians wanting to do the same thing. We had more people there to greet our team even though they lost than most teams have when they celebrate a Super Bowl win. The city wanted to make sure that we showed these players how much they meant to us, how much we wanted them to keep trying the next year, and how much they were our voices to the rest of the world that said, "We are back. Our buildings may have been destroyed, but our spirits were not lost."

Two years later the Saints did win the Super Bowl against the Indianapolis Colts, who had a New Orleans native, Peyton Manning, as their quarterback. It was one of the most exciting times for the city, especially after such a devastating disaster. There were fireworks being popped around the city, and all the party spots were flooded with natives. Bourbon Street was as crowded as it normally gets for Mardi Gras. The parade the city threw for the Saints was attended by an estimated 800,000 people, which is pretty impressive because the entire Greater New Orleans population at that time was around 1.2 million. Nothing dries tears like a good celebration, and New Orleans invented celebration. As we say in New Orleans, "Laissez les bon temps rouler."

The Saints were always so important to the city. Our dad even made a joke not long after we won, speaking as if he were addressing his father about current events since his death. He said, "Dad, you wouldn't believe what has happened since you left us. First there was a hurricane that wiped out the city." He spoke for my grandfather and said, "Nah, I don't believe it." Dad continued the conversation with my grandfather, "Yeah and then the Saints went to the Super Bowl and won." He spoke loudly like my grandfather would and said, "Now I know you're pulling a fast one on me. That is impossible!"

Our sports team success was not the only force helping New Orleans recover from Katrina. Many famous persons came to New Orleans to be supportive including movie stars, entertainers, and performers. One was Paul Simon, a favorite of Randy's and an inspiration for his own music career. The special way in which Paul Simon supported New Orleans and inspired my brother is best illustrated by Randy's own words in a letter he wrote to Mr. Simon:

Dear Paul,

You are the most gifted songwriter in my knowledge of music's existence. You are one of my true inspirations, not just in music but in your heart as a person. I feel your feelings that you pour into your songs. I use the same platform for my music, words, and emotions.

Being a resident from New Orleans, I was deeply touched that you would come and light up our wonderful air with your music; especially after such a hardship and tragedy our city encountered. It was especially moving to me because I had been a fan of yours and had never seen you in person. My best friend introduced me to you and he is no longer with us in body. It was very uplifting and something I will never forget. This past year I saw you and Art at Hang Out Fest. I was moved and inspired!!

If time is not in your court, please skip to the next paragraph, this section is about me and my discovery into this existence. I remember my first deep memory was why was I here? Why do I look out of these eyes? I know it had to be for something. I went to a concert in the Superdome as a kid and when the band was playing and the lights shined on the crowd, I looked and saw thousands and thousands of people. I said to myself that all of these people are here to see them!! I immediately knew what I was here for and so my journey began.

I speak of things in nature, in experience, in teaching, in leading, and I use a humble pen, at the least I never stop trying. It speaks the same about my desire for a career in being a writer, musician, and inspiration for some kid to do the same, etc... I will never stop trying because I believe I was made to do it, created to move people in the positive, and teach humanity how to love, and live. "What if you could teach these people something great, and do it through music."

I am now recording my first ever album and it has been a magical experience. I am creating my dream one song at a time, each show I move in time towards it. I would love the opportunity to collaborate with you, to even play you three songs in person, to share a stage with you, to have you listen to my songs, to just shake your hand and say, "Thank you so much for being who you are, who you inspire, who you love; because that is enough to move a crowd, that's enough to help a person, a country, humanity as a whole. Thank you for creating me, as indirect it seems, when you create songs from love, you create children who spread it out for the good message you portray."

I am Italian and from New Orleans, I would love to meet you, entertain you, show you my beautiful city and see the person who writes to you. Bienvenue a la Nouvelle Orleans!!

I have attached my website and band stuff, thank you for taking your time to read this. I hope it finds you with kind eyes!

Sincerely,

Randy Perrone
www.zamaparamusic.com

P.S. The name of the band, ZamaPara, comes from the Sanskrit language and means, "Internal Quietness & Peace of the Mind."

Life is a series of storms, some larger than others, and some larger than life. It is humbling how storms that change so much can be so brief, how an eight-hour storm can alter all the years that follow. Katrina, a large storm, was one to remember, all eight hours of it; however it wouldn't be the last of my own storms. It's amazing how that eight-hour event changed life so drastically from what had come before and what would follow in so many ways.

Chapter 21

Post-Katrina Trauma

The months rolled by like a river, and life seemed to get back to normal. Randy and I found ourselves again looking for the next business opportunity. We had a sweet taste from the amount of money cutting trees generated, so we were looking for something similar in work and payout. We both enjoyed photography, and Randy had purchased a nice camera with his Katrina money, so logically we landed on starting a photography business. We purchased a professional Nikon camera, and put an ad on the internet to offer our services for free to build a portfolio. The first wedding was done during Halloween in the French Quarter, and because skull and crossbones painted fingernails weren't our idea of a good portfolio, we opted to do several more free weddings to put together a really professional-looking portfolio.

Once we had established our portfolio we created our photography company, R&R Photography. We scheduled our first paid wedding gig but had no backup equipment in the event we had an issue. We were nervous about this so I chose to go to the store quickly to buy another memory card. Good thing I did, because while I was out Randy called and said that the memory card wasn't working. I told him to do his best to stall them because I wasn't far away. He improvised and snapped pictures as though he had a card, as to not lose the confidence of our clients. "Phew. That was close," I said to myself.

Fortunately it got better and we got smarter through our professional photography occupation. We kept this project going for several years, and amassed more photography equipment in the process. We were booking weddings every weekend and making decent money at it. We even traded our services for a trip to Miami to shoot a wedding of a close friend's daughter. It was a great experience for both of us solidifying of our business partnership. We did this through our senior years in college before we would graduate and start working in the family business full time.

One evening I was heading home, and as I was crossing a major intersection that seemed to be empty, I noticed headlights directly to my left and in a split second I said to myself, "Those lights aren't supposed to be there!" I grasped my steering wheel as hard as I could then heard this loud bam and felt myself being held down by my seat belt, which prevented me from flying out of my window. Once I came to a stop in the neutral ground (the roadway median), I quickly evaluated the major parts of my body to ensure that I was still intact and not bleeding or broken, and then tried to get out of my door. It was jammed. I wanted to get out of the car as quickly as I could, fearing the car might catch on fire, so I crawled to the passenger side and exited the car practically on my hands and knees.

As soon as I got out the car someone greeted me and said, "Thank God you're alive. That guy was running red lights and we just said to each other that he is going to kill somebody, and then your car just appeared out of nowhere." I was so relieved that someone else had witnessed the accident in fear that the other driver would try to say it was my fault. "The other driver!" I said to myself, "I hope he or she is okay," and I looked toward his SUV. The front window was smashed, almost as if someone had flown into the windshield and I immediately thought someone was dead. Just then the door opened and a tall man looked at me and said, "It's okay, it's okay," and I was relieved that he was alive.

I then called my mom and told her that I had been in a terrible accident but was okay, and I needed her to come for me. When I got off the phone, the witness came back to me and asked if I knew where the other driver was. I pointed in the direction of his SUV and realized that the driver had run off. "Great! He is gone!" I blurted out. A hit and run was the last thing I needed at this time. Randy and my mom pulled up and Randy ran over to me and hugged me and said, "Russ, I am so glad you're okay. I don't know what I would have done if you had been killed." We hugged there for a minute and didn't say much. I looked at my car, and it was so mangled that I was amazed I had made it out alive, similar to the way I felt after the storm of Katrina, but not like the storms that were yet to come.

The next day I woke up in a world of pain. Fortunately it was nothing major but just soreness from the seatbelt which is what the doctor at the hospital had warned would happen. Our mom came up to me and Randy and said, "You see how life can just change in an instant. You two should not be giving each other a hard time over each other's girlfriends and enjoy the life that God has granted you."

My mom's words really got my attention, and I was starting to realize that my relationship with Randy should be respected by whomever I might choose to be my wife. I started the process of accepting that my current girlfriend wasn't going to be that person. The process was a long one, though, because I had never had the task of breaking up with someone, and the heartbreak I suspected my girlfriend would experience prevented me from acting on my feelings right away.

One of the first signs that I was getting closer was when my dad bought me a Volvo and offered to fly two people to Sweden to sign the papers and stay one night in Sweden, and I chose Randy to be the person to go with me. Naturally my girlfriend wasn't happy at the time about my choice, but I knew that this trip could be a good opportunity for Randy and me to talk about life and get back on track with our relationship. That trip was special for Randy and me because it allowed us to do just that, get back on track.

I was still working on myself to gain the courage to break up with my girlfriend, but there were other events that would keep me busy and allow me to delay the inevitable. About two years had passed since the storm, and my grandmother, Maw-maw, whose house had been damaged in the storm, was not in another house yet, nor had she started repairing her house. My dad was really pushing her to buy a newer house that had been gutted and was ready to make new again. She finally agreed to buy one and my dad submitted an offer for her. The person selling the house accepted the offer, and as my dad was going to tell my grandmother that he had bought the house, she began to get cold feet and chose to redo her house instead. To me it made sense, especially considering that she had raised her whole family in that house; therefore, her connection to that house was too great to leave, even though it was completely gutted of the original features. I don't blame her as she was so connected to her house and cherished the life she lived when there. After the storm she spent days and weeks trying to salvage letters that my grandfather, Pawpaw, had written her from Europe during World War II. With his death not long before the storm, these letters were all she had left to hang on to his memory.

Even though Dad understood why she changed her mind, he was still a little upset as he was explaining what happened at dinner that night when Randy jumped up and said, "I'll buy the house, Dad." Our dad took him up on his offer, even though Randy didn't really have the money to buy it. This was the first big endeavor for Randy that he took on his own, which made me feel left out in a way, but at the same time I realized that we were becoming adults and eventually we would have to create our own lives.

Randy jumped on repairing the house really quickly, and I tried to help him as much as I could. He and I did as much of the work ourselves as we could, including running the internet wires, speaker wires, putting in the floors, insulating the walls, putting in the cabinets, and painting the house. It seemed like it took forever to finish the house, but as soon as we did both he and I moved out of our parents' house and into a deserted neighborhood that was far from having recovered from Katrina. This was a good bonding time for Randy and me and it gave me time to find more courage to break off with Isabella, but not enough time had passed yet.

The first night was precarious because our street still didn't have street lights, and we could go thirty minutes before seeing someone or go all day without seeing the police patrolling. I came home one day from work and Randy showed me his gun. He said, "I bought a gun because of all the reports of break-ins in the neighborhood." I thought to myself, "Well I could use a gun, too, in case he isn't home and I need to use one." Randy and I were loving living in our own house in Lakeview. It was the same neighborhood where our dad had grown up. Randy's house was right next door to my parent's first house, and City Park was so close that Randy and I would ride bikes there. It was great because there were miles of golf cart paths that were overgrown but still rideable, so we would ride deep into the park, throughout the overgrown brush and around the bayous. It was exciting because we felt like kids again exploring parts of the city we had never known.

Chapter 22

Discovering Sweden, Germany, and Holland

Several months later Randy was to get a car for his upcoming graduation, and he, too, chose a Volvo in order to repeat the experience we had with my car, except this time we would make a vacation out of it, staying in Europe for fourteen days and driving Randy's car to our destinations. Randy and I invited Ben to come with us, who quickly jumped to accept the invitation and booked his tickets. It's important to note that obviously Ben had become a very close friend to both Randy and me. We were all excited about this trip and planned to visit several cities including Stockholm, Berlin, and Amsterdam.

The trip was amazing. We started out in Stockholm and hung out with some people we had met in Sweden during Randy's and my prior trip. We went to the Stockholm Zoo and learned a lot about Sweden and its unique climate and geography. Two days later we were to catch a train to Gothenburg which is where we would pick up Randy's car at the Volvo factory. Once we picked it up we hit the road to Berlin and saw some amazing sights along the way, including wind turbines, exotic cars, amazing bridges and tunnels, and then the ferry that would take us from Denmark to Germany.

When we got to the ferry, the attendant asked us if we had a reservation, and he informed us that the ferry was booked but we could wait in standby to see if a spot would open for us. There was one car in front of us and one car behind us. The ferry started to fill up when we noticed that there were two spots left on the boat and no other cars in the regular lines. This meant that the car in front of us and our car would be able to board, which was great because the next ferry would be two hours later.

It was dark when the ferry arrived in Germany, so we started our three-hour drive to Berlin. The roads were fairly empty and it was darker than we would have liked for driving on foreign roads. We were curious about the Autobahn's speed limits or lack thereof but noticed signs that appeared to suggest speed limits. We were puzzled by the different types of speed limit signs. Some were written with red letters and some were written in black letters with slashes through them. We didn't know it at the time but the slashed numbers meant that there were no more speed limits. This was okay to have found out later because it was so dark; it would have been extremely precarious being so late and so dark to drive faster than we did. It was a long drive and tiring, but Randy was able to do the whole stretch from the coast of Denmark to Berlin.

We finally made it to Berlin and went to a hostel to see if there were any openings. Unfortunately there weren't any openings that night, but there were openings the following nights that we were to be in Berlin. We booked our rooms and started to hunt for another hotel room for the night. We drove for about forty minutes and found a rundown hotel. We got a room and wanted to go back to the area of the hostel to visit a bar we had noticed on our way. We found the bar around midnight and started having some drinks. Naturally being Americans we stood out as soon as we spoke. The bartender started to talk with us and we wound up talking to the bartender and a friend of his for a while. Suddenly the bartender announced last call to everyone in the bar. We were sort of bummed that we would have to go back to our hotel. He looked over at us and said, "Last call applies to everyone in the bar except for you. If you want to stay and drink, we can enjoy more conversation."

We were ecstatic to hear that and felt obliged to stay and have drinks. We talked about everything from politics to World War II. The most interesting though was talking about World War II and how Germans viewed it. Needless to say, being in Berlin, walking on the very streets that Nazis walked, and now talking to Germans who had ancestors who had participated in the war was amazing. I was hesitant to talk about it at first because I didn't want to appear to them that we were boastful about winning, but as soon as the ice was broken we were deep into the conversation. It was great to get a perspective of a native and how he was told by his parents that the Americans were to be praised for saving Germany from Hitler. To hear that made us proud to be Americans and appreciated, which we hadn't felt until this point. To know that the people of Germany weren't all bad, and that it had been only a few who had controlled the minds of the masses through intimidation and violence was a relief. It wasn't lost on me that my grandfather fought the grandfathers of the very people drinking and having friendly conversation with us, a miracle of changing times.

Our conversation lasted so long that the sun was starting to come up. We decided to all go get some breakfast down the street, but before we left, they poured us some absinthe as a special treat. Although I was aware that some accomplished and notable persons had once partaken (Van Gogh and others), I hadn't had any before, and I was a little leery about it knowing that it may have led Van Gogh to devour the turpentine and oils used in his paintings. Once I tasted it, I knew that I wouldn't be able to finish it. I felt like I let our New Orleanian ancestors down as absinthe was very popular in the late 1800s. After our sips of absinthe and our breakfast with new friends, we needed to return to the hotel room in order to gather our belongings, a room for which we had had paid but in which we had never slept. The hotel desk attendant laughed at us as we came back to get our things. We tried to get a partial refund for not even staying in the room, but he wasn't buying our story. We gathered our things and headed back toward the hostel, hoping to be able to check into our room early. Unfortunately the room wouldn't be ready for another eight hours, so we decided to go to the park across the street to lie out in the sun and try to get some sleep.

It was funny to be outside in a foreign country sleeping in a park. We were so vulnerable all three of us sleeping there. Needless to say, I didn't sleep all that much or all that well. I remember the wind started to pick up, and I was awakened by Randy saying, "Turn the fan off! Russ, turn the fan off!" I woke up and realized that the fan he was dreaming about, and the one I was starting to dream about, was the air blowing over our heads. When I woke him to tell him there was no fan, I realized we had fallen asleep for a couple of hours. I walked over to the hostel to check on our room, and to my relief it was ready. We all gathered our things and went to the room to get some more sleep.

The rest of our time in Berlin was amazing. We met two girls; one was from Germany and the other from Poland. They became our tour guides for the two days we were there, which was great because they spoke English well, and they were really knowledgeable about the sights. We went to the Tiergarten, which was a roundabout down the main boulevard, and climbed up the monument. The monument was made of marble and there were remnants of bullets and mortar shells that had carved out craters in the marble. From the top of the monument we could see a church in the distance that still had a partially blown off bell tower. This was a photographer's paradise with all the photographic opportunities. All over Berlin were signs of the old and the new. One particular sign of the old that struck me was a sign that at one point had lights and said, "Kapitalismus zermalmt," which I was told translated to, "Capitalism Crushes." Seeing this old building that obviously hadn't been occupied since the war was eerie. Another interesting sight was to see the Berlin Wall still standing in parts of the city, and where it had been demolished, its brick pattern footprint could be seen throughout the city. Berlin was so majestic and full of history, a history we had read and heard about practically our whole lives. I was finally walking the same grounds my grandfather had walked decades ago as he helped our country defeat the Nazis.

On our last night, the girls had retired early so we decided to find another bar to have more conversation before we called it quits. We found a bar and noticed as we entered that there weren't too many men there, but the patrons were mainly women. It didn't take long to figure out that we had landed in a brothel, which wasn't too obvious from the outside, but the women who flocked to me, Randy, and Ben were giving us obvious signs that they wanted more than just a conversation. The language barrier was quickly broken when one pointed to a curtained portion of the bar and tugged on my shirt. I quickly looked at Randy and Ben and said, "Um, guys, I think we are not in a regular bar. We should probably pay our tab and get out of here before it turns bad." The bartender picked up on our mistake and smirked. He handed us the bill and pointed to the door, which we were happy to see. After this little mishap, we all decided it was probably best just to head back to the hostel and get some rest before the last leg of our trip to Amsterdam.

We were excited to be leaving for Amsterdam for two reasons: one was that we had always talked about going to Amsterdam, and the other was the ability to drive on the Autobahn. Our friends who toured us around Berlin told us about the speed limits and how they worked, so we were ready to legally go as fast as we wanted while driving across Germany to Amsterdam. All I have to say is that driving on the Autobahn was one of the most exciting experiences of my life. We didn't go past 125 miles per hour because we didn't want to redline the brand new engine, but even at 125 mph we were being passed by others as if we weren't going fast at all. One of the rare moments when I actually followed the hand placement advice of ten and two o'clock on the steering wheel was when I was going 125 mph on the Autobahn, especially when we would pass a truck and the wind turbulence from the truck would be pushing us into the guardrail. We certainly covered some miles in a short period, so getting to Amsterdam didn't take long at all. The Autobahn takes minutes off one's drive, and years off one's life.

Arriving in Amsterdam was like a dream come true. The city's look and feel reminded me of New Orleans. Everything seemed to be as it must have been 400 years earlier. The young crowd even resembled that of New Orleans. We quickly felt at home there. Our first stop was a coffee house where we saw what happens in the legal trade of marijuana. The shops had menus for different types and styles; it was truly a weird sight to see. Amsterdam is also known for its bike paths and museums among many unique things other than their coffee shops.

We rented bikes one day and really immersed ourselves in the Amsterdam culture. It was great riding around looking at all the different houses and parts of the city. We also got to experience what it was like during rush hour; however, the rush hour in Amsterdam involves bicycles instead of cars. The bike paths have traffic signals, and the amount of bike traffic left me awestruck. It wasn't long before I was wishing New Orleans were as bike friendly as Amsterdam.

Naturally the first full night we were there we wanted to see the red light district. This reminded me of Bourbon Street in so many ways, except here in windows that were lit up with red neon lights were women ready to take money from the sexually desperate. It was a sight to see, but at the same time, I was not too comfortable being there. It was certainly not something that we were interested in being around that much longer; it was enough that we could all say that at least we witnessed this well-known piece of Amsterdam.

The next day we visited one of our family company's suppliers, a company called Beemster that produces aged Gouda. Anytime we travel abroad we have always tried to visit with customers and suppliers, companies with whom we do business. The experience is just as memorable as the museums and other attractions that traveling abroad has to offer. One of the most unique things about visiting the cheese company was the fact that their grazing land for the cows is reclaimed marsh land, which is the same civil engineering practice that makes possible most of New Orleans. Having experienced Katrina and massive levee failures, it was really a good experience to see what types of systems were in place there, being that they are below sea level like us and fight flooding like we do in New Orleans.

The entire trip was a great experience for the three of us. It would be one of the last trips we would all be able to take together, and I am forever grateful that I was able to experience it. As memorable as it was to me, it was enough for Randy to write a song about it. The song is called "Driving Song":

> *Rolled out of bed, shake the night from my head*
> *Throw on my shirt and grab my shoes*
> *Fixin' up some grub, get my belly full*
> *Walk out my door into the world*
> *Sun shines, I hide my face real well*
> *Then I jump in my car and I can go anywhere I want*
>
> *Driving with the windows rolled down*
> *All the wind blowing me away*
> *With every pass and breath I take*
> *I'm so alive*
> *Miles of open road ahead*
> *Losing time I don't want to look back*
> *To see the storms I left behind*
>
> *Run my hands through my hair*
> *Wondering how I got here*
> *The past is forgotten history*
> *Feel the breeze grace my spirit's hand*
> *Pulling me to walk again*
> *Closer to seeing belief*
> *Holding nothing but this dream*

"Driving Song" by Randy Perrone

    The trip also gave me a lot of time to think about my situation with Isabella and come to the realization that I wasn't completely convinced that she was the person with whom I wanted to spend the rest of my life. When we got back to the States, it was even more apparent that I felt this way, and I am sure this is when she noticed that in me as well. I am a personality type who just wants to make sure everyone is happy around me, and by breaking my relationship with her, I would be the very reason she might be unhappy.

    It took several more months of being together before I went ahead and did it. It was crazy because one night I had a dream that I was breaking up with her. When I woke up, she had called me and said that she had a bad dream that I broke up with her. To me it was the proper premonition to what needed to be done and I went to her house to talk to her. I sat down with her and had to tell her that I had the same dream as well, and that I felt the dreams we had in common were my unconscious and her unconscious saying what needed to be said. It was the hardest thing I had to do, but when you know deep down that the right path is a separate path, there is no other way to handle it. So all that unconscious talk became very conscious after all. Our paths parted.

    The good thing through this was the support I received from Randy. He knew deep down inside that she wasn't the right person for me, and to see him happy that I wasn't going to make a mistake was all the support I needed to maintain my position. There were several weeks after the breakup that I acted out by going to bars and talking to women. I didn't have any real intentions to find another girlfriend because I knew that if I were not looking, I would be more likely to find the right one. I also realized that bars might not be the best place to look. It's hard to find water in the desert.

Chapter 23

Love: A Different Kind of Music

Randy and I were getting used to being full time employees of the business. We both started out on the ground level, even though we had already been doing that type of work our entire lives. I was producing our olive salad, grating cheese, driving trucks, and doing warehouse work. Randy was in full swing in the retail sector. Slowly but surely I started to get into restaurant sales and also retail sales. Our cylinders weren't all firing yet, but they were certainly  getting ready. Without having a girlfriend to take my time, I really started to excel in the business and Randy was feeding off of my ambitions. We took what we learned from school and started to apply it to business, going after the accounts that we already had but making them better accounts by selling more to them. We were really starting to make waves for ourselves. One evening I went to get pizza by myself at a restaurant not far from Randy's house, and as I was leaving I ran into Christine, a friend since eighth grade. She and her husband had been together for quite some time and I had always enjoyed being around them. We went to Our Lady of Holy Cross College together and I would often ask her to introduce me to her friends, but she never had any who were available, so when I mentioned that I was single again, she perked up and said that she finally had friends for me to meet. She invited me to her birthday party to be at their house in a couple of weeks and I quickly accepted the invitation. Randy and Ben came with me to the party, and we hung out there for a bit. I remember seeing a lot of her friends and she introduced me to all of them except one. I noticed a pretty girl who was still in her nursing scrubs. I was immediately drawn to her and asked Christine who she was. She said that she was in a relationship but wasn't sure she would be with the guy much longer. I asked her to introduce me, but for whatever reason she got pulled away and I was too timid to go there on my own. Randy and Ben wanted to leave to meet our friends at a bar, so I missed that opportunity to find out who she was.

A couple of weeks had gone by when I received a late call from Christine saying that Cristy, her friend I had admired at the party, wanted to go out with her and Jon, Christine's husband. It was a Thursday night and I had to work the next day, but I was ready to get out of the house to join my friends and Cristy. I went alone, and when I got there the chosen bar was pretty empty and Christine and company were nowhere to be found. I ordered some drinks and then out of the corner of my eye, I noticed the most beautiful girl in the world walking in with Christine and Jon. At that moment, I knew that tonight was going to be a good night. I bought drinks for everyone and we all sat down and talked and talked. Throughout the entire night, Cristy and I talked almost exclusively to each other. I could tell that she was special, and I even suspected that she could be that one special girl for me. We stayed out until 5:00 a.m., which was great but bad at the same time. It was great because Cristy and I had hit if off so well and I was so excited, but bad because I was supposed to be at work in two hours. We wound up going back to Christine and Jon's house and I fell asleep on the sofa while Cristy slept in the spare bedroom. I woke up at 7:00 a.m. and called my dad to tell him that I wasn't feeling well and that I wouldn't be coming into work. He was so concerned about me that he was going to send my mom over with chicken noodle soup. Lots of problems are cured by chicken noodle soup, but being late for work because of an exciting evening is not one of them. I quickly shot up from the sofa and told Christine that I had to go. I didn't even get a chance to say goodbye to Cristy, but I had already gotten her number the evening before, so I knew that I would be able to see her again soon.

Cristy and I started to see each other a lot and I was becoming more and more convinced that she was going to be the one I wanted to spend the rest of my life with. We started our relationship going out with our friends Jon and Christine, which was almost every weekend. All I could think about during the day was Cristy. I would send her text messages throughout the day and get a glow on my face when she would reply. Everyone at work could tell when I would get a message from her. Before long it came time to introduce her to my family, which was a big deal because of how close we are and how much I wanted them to accept her.

I arranged an introduction to occur at our traditional Sunday lunch. I figured that this would show her how close of a family we were and hopefully impress her that I was a family man and not someone who didn't have a good foundation. We all sat at the dining room table and the questions were being shot out to her. She feared something like this happening, being bombarded by my large family with all kinds of questions. She did great though answering pertinent questions like, "Where did you go to school?" which in New Orleans means where did you go to High School, and "How do you like being a nurse?" She became more comfortable with each question, and I became increasingly proud that she had the right answers to the questions. They instantly fell in love with her, and most importantly, Randy liked her, which felt good. When it came to relationships with girls, Randy and I were very much standoffish and watching from the outside to observe each other's girlfriends to make sure that they were right. We didn't have to say anything about approving or disapproving, it was something we could pick up from each other with just body language. With Cristy, I could see from Randy's body language that he approved.

Next came the time that I would meet her parents. I was nervous about this because they were from the Bayou area, which is outside of New Orleans in Cajun Louisiana. (The language spoken there, *cadien/Français, cadjin,* blends African, Spanish, Native American and English words. Cajuns are an ethnic group who descended from Nova Scotian exiles from Acadia in the Maritimes of Eastern Canada and who immigrated to Louisiana in the late 17th century.) I, being a city boy, admitted to some city boy prejudices, all of which were amenable to correction by getting to know Cristy's family. We first met at the Angola Prison Rodeo. This is an event that the prison holds twice a year where the prisoners partake in a rodeo of sorts, entertaining the crowd with crazy stunts and events. One of the events included four prisoners sitting at a table playing cards while wearing red. The last prisoner to remain at the table, facing an enormous bull ramming its weight at them, would win some money. This was a great way to take the edge off, because we all had something to laugh at or pay attention to other than drilling me like my family did Cristy. What better way to enjoy time with my future in-laws.

As we left, I felt that I was able to gain their trust, plus I felt that I wasn't seen only as a city boy, but also as a man who could adapt to my surroundings. I surely proved this the second time I met them. It was Easter, and Cristy's two sisters (Tricia and Maegan) were visiting her along with their significant others, Joey and Carl. Her mom, Sherrie, and her dad, Clyde, and several aunts, uncles, and cousins and I made good conversation, talking about where I was from, what school I had attended, and what I did for a living.

"Rusty, you think you can be like a Cajun?" Mr. Clyde interjected in the conversation.

"Sure, Mr. Clyde, what do you have in mind?"

"Let's go get my dug-out pirogues and take them for a dip in the bayou out back. It will only take a minute and it will give you an opportunity to see some authentic 150-year-old dug-out cypress trees that my grandfather carved."

I knew this was going to be a special treat being able to see these antique pirogues which would also give me an opportunity to show them I was not just a city boy. Cristy instantly told me that I didn't have to go, but I knew that this was my right of passage into her family, and I got up to meet her dad, Joey, and Carl at the door. We jumped into Mr. Clyde's car and went to his barn up the road to get two nice pirogues. We loaded them into the car and went to the bayou. Cristy followed and was continuously telling me that I didn't have to go. As soon as we got there Joey got into the boat like a pro, being from Vacherie, another Cajun town up the Mississippi River. When Carl boarded his pirogue, it started to wobble, and he almost went into the bayou. When I saw this I said to myself, "Oh boy, do not tip and fall into the water. That would be really bad!"

They paddled down the bayou a good bit and Mr. Clyde, Cristy, and I stood on the bank talking. The whole time, though, I was starting to get nervous about this test. I really didn't want to be the only one falling into the water, plus

I didn't have any change of clothes in the event I did. This could be really embarrassing. Joey and Carl paddled back and Carl, a bit of a teaser, started to warn me of the dangers involved. I made a smart remark back to him, and put my chin in the air with confidence. Mr. Clyde got into his pirogue first and pushed off the bank. It was my turn, and all eyes were on me. I observed Joey, Carl, and Mr. Clyde getting into their pirogues and mimicked them as best I could. I got into mine next and could feel right away how unstable it was. I slowly moved backward from the bank into the pirogue and scuttled my way to the perch of the pirogue. I paddled myself off the bank and got on the water successfully. It took me only a couple of seconds before I had the hang of it and I was off.

Both Mr. Clyde and I were down the bayou in no time when I saw an alligator right off the side of my pirogue. As I put my paddle in the water the gator submerged himself and disappeared. This was more of a reason to not go into the water: I didn't want to be eaten alive. As we were coming back I wanted to show off my skills so I let Mr. Clyde get a pretty good distance ahead of me, and then I paddled hard all the way back. By the time I came into sight, Joey, Carl, Cristy and Mr. Clyde could see me zooming back up the bayou. I yelled out to Mr. Clyde, "Now does this make me Cajun?" He laughed and said, "Yeah, I guess that makes you Cajun." After that point there was no question they were going to like me, and I was going to like them.

The weeks went by quickly and before we knew it we had been dating for over two months. Cristy was coming over to Randy's and my house a lot, and one afternoon when she was over, Randy came into the room and said to me, "You want to be in a movie?"

I looked at him and kind of laughed. "A movie? What kind of movie?"

"I was messaged on Facebook from a twin who is going to UNO Film School and somehow he found out we were twins and wants us to audition," Randy said.

Growing up, Randy and I had done many talent auditions being that we were twins, and my mom even had us join a talent agency. We had only a couple of jobs, but this one could be a really neat job. I looked over at Cristy and she seemed really interested in what it was going to be about. We set the audition date, and both Randy and I went to it. We were used to this type of audition in which several people in line waiting to go in front of the casting director would strike up conversations about what they had done so far, sizing up the competition. We were a good tag team for this type of sizing up, and as we did we started to realize that we had a good shot at it, because the people auditioning didn't have much experience.

They called us and asked us to do some lines. It had been a while since I had performed, but once we got into it, the audition flowed well. As usual, they would take a couple of days to get back with us, and after two days we got a call that they wanted us to be the twins for the main part. This was so exciting, but then I quickly realized that I would have to spend time away from Cristy doing this movie. Randy said, "Don't worry; it wouldn't be too bad; they will shoot over two weekends." He talked me into it and I was starting to get excited about it. We were given the script to read. The movie was going to be about the director and his twin brother and their different personalities. I was going to play the smart brother, who had no social skills, and Randy was going to play the smooth-talking brother who had all the social skills but no book smarts. The crazy thing is that we almost were just that; Randy was more sociable but always struggled with school, and I would become good at school but not as sociable.

The first movie shooting weekend came and it was really neat to be part of the project. We had someone who did makeup, real film equipment everywhere, food for the cast, and people running all over the set just like a real movie. We quickly got comfortable with all the crew and with our lines. It was such fun to experience other actors and to work with a director who really gave us direction. The idea that this would be forever recorded and that others would be seeing Randy and me on a big screen was exhilarating. It would be "big" as in a movie theater for one viewing. The first weekend and the work week that followed flew by quickly. The next weekend got even better than the first and we became more comfortable with our parts. At times I would get frustrated, though, because it was going over the scheduled time and I wanted to be with Cristy. Looking back on it I am glad that I did it. There were several sessions after filming that we had to attend, and one of the cool parts of doing the movie was that Adam, the director, was going to put some of Randy's music in the movie as well.

After we finished the movie, it seemed that time was moving quickly. I was spending a lot of time with Cristy, both around the city and also at Randy's house. I started to really feel that Cristy was going to be the woman I wanted to marry. Randy's and my relationship was great, but I was starting to prepare myself consciously and subconsciously for the day that my life would be devoted to a woman and not so much to Randy. Such thoughts often occurred at Tuesday night band practices. *ZamaPara*, Randy's band, would practice in the house every Tuesday night which created a hindrance for me to visit with Cristy there. I was always around when the band got together, so this presented a conundrum. Sometimes we would go out while they practiced, but most of the time we would stay in the room with the TV volume up as loud as it could go. This however didn't create a bad relationship between Cristy and Randy, which made me more and more love the thought of making a life together with Cristy as my wife. All kinds of music was being made.

Randy and Jailin were starting to have some problems in their relationship. They would be on again off again, and Jailin was acting differently, since she graduated and started working in a law firm downtown. They would break up and then get back together again. I warned him that it seemed as though she was doing to Randy what she had done to her previous boyfriend before they started dating. I was trying to convince him that she was too afraid to do the right thing when the right thing was something that was hard to do.

That year for Halloween we went to a party at my parents. Jailin was too tired and did not join us. Since we weren't too far from her apartment, Randy wanted to go and surprise her and pick her up to go out with us to the Frenchman Street Halloween block party. He called her when we got out front and said that he was outside and he wanted to come inside to get her. I could hear on the phone that she frantically said not to come in, and I saw someone looking out the front window. He slouched in his seat after failing to convince her to come out and told us to go without him. I felt so bad because I had a suspicion that she had someone in there that she didn't want Randy to see. I wanted so badly to insist that we go inside, but didn't want Cristy to be in the middle of it. We went out and had a good time, but I could tell that Randy was concerned about it the whole time.

The next morning he went over to Jailin's place to see her and talk. When he knocked on the door a guy answered and told Randy to stop bugging Jailin. He said that she felt he wouldn't leave her alone and she wanted him to go away. I happened to be at the warehouse that morning when he came in and was crying out of control. I knew he didn't want me to see him like that, but there was no one else to talk to him other than me and our dad. I convinced him that it was for the best and that we should go to City Park so he could clear his mind of it. It was in the days and weeks that followed that he wrote two of his best songs, one called "Beautiful Riddance," and the other called "Jail-in." To this day they get my blood flowing, especially when I am facing adversity like he did then. I did not know then that "Beautiful Riddance" would have special meaning down the road.

So here we are you are so ashamed
Covet you all the blame for this mess you brought to my taste
There I slipped out your window,
I watched the rain fall down right on my face
Open up the door,
Standing there with all my time wrapped inside your mind
I don't think I deserved to see what I had seen but all fell in me
As I walked away from you my friend you know that was not the way to go

I can breathe now that I'm on my feet
'Cause I walked away from the fire you've made
Then I open up and let the new breeze in
'Cause you found a place that I am not in
Welcome to the world of not being my home, being alone

So come again I don't hear anything,
you have not said a word to me
What is wrong, the cat has got your tongue
Or is it the devil of lust holding down on you keeping you from opening up the truth
Taking what you know was wrong or right
I don't know you had ever seen the sun burn for you but in me you never will
So go away from me now, take it away the blood you've shed

Do you know, do you care for anything, do you feel, is there a heart
In there, medusa shares your ground, don't think you know what it feels like

> *You know I can't take you anymore my friend*
> *I don't think you thought this through, so go away from me now*
> *Take the world that you left behind.*
>
> "Beautiful Riddance" by Randy Perrone

An intimate video of Randy playing this song can be seen here:
https://www.youtube.com/watch?v=Y9W4R-OGjtU

  Randy was crushed by this breakup, and all I could hope was that someone would come along that would erase the hurt, and when that happened he would know that all of the pain he experienced would have taught him to be more cautious about lending someone his heart.

  I felt bad with Randy being single and having gone through what he went through, especially because my relationship with Cristy was getting stronger. One day my mom called me and said that the Jewelry Show was coming to town and asked if I wanted to go with Cristy. We were already dating for a year, and I was feeling more confident about asking her to marry me because I had known from the day I met her that I wanted to be with her forever. At the show Cristy didn't want to seem like she was pushy or that she might want something too extravagant for my price range. I had an idea, based on prior observations, what she liked. We found a merchant we recognized and I saw a ring I thought she would like. Sure enough after some looking around I noticed her eyes attracted to the same ring. I didn't give her any inclination that I noticed the ring she liked, but I broke away once we started roaming around the showroom. I told Mom and Cristy that I had to go to the bathroom but ran back to the booth. With some back and forth with offers, I finally made the decision and purchased the ring. "Whoa!" That was a big step. I had the ring in my pocket for the remainder of the day and continued to act interested in looking at rings to throw them off.

  Once we got back from the show and Cristy went to her parents' home, I nervously went to Randy and showed him the ring. I could tell he was happy and sad at the same time but tried to hide his sadness. I knew what this meant and he knew what it meant. For the first time in our lives, I was going to openly devote my life to someone else, and the uncertainty of how much time he and I would have together was unavoidable. Nonetheless, he was really happy for me and asked me how I intended to propose and how the purchase went. At this point I wasn't sure exactly how I was going to propose, much less when I was going to propose, but I knew it had to be unique and memorable. Randy was good at being creative so he offered me plenty of ideas, but I wanted to make it my own, something Cristy and I wouldn't forget.

Chapter 24

Aloha: Miles to Go and Promises to Make

My brother John came into my office at work a couple of days later and asked me if Cristy and I wanted to go to Hawaii with Yvonne, John's wife, and him. I knew Hawaii would be the perfect place to propose to Cristy. I told Randy and he was all ears. Finally I had a plan and a date which wasn't that far away. I started getting nervous that I had to tell my parents and also ask Cristy's parents if I had their blessings to marry their daughter. I wanted to plan a meeting with Cristy's parents in a way that would be unique. I thought long and hard and time wasn't on my side. I wound up having to ask Cristy's dad after a Sunday lunch at her parents' house. I was able to get him outside by saying that I had a hat I wanted to give him from a recent trip to Callaway Gardens. I was so nervous as we walked out.

"Mr. Clyde. I didn't really bring you out here to give you a hat, although I have one for you."

"Really? Well then what did you want to tell me?"

"Well…" and I lost my words for a second. "Well, I would like to ask your permission to have Cristy's hand in marriage."

He stood there in silence for a moment. I started to think to myself that maybe he was going to say no. He loved to mess with me.

"I would love nothing more than to have you as a son-in-law and to marry my daughter. I want you to know that she is my little girl and I trust you with her life."

"Thank you, she means the world to me. I will love her for my whole life, and make sure she is safe with me."

Now that I had accomplished that, I could start to figure out how I was going to propose to Cristy in Hawaii. Just the fact that we would be in Hawaii should have been good enough, but I wanted to use the setting sun, with the view of the water, before just the two of us went to dinner. After all I am a New Orleanian and I am Italian! I looked at the hotel restaurant and the views were great, but I didn't want to do it at the restaurant itself. I was going to have to scope out the area when we got there to find a perfect spot. I planned the day and made dinner reservations for the third day of our trip.

Our trip was fast approaching and we were all excited to be going to Hawaii. The plan was to have Randy bring Cristy and me to the airport at 6:00 a.m. where we would meet John and Yvonne. Well the evening before we left, Randy and Ben went out to a party. They stayed out until 5:00 a.m. which meant that trying to get Randy up was a task. Several attempts to get him up were met with his agitation and lack of desire to get out of bed. I told him that I would drive his car and leave it at the airport for him to get later. Well that got him up and hit a chord with him that set him off. We argued the entire way to the airport and at the airport, and then we picked the argument back up by phone when I landed at our connecting airport in Dallas. The fight was so intense that Cristy asked John if we were going to be okay.

"They will be good. Their fights are sometimes like this. They go around and around in a circle, each trying to convince the other that his position is the right position. It's like having a fight with your own self. How do you make yourself believe that you are wrong when you think your right?" John said to Cristy. "Randy and Rusty will get over it like nothing ever happened. That is just how it works. It's not often, and it never lasts."

I finally was able to realize that we both were wrong and right. He apologized to me for making an exciting trip begin with a huge fight. I apologized to him for threatening to leave his car and assured him that I appreciated his bringing us to the airport. In a way I think that the fight had a lot to do with knowing that our relationship would be changing with Cristy and me becoming engaged. It wasn't just a trip to an airport, and it wasn't just Randy's car that would be left at the airport. It was a trip that would be the beginning of a new way of life for us both.

The trip to Hawaii surpassed expectations. It truly is paradise and we tried to enjoy every minute of it. The people were great, the weather was always perfect, and the scenery was beautiful. A sugar cane refinery on the island was burning sugar cane, which we noticed gave a more pleasant odor than what we were used to smelling back home when sugar cane is refined. In Louisiana it is somewhat of a foul smell, while in Hawaii it was a pleasant aroma that etched a sweet memory. We drove to Hana on a winding mountain road that took all day. We went to see the sunrise on top of Haleakala Volcano, and we spent a lot of time on the beaches. If you're a tourist in Hawaii, this is what you do. But I had other things to do as well.

The day I was going to propose to Cristy was a relaxing day spent at the hotel and on the beach. That evening I had John take pictures with Randy's and my professional camera using a good zoom lens from our balcony which had a great view. I took Cristy for a walk along a path that was above the beach and this is where I was going to propose with the beach behind her. I was so nervous about proposing but I knew that now was the time, and the setting was perfect for asking for her hand.

I presented her with the ring and said, "Cristy, ever since the day I met you I have always known that I wanted to be with you. Will you do me the honor and be my wife?" I was so nervous that I almost forgot to get down on one knee.

"Yes. Yes, I will be your wife," she said to me as I remembered to get down on my knee. I got back up and gave her a big kiss and we both were smiling from ear to ear. I pointed at the balcony where John and Yvonne were waving and jumping up and down with excitement. I was finally able to feel some relief and not be so nervous about the proposal, which allowed us to really enjoy the remainder of the trip. She called her mom and dad and told them, and then we both called all of our family and told them. When I called Randy I knew that he would be happy on the surface but sad underneath. The conversation wasn't long at all, about 30 seconds, as I didn't want to rub it in his face and he needed time to decipher his emotions.

The trip as a whole was a great experience and we were all very excited to get back to our families and tell them all about it. I wanted to show all the pictures to Randy and tell him all about it, especially photos of a helicopter ride as his interest in flying was as strong as mine. On our return we had a big family dinner at my parents' house and everyone celebrated our engagement. Cristy and I had already discussed who would be standing in our wedding. We would have

John and Randy as best men, Tricia and Maegan as matron and maid-of-honor, and then would have my sisters and their husbands as bridesmaids and groomsmen. All in all we would have a large bridal party with seven men and seven women. We do know how to celebrate weddings in New Orleans!

Chapter 25

Significant Others and Significant Changes

The wedding planning was in full force and Cristy did such a great job of it. My job was to plan our honeymoon and start searching for housing. During this time I wanted to make sure that Randy and I were spending time together, and it seemed that his fears of losing our closeness had waned. Work was becoming a place where Randy and I were excelling together as a team. We understood the business and were creating growth, both of which up until this point were non-existent for several reasons which included Hurricane Katrina, growing competition, and the fact that our dad was getting burnt out after running the business for thirty plus years.

One day at work, Dad came upstairs to our office and told me that one of his tenants was moving out and he was going to have to find a new tenant. He wanted to know if I could help him post an ad. I jokingly told him that we would buy the apartment and occupy one side and rent the other side out. Before I could think about what I had just said, he said, "You have a deal," and it was done. I called Cristy and told her that we had a place to live. I caught her off guard with that phone call, but she became relieved that we would actually have a place to live as a married couple.

In the next month or so we had signed the deal and had access to the apartment. Cristy was going to move in as soon as we had done some minor updates. We went to a place called The Green Project and bought some recycled paint, added some heater vent lights to the bathrooms, changed out the toilets, painted the vanity in the guest bathroom and replaced one in our bathroom, glazed the tub, and put brand new carpet in the rooms. The apartment was starting to look cozy. We put a lot of effort into the apartment to make it feel like our home. Cristy moved in about three months before the wedding and I found myself spending a lot of time there. I felt guilty doing that because I felt like I was abandoning Randy at his house. I really struggled with trying to split my time with him, and I know he was noticing it too. It was at this time when I realized that sometimes being a twin came with great sorrow, especially when you have to make that rough decision to start a life with a different kind of significant other while everything I had done before I met Cristy had been with Randy.

My struggle seemed like it was about to ease up because one evening Randy and Ben went out to eat, and Randy spotted a girl waiting on a table next to theirs. Randy was instantly drawn to this girl and gave her his number with a stroke of confidence. Mara was her name and they started to text each other not long after the restaurant encounter. When I heard this I was very happy for Randy. I hoped that this girl would be a good person for Randy. Mara had just become a presence in our lives, and I had no idea how much more of a presence she would become.

I started to have concerns when he told me that she didn't want to talk on the phone, but only text. I didn't say much, but I knew he felt my suspicions. This went on for about two weeks until he came into the room with Ben and said, "I finally talked to her on the phone, and we talked for two hours." At this point I just wanted to hear what he had to say. She was telling him all kinds of things about her life, and Randy was upset by the way she portrayed her father and his absence. I was just not getting a good feeling about the direction of this, but I wanted to stay back and not give the same grief to him that he had given to me with Isabella.

They were talking a lot and spending time with each other more often. Ben was kind of kicked to the curb by Randy because of Mara. When it came to girls, Randy and I didn't discuss much. It was our way of keeping at least that part of our lives private. One weekend Ben and I went out to get some beers and the subject of Randy and Mara came up.

"What do you think of Randy and Mara?" I said to him. "It seems they are spending a lot of time together. I guess that is good but I don't hear much about what they are doing or how she is. I have only seen her a couple of times."

"Well, I am glad you asked because I am not so sure that she is doing things that are in Randy's best interest," he said in a concerned voice. We shared some sentiments and didn't discuss them further. After we spoke I was convinced that something just wasn't right. It was almost like he had found another relationship that was just like his previous one.

Based on several things that I had uncovered, I feared that Randy was in a relationship with someone who was not right for him. I didn't know what to do or how to handle it, because I didn't want a repeat of what happened with Isabella. I went to my parents and my siblings and told them my feelings, but my parents didn't want to make a big deal of my suspicions which might cause Randy to avoid us. My siblings all were on the same page with me, but none of them wanted to step in or do something drastic that might push Randy away.

Randy was starting to get really head over heels for Mara. He wrote one of my favorite songs that showed just how much he loved the beauty of love itself.

Tell me all the secrets you never want
To share with them,
They don't ever have to know
What's underneath your eyes
Look me in my mind and tell me if
You can see me flying
'Cause I feel so light that nothing
Could keep me from trying
The night comes and we are so far away
The night comes, a candle will light our way
I will lay with you if you would want me to
Take my hand and we can walk so far away
That everyone will never know that we had ever
Touched down on the plane
And I wonder if you would stay
If we're falling down we're falling in and
I don't want to fall out of this
'Cause it's so nice to see us living just for the night
Close your eyes and lean back then jump out
So we can see where we land
The unknown is the best leap that I have ever known

So fall into me now
So fall where we are nowhere to be found
I will lay with you if you would want me to
Take my hand and we can walk so far away
That everyone will never know that we had ever
Touched down on the plane
And I wonder if you would stay with me
If you would stay with me, tonight

"Stay" by Randall Perrone

An intimate video of Randy playing this song can be seen here: *https://www.youtube.com/watch?v=GRYIu13FXyI*

One afternoon at work Randy told our dad that if his music were to take off, he was going to leave the business. Randy had previously told me this, but I could tell, when he said it, that it was his way to be able to spend all of his time with Mara and not have to worry about money. I knew what it felt like to eat, breathe, and sleep a significant other. The thought of Cristy always danced around my mind endlessly, and because Randy and I shared those types of emotions and thoughts about someone we loved, I was able to identify with his situation. Our dad was very upset over the conversation with Randy, and I felt like I was the only person who would be able to bring Randy back to reality.

Randy and I went to lunch and during lunch I brought up things of mutual interest, but had no intention of bringing up my concerns about his relationship; however, my plan to not get too deeply involved backfired, and we were in a full-fledged fight, similar to the fight before Hawaii.

The fight went round and round for hours. I kept telling him that he didn't have to focus so much on whether he would be getting out of the business. If his music took off, then great, but he couldn't plan on it happening just to be able to spend all his time with Mara and not have to worry about money. That was not the answer. She should want to be with you for who you are now, not what you can give her monetarily. The fight ended in a stalemate, which was hard for both of us because we both had our feelings concerning Mara, and unlike twins they were not identical.

It was a hard couple of weeks for Randy. I could tell that all he wanted to do was be with Mara. The problem was that sometimes I didn't get the same feeling from Mara about Randy. Nonetheless, we never spoke about Mara or his work situation again in depth like we did in this instance. He could sense my true emotions and feelings about her, and that was good enough for me to have him keep at least one toe on the ground.

Chapter 26

Wedding Bells and an Italian Honeymoon

Love comes in many forms and that shared by twins has much to teach a husband and wife.

The wedding was upon us, and all the planning Cristy and I had done was finally starting to pay off. The rehearsal dinner was a memorable event. I knew that when it came time for speeches, my family would surely try their hardest to embarrass me. I already knew that Randy would bring up our bedwetting past, which we had both embraced and made light of as adults even though it was terrifying and aggravating as children. He stood up and made a great speech, using words so eloquently and heartwarmingly, and at the same time making a good attempt to embarrass me with our stories. He raised his glass to Cristy and said, "Cristy, you are such a great person, and I am so happy that Rusty found you. I love you like a sister and I want you to know that Rusty loves you so much. Y'all make such a great pair. Please take care of him as I know that you will." His speech meant a lot to me, so much so that I started to tear up as he spoke. I looked at Cristy and she too was tearful as she understood how hard the moment was for Randy and me. I got up and walked across the room to give him a big hug, as did Cristy. After the rehearsal dinner, a bunch of us went out for some more drinks. We all had such a great time, this being one of the most joyous occasions we had experienced as family and friends. The wedding likewise would be no exception to this.

Our wedding was officiated in an historic Catholic New Orleans church not too far from the French Quarter. The church was filling with guests, and I  was with all my groomsmen trying not to show my nervousness. As the services started, Randy leaned over and said, "I hope she comes," and then leaned back. This took off some of the nervousness, being able to joke as we always had. As all of the bridesmaids walked up the aisle, I saw a silhouette of Cristy through the door windows and then they opened. She looked so beautiful in her dress and her perfect smile. I couldn't keep my eyes off her as Cristy's dad walked her down the aisle to me. As soon as we were joined hand in hand, my nervousness vanished and nothing but happiness was remaining in my being. The priest officiating our wedding was someone John, Randy, and I admired because we had been altar servers for him in grammar school. His sermon was special to me in that the message was meaningful. Also special was the fact that he knew us as children and was able to include some of our past in his sermon. It was surreal to think about being a child serving for him and now as an adult he was officiating at my marriage. The ceremony led to a reception in true New Orleans style. Our weddings, like many other traditions here, are not like weddings in the rest of the country. Our groom's cake was a Muffuletta, an Italian sandwich tradition inherited from Sicily; we had many types of delicious Italian food, a live band, and we "second lined" with the Stooges Brass Band. There is nothing like

having a brass band play the "second line," which is a New Orleans tradition where party goers wave handkerchiefs in the air while following the band as they play their instruments. The second line closes out a wedding, and I have to say that there couldn't have been a more perfect finale to our wedding.

Following the wedding, our honeymoon would soon begin. It would be the first big trip I had ever made without Randy, but only his physical presence was missing; he was never far from my mind. Our honeymoon was one out of a combined comedy, mystery, and suspense movie, filled with lost luggage, missed planes, getting lost, and being stressed by events out of our control. We started our trip after only four hours of rest and after a large family gathering with breakfast, after which we were carted away by my parents and sister, Andi, to the airport. We flew first class from Miami to Europe, which was a wedding present from my parents. We felt like Hollywood movie stars, which helped us cope with delayed flights and some upcoming unexpected adventures.

We arrived in Spain the next morning too late to make our connecting flight to Venice. First a seven-hour delay, then we were off to Venice to start our honeymoon adventures. Iberia Airlines had special plans for our bags, which didn't make our flight. Once in Italy we were off to Venice via a private water taxi, minus luggage. On arrival at our hotel, Cristy was feeling under the weather, and soon was practically under water as well. While I was out searching for food for us, my new wife took a bath, and the bath fought back, spraying water all over the place. Venice included some brief illness and plumbing issues but no luggage. Christopher Moore summed it up:

"Everything in Venice is just a little bit creepy, as much as it's beautiful."

On our last day in Venice we awoke to a flood where San Marco Square was only traversable by planks used as walkways. I have come to realize that for whatever reason I am drawn to places that are below sea level, and I have had opportunities to experience flooding in other parts of the world and see how the natives deal with rising water, storms and floods. We were however humbled by Henry James' words:

"Though there are some disagreeable things in Venice, there is nothing so disagreeable as the visitors."

We accepted a manual transmission rental car that provided some amusement on the hilly side roads of Italy. We declined the extra insurance emphatically offered, and about thirty minutes from Venice, our windshield took on a golf ball sized boulder and lost. It leapt in slow motion from the truck in front of us and took aim at the windshield, causing an artistic star about an inch and a half in diameter to form. Throughout the ride the crack in the windshield started to take on a life of its own!

Finally in Florence we found the Continentale Hotel right in front of us with the help of some Politzi, or police officers. It's amazing how mispronouncing vowels can keep two "stupid Americans" from locating a hotel right in front of them. Italian police officers can help you and humble you all at the same time.

As Cristy and I discovered Florence's wonders, including Michelangelo's David and the Cathedral of St. Mary of the Flower, one of the most beautiful churches ever built with its green and white marble, I couldn't help wishing Randy could be seeing it too. With this trip I was launching a new life, but with some cherished and familiar mental baggage. As I crossed my mental bridges, Cristy and I crossed the Ponte Vecchio, the well-known medieval closed-spandrel segmental stone arch bridge over the Arno River in Florence noted for its many ancient shops built along it.

One day we chose to visit Sienna, whose clock tower is replicated in Waterbury, CT. Siena is built on top of a mountain and surrounded by a wall that was used for defense centuries ago. The cathedral boasted white and pink marble, yet another breath-taking structure. We made our way to the famous square where once a year horse racing attracts hundreds of people. When not racing horses the town's people worship at the Basilica Cateriniana San Domenico, a church built around A.D. 1100 which houses the head of St. Catherine on display. The story is that she was beheaded and her face and head never decomposed, providing one of three miracles that a holy person must complete to become a Saint. It was amazing to see, not only because of the miracle, but also because the school I attended from kindergarten through seventh grade was named St. Catherine of Siena. They never mentioned her head in kindergarten: good judgment by the curriculum committee. All of this when shared with someone you love is so much more special than it would be otherwise.

Morning found us heading for Assisi on our way to Bari. Assisi, a town built into the mountain, has a defense wall around it much like Siena, Florence,

Venice, Milan, and other towns in Italy, remnants of the Italian city-states of the fourteenth and fifteenth centuries. Assisi was an exquisite ancient village and we lingered as long as possible. Did those walls keep them safe, or just separate?

The hotel in Bari, old and charming, was on the Adriatic Sea, and the postcard view out of our hotel window that evening overlooked a marina with beautiful sailboats all docked in a row. A pasta factory and an olive oil factory with whom our family in New Orleans had long done business awaited us in the morning. I was across the Atlantic but surrounded by family connections.

The next day, the pasta factory owner arriving at the front desk called, "Oh Mista Paronai, Mista Paronai." He was an old man waiting for us in the rain with his Mercedes to drive us to his factory, where we met his son over some espresso before we started our tour in the warehouse where all the pasta was stored, most of which was labeled for Italian customers, but some for China, America, and some even for the Italian government. We were introduced to the warehouseman as "Mista Paronai" as if they knew who we were. After thirty years of business our names on their shipping containers were remembered. I was with family!

The manufacturing portion of the plant smelled like fresh semolina and pasta. They were having some trouble with the long cuts packaging machine, which appeared to be jammed because of a power surge. We saw huge half football field length dryers, which dry the fresh pasta in twelve hours. We soon were off to see the olive oil factory. I couldn't help thinking my business partner brother should be seeing all this with me.

It seemed like an eternity before Luglio, the owner, finally arrived because he was late finding small wedding presents for us: a money clip for me and a beautiful silk scarf for Cristy. Back in Bari, Luglio in typical Italian fashion went all out. Dinner included appetizers, octopus, anchovies, fish of all types, and glorious clams on a half shell, as well as mussels, prosciutto di Parma, mozzarella di buffalo, and many more great Italian favorites. We thought we were in heaven, or maybe just back in New Orleans at Perrone and Sons. After seeing the plant, Luglio offered to lead us back to the autostrada but we declined with thanks saying, "We have a GPS." Like those hip-wader boots during Katrina, we probably should have taken that gracious offer, because two hours later on the opposite side of Italy our GPS failed.

We eventually made it back to the hotel in Bari to find the doors locked and no one there. A phone number on the door put us in touch with a nice lady saying, "Oh we were waiting for you. Give me fifteen minutes to let you in." We were the only couple staying in this hotel, a welcome sight.

Rain and a great view of the Amalfi Coast greeted us the next morning, as did delicious sights and smells of Italy. Travelers are forced to stop and enjoy a moment, which we did over and over on our honeymoon. We headed back to Salerno along the same winding road that hugged the mountains on the Mediterranean coast. We gave up on a GPS and attempted to get to the autostrada and head to Rome. I was learning how to work through obstacles, lost luggage, and just plain ole bad luck with my new wife as I would have with Randy.

En route to Rome we did attempt to view the ruins of Pompeii; however, the closest we came rumbling over cobblestone dusty roads to what should have been the ruins was a park with a "closed" sign, but no sign of any ruins. Sometimes discretion is the better part of valor, so we used some discretion, having expended all our valor, and with the help of a gas station attendant found the autostrada and proceeded toward Rome. Poor Pompeii—once again left in the dust.

We headed back toward the Rome airport where we returned the car, and much to my surprise the guy checking the car for damage didn't notice the windshield's rock artwork, a plus for us after a frustrating day. Ah, but Italians are fond of art, and the windshield wound was artistic. We got our luggage and found a taxi to go to our hotel, one with a great location, friendly staff, and a great room with a private terrace. Our navigation nightmare being over, now we could enjoy the end of our journey in Rome. We visited all of the great sights of Rome and were happy that our honeymoon had ended on such a good note. Arrivederci Roma!

This first trip without Randy was something that prepared me for the future. I felt that it brought Cristy and me closer to each other and taught me how to make it in life with Cristy as my problem-solving partner and wife. I knew there would be room in my life for both Cristy and Randy. La dolce vita.

Chapter 27

Your Eyes May Look Like Mine

Lyrics taken from Randy's song "Julien"

We were married a little over a year when one evening while I was fixing dinner, Cristy called me into the bedroom. I was washing dishes and was reluctant to stop before I finished. She called again, and this time I knew there was something up. I walked to the bedroom and didn't see her. She called again and her voice came from the bathroom. I walked in and she was holding a pregnancy test. All of a sudden I knew what was going on, and she said, "I think this thing is telling me we are pregnant." I took it and looked at it and sure enough I could tell there was a faint line on the test. "Oh boy," I thought to myself, "Ready or not, here we go." We were both excited. Our first child. That evening going to sleep I was thinking of how much I was looking forward to being a dad. I imagined if it were to be a boy I would love being able to do the things with him that my father had done with me: camping, fixing things, building things, things that a boy would want in a father. If it were to be a girl I would be the best and most supportive dad around, along with a tendency to lean toward the strict and inquisitive parent type. I imagined there might be some wishes for us to have a boy. My older brother had just had a girl. Randy was not in a position to have children as he wasn't married yet; so I was thinking, "Out of five children, it is up to the last one to carry on the family name?" Wow, this was heavy thinking! I stayed up late that night with my mind going in every direction. One of my thoughts was, "How is Randy going to take this?" I was really nervous about telling him because as kids we always talked about one day having children at the same time so that they could grow up together.

Unfortunately that wasn't in God's plan, but at the time I was still nervous about it.

Cristy had scheduled the first ultrasound a day before Randy's and my birthday. In a way I was hoping for twins, so, as we were on our way, I kept joking with Cristy about that thought. She always said, "Well if it's twins, I hope they are healthy." She said the same thing regarding all my wonderings: twins, a boy, and possibly twin boys. Arriving in the obstetrician's waiting room, I looked around and noticed all the posters of pregnant women, and other things that such an office would have, and I remember saying to myself, "Wow, this is the real thing." There was another couple there and I wasn't sure if it was their nervous faces that tipped me off that they were pregnant or the fact that men usually don't go to gynecology visits with women. The nurse called us back, and I was unsure if I was supposed to go. Cristy looked at me and said, "You're coming in, right?" I just stood up and shrugged my shoulders as a way of saying, "I don't know, is that okay?" I was so nervous about the visit I didn't know what to do with myself.

We got to the room and the doctor came in and started asking questions. The first question I asked her was, "Is this the visit when you can tell if there are twins?" Cristy quickly laughed and told her that I was hoping for twins. She looked at me and said, "You are probably the first person I have met that actually wants two crying babies at once." Cristy explained that I was a twin and the doctor quickly understood my anxiousness. She started using an ultrasound and I was trying to decipher the sonogram like a foreigner tries to make heads or tails of a language he doesn't understand. The screen started to show things a little more clearly, and I could see one baby in there. The doctor looked at me with somewhat of a disappointed face and said, "Nope, just one baby this time." I wasn't too upset, I just said to myself, "There is always the next one." The doctor printed some pictures of the sonograms and sent us on our way. In the car we started to wonder how we would cleverly tell our families. I told Cristy it would be great to tell them on my birthday, because we would have them all together.

Two days later on my and Randy's birthday my parents were cooking lunch for us. Growing up we always sat at the dinner table as a family to eat. We all had our places at the table and they never changed. We would say our grace and then, as we ate, we would talk about the day, everyone conversing together, enjoying each other's company, learning what it meant to be a family. On Sundays, however, we had a ritual of eating a large lunch which our dad would cook, usually consisting of five courses and almost always revolving around our Italian heritage. We would sometimes have guests, be it our larger family, grandparents, priests, cousins, aunts and uncles, or friends. On our birthdays we would all get together and the one(s) having the birthday would get to pick what to eat. It was just another way that my parents made us feel special on birthdays. Over the years as our family grew, we couldn't eat in the breakfast room any longer because the eight-chair table wasn't enough, so we started eating in the dining room where we had a table that could seat twenty-two, with no trouble filling it.

My parents and my siblings and our significant others plus my grandparents were there, and I wanted to wait until we were all sitting before I would cleverly show our mom the sonogram. I wanted to show Mom first because she was always the caring and loving mother who would do anything for her children. She was so proud to have grandchildren of her own and would do anything for them. I was so excited we were able to give her another grandchild to love. As we all sat and said our grace, we started eating and I pulled out my phone that had the picture of the sonogram. I made up this story about working on the apartment and how proud I was of the work I had accomplished. She seemed somewhat intrigued but I could tell her attention was on something else. I stood up and walked over to her to show her the picture. I said, "I want to show you my progress on the apartment," and I put the phone in front of her.

She immediately said, "Oh, my God, this isn't a joke right? Rusty, please tell me you're not joking?"

I said, "No, this isn't a joke." Our dad became interested in what was going on. So I showed him the picture and he was immediately smiling and said, "So y'all are going to have a baby?" As he said that I looked at the rest of the table and could tell instantly that Randy wasn't excited about it.

Just what I feared: he would be upset that we weren't having children at the same time. I didn't say much to him nor did he say much for the remainder of the dinner. In a way I was a little upset that he didn't, but I understood why he would be quiet. Everyone was so happy for us, especially my sister, Dayna, because she was also pregnant with her third child. My sisters, Andrea and

Dayna, had children at the same time, except with Andrea's second pregnancy she had twins. So I was excited that John, Dayna, and I would have babies all around the same age. I think this was even more of a reason why Randy was upset, knowing that he would be left out altogether because Mara wasn't wanting children for five or ten years after they got married. The remainder of the afternoon went on as it usually did, every now and again someone would make conversation about names, or what gender, but I didn't want to entertain those conversations too much for fear of hurting Randy.

  A couple of days later at work, Randy came up to me and apologized for being quiet at lunch when we announced we were pregnant. He said, "Russ, not sure if you knew I was upset but I have to apologize for not being happy and excited for you when you told us. I was upset because we had always talked about having kids at the same time, and I just realized that most likely won't happen because I am so far away from being ready to have kids."

  I said, "Randy, I knew you were upset and I don't blame you for being upset. It's just that if we were to wait for you and Mara, Cristy would be much older and it wouldn't be as safe for us to have kids." Mara was six years younger, so she had plenty of time biologically to wait to have kids. Cristy is my age, and because we wanted at least three children, we didn't want to chance having a baby at an older age. He understood and we hugged and he said how excited he was for us. We talked about what I wanted, and what I would name him or her, and he wanted to make sure I wouldn't take his boy and girl names that he had already picked out. I assured him that we wouldn't take his names and that we had not decided yet on names. It felt good to hear from my twin brother that he was excited for me, that this was a happy time, and that the last thing he wanted to do would be to take any of that joy away.

  I had a tough decision to make: who would be the Parrain of our first born child. In Louisiana some families use this term which is French for Godfather. I didn't want John to feel left out if I picked Randy, and I didn't want Randy to feel left out if I picked John. If we went in birth order, John would be the first to be Parrain. This was a hard decision to make. Cristy and I discussed this, and she guided me on this dilemma; however, telling either of them was going to be the hard part no matter what decision I made. I talked to my entire family except John and Randy about it, and the consensus was all the same: "Do what you feel is right, and neither will be upset if you don't pick him." I chose

Randy being that we were twins. I wanted to pick Randy because of our special bond, and I knew that Randy would truly look at my child as if it were his DNA, because it really was his DNA. I put off telling either of them until Julien was born.

Cristy and I were torn between learning the sex of the baby right away or waiting till the baby was born to find out. For me, I wanted to know in the worst way if it were to be a boy. With all my siblings, two being girls and two being boys, I was the first to have an opportunity to have a boy and carry on the Perrone name. John had already had a girl, so my wish was to continue the family name. We finally agreed that we were going to find out before the birth, but not when we first saw the ultrasound. We wanted to have the nurse write the ultrasound result on a paper and put that in an envelope and seal it, and then we would deliver it to the bakery to make a cake specific to the gender. If the baby were a girl, the cake would be pink on the inside, if it were a boy, it would be blue on the inside. When we told the nurse this, she thought that was such a great idea, she said she was going to do that for her next child. When she gave us the envelope we were both so curious to see what was written on the inside. It was like being a child again, looking at wrapped presents under the Christmas tree. We were very careful not to look at it too hard so neither of us would see what it said and spoil the surprise.

After the appointment we ate at a Chinese restaurant near my work. We sat at a booth and Cristy pulled the envelope out of her purse and we both looked at the envelope. Just then my heart sank. I thought I saw the letter "I" and I told Cristy what I thought I saw. She told me that she thought she saw the letter "y" and we both laughed and put the envelope away quickly. We sat there and looked at each other with big smiles and I said to her, "We had better plan this reveal-the-gender party pretty soon." She agreed with me and we started planning the date. It was going to be three weeks away, and all I could think about was how long those three weeks would seem.

Time creeped along and we were finally preparing my parents' house for the reveal-the-gender party. Their house was naturally bigger than our apartment, so it only made sense to have it there. The decorations were pink and blue, and everyone was supposed to come dressed in the color they thought the baby would be, except Cristy and I would wear neutral colors so it wasn't obvious which sex we wanted. We had made up mustaches and lips on sticks for everyone to hold up for a picture. We probably had about fifty people there who were family and our group of close friends. It was a great time, but throughout the entire party, I was just filled with such anticipation for the moment we would cut the cake. I had to coach myself on how to still be excited if it were a girl. People would ask what we thought, and I would tell them my gut feeling: a boy. Well a majority of people thought the same way because there were more blue shirts and dresses than there were pink. It was definitely a little relief to think that this many people were thinking the same as I was.

Finally the moment of truth arrived. We all stood behind the cake, Cristy and I holding the knife to cut it. Randy was taking some pictures of all of us and was going to snap the pictures of the cutting, revealing the answer. We all counted down and as everyone yelled, "3, 2, 1," we started to cut. From my viewpoint, I could see directly into the cake but no one else could. With my nerves jumping like atoms and the first glimpse of blue, I couldn't control myself and I yelled out in excitement, "It's a boy!" My brother caught that moment on camera, but it wasn't my face that was the funny thing: it was Cristy's face that said it all. It was a face that said, "Wait I didn't get a chance to see it yet!" I couldn't help it, I was so excited that we were having a boy and was happy that I was going to be passing the family name down to the next generation. It seems this scenario has played out generation after generation starting with my grandfather, who only had one son out of three children to pass the name, and my father starting out having two girls and looking like the name would stop with him until John, my older brother was born. It seemed that each generation would come close to surname extinction, but not my generation yet. Having a family business that carries the family surname provides some special pressures. The revealing wasn't over yet.

Cristy and I had already picked out names in the event we would have a boy or a girl. After the cake had been served, we all gathered again to reveal the names. As we were getting ready to reveal, everyone was blurting out names, funny ones and serious ones, but the one that our dad blurted out left us all in awe.

I heard him shout out in a joking manner, "Julius."

I quickly said back to him, "No, it's Julien."

He was caught off guard and said, "No I said Julius!" still keeping up with the joke.

I said back to him, "No Dad, his name *is* going to be Julien," and everyone just stopped talking to look at both of us. The look on their faces was priceless.

Out of thousands and thousands of names, who would have thought he would guess so close. I was so much in awe that I almost forgot to mention what the baby's middle name would be. Julien's middle name was very important to me and to our family. His middle name was to be after my Great-Grandfather Bartholomew who started our family business. It was the business which was the main reason I was so concerned about passing the name on to the next born, becoming the 5th generation. When my dad heard that, I could tell right away he was honored, not only honored for himself, but for his grandfather, someone I had never met. I was so proud we were able to give that to my father.

Shortly after Randy found out that we were having a boy and we were naming him Julien, he wrote a song titled after him. The song explains how Randy's mind was so intertwined with mine and how the announcement of his conception, gender, and name made his emotions go wild.

Oh little baby, you're just a portrait
Soon to be in the arms of a mother
She is with child and the likeness of me through my brother
As two have made another

Oh how your eyes may look like mine,
Keep them stretched across the sky
Two were made from one, we're grown alike
Your father is my brother

Oh little one walk softly
Watch all the comets fly and the only thing to worry
Is their dust hitting the sky and flaring all the lucky
On your patient little face shall it light a smile.

Then there would be the day
Where you won't be the same
You will grow with every move you make

Hush little Julien you will inherit to be okay

Oh when you come into this life you will cry
Screaming loud because you're alive
Oh my curious eyes will watch
Through those two who've made you, one looks like me

"Julien" by Randy Perrone September 11, 2012

Chapter 28

A New Home Sweet Home and Warehouse

"But I don't want to go among mad people, said Alice. Oh you can't help that, said the Cat; we're all mad here." from **Alice in Wonderland,** *by Lewis Carroll*

The business was growing because of all of the hard work from Randy, John, and our dad. One day Dad had a call from a real estate agent who was looking for a new warehouse for our business; the agent was letting our dad know that he had found the perfect spot. We took a tour of the facility together and instantly knew this was meant to be for us. Our dad put in an offer almost on the spot and without much negotiating back and forth we had an agreement. This was going to be a project of massive proportions that would envelope Randy, John, our dad, and myself. All of us were excited and ready for the challenge.

We took possession of our new warehouse in February of 2012, but we had to build it out. That meant adding walk-in coolers and freezers, processing rooms and warehouse pallet racking. A complete remodel of the office space was needed. Money was tight so we subbed out all the work that we could not handle. This left us with the office remodel. True to form, Randy found ceramic floor tile for the office at half price. We bought pallet loads so that we could lay the tile in the 3000 square feet of office. I used to love getting off of my everyday work to go to the warehouse and work there. Sometimes Randy would be there the whole day when I wasn't able, and other times it was the other way around. One time I remember going at the end of the day to see that Randy had already started putting up pallet racks by himself. In our short time in the businesses we had done much assembling and disassembling of pallet racks, but never by ourselves as this was difficult. He found a way to use the fork lift to aid in his solo act. I remember yelling at him that what he was doing was dangerous, but I think mostly I was upset that he was getting started on the fun work without me.

While all of the warehouse work was going on, Cristy and I realized that we had to move into the bigger side of our duplex with the addition to our family. Cristy and I had bought a duplex from my parents and our unit was a two-bedroom, while the back unit was a three-bedroom in which we had a tenant. We didn't want to kick the tenant out, but we knew that it was going to be a tight fit in our little two-bedroom apartment. Fortunately things seemed to work themselves out. We got a notice from the tenant in the back that they were going to move out in one month. Perfect timing! This gave us a month to get our apartment rented, and a month to work on the three-bedroom apartment. I took photos, put the ad on the internet, and within five days I had our apartment rented. I gave myself a month to work on the three bedrooms and move out, while also working on a new warehouse for the family business. Sometimes I can be too ambitious with my schedule, and in this case I was. Multitasking is another name for partial doing.

I would go to work at 6:30 in the morning and get my regular work done about noon, then head over to the new warehouse to lay flooring, put up pallet racking, paint walls, or do whatever else needed to be done until about five o'clock in the evening. Then I would head home, eat dinner with Cristy, and then head to the back apartment and work until about ten. The back apartment needed new paint and new floors, and I wanted to redo the bathrooms. I was making great progress on the apartment and seemed to be on track when one evening I was working in the bathroom and noticed that the tub surround was coming apart from the wall. I looked back there I could see mold growing on the sheetrock. "Oh boy," I said to myself. This would really put a damper on my schedule. I was so disheartened by this that I stopped working a little early and turned in for the night. I told Cristy of the issue and she started to get worried about the timing. We had two weeks before we had to move out. I said, "Don't worry, I will order the tub surround, get some moisture resistant sheet rock, and the bathroom will be better than it was before." As always I asked her to trust me and everything would work out. Timing couldn't have been better with doing the sheetrock, because we were having sheetrock done at the warehouse. I was able to learn from one of the workers the proper way to do it. I finished the sheetrock on the walls, and just pushed forward on the floors.

We were one week away from having to move out, and I had three rooms of wood laminate flooring to install. I put in my headphones and started on the rooms we would need right away. In three days I put down 800 square feet of flooring in the bedrooms, and tiled the two bathrooms. Randy helped me do some of the flooring, and if he hadn't I wouldn't have gotten the floors down in time. Two days to go and everything shifted from renovating the apartment to packing and moving. Fortunately, we were only moving a short distance, but nonetheless it was still very stressful having to move out so quickly. I could just see the stressful look on Cristy's face and just kept telling myself, "She is pregnant, so I have to push through my fatigue and get us moved." We literally moved the last box at 3 a.m., and the new tenant was supposed to arrive at 8:00 a.m. to pick up the keys and start moving in. It was so close that I had to warn them that touch up paint may still be wet and if anything was left undone to let me know as we were trying hard to get out of there in time. Looking back I am proud of what I was able to do, but at the time it was one of the most hectic times of my life because we were simultaneously moving our business' warehouse and moving our private lives. Time, deadlines, and priorities are all fanciful inventions to which we fall prey.

The warehouse on the other hand took a joint effort by Randy and me on a level that was new to us. It was grueling all the work that was required to get our new facility up and running. John also was big into the task, doing all the wiring and electronics tasks that were needed to start the operation. Even our mom was in there painting walls and helping pick out materials for the offices. There wasn't an inch of the place that didn't have the input from and hard work by Randy, myself, John, our mom, and our dad. Randy and I with the help of our good friend Bobby tiled the offices practically every day after work and on the weekends. This was a gruesome task as we had to rip up carpet that had been there for over 30 years, lay a thin set on all of the floor to cover up the glue remnants from the carpet, and then tile the floor, which is back-breaking work. At the same time Randy, always the aggressive businessman, stretched our delivery limits and started doing business with a supermarket chain in Hattiesburg, MS, about an hour and a half north of our closest delivery point. Many times he made the two hour trip on his own, sometimes even making the deliveries himself, and then would come back to work on the warehouse with me.

Moving into the new warehouse was exciting and stressful at the same time. To move a business that is still trying to operate and do it flawlessly was really a tough task. As a family we were prepared to put in the time and effort to do it without interruption to our customers. Randy and I were the first to permanently move offices, and it felt great. This facility was so much bigger and nicer than our other facility. We each had an office and between our offices there was a door which we removed so that we could constantly be in sight and communication with each other. It really felt like the new facility would open up other doors for us and allow the company to grow to another level that Randy, John, and I had envisioned. It was really an exciting time for our family business. I can remember being so excited when we took over the building from the previous tenant that I went after my regular work day to run an industrial vacuum through the entire warehouse. I was all by myself in a 30,000 square foot warehouse, and just went back and forth the whole way. I knew that I wasn't alone in my excitement, for sure enough Randy arrived and saw me with the vacuum. He quickly took the magnetic nail sweep and followed behind me.

At this point with all the work we had done, we were finally able to sit at our desks and look at each other with smiles from ear to ear, somewhat like the Cheshire Cat. We didn't say much, but we knew how proud we were of each other to have accomplished something like this. It was our world. It was our time to take the family business to the next level. It was sort of our Wonderland.

After some strenuous times of moving into the warehouse and moving into our new apartment, Cristy and I made a last-minute trip to Chicago. This would be our last trip without a baby. I was a little nervous because it was August, and Cristy was due in October, but that's how we were, spontaneous and adventurous. We had a pretty laid back trip planned, staying downtown and just living like Chicago natives. We did, however, plan a visit to a cheese grating supplier with whom we were doing business. Whenever we travel, I try to make a point to see what suppliers or potential suppliers have businesses in the area. Growing up we frequently did this, and I remember being quite fascinated at some of these factories as a young boy. After our honeymoon, Cristy understood and was hooked too. We toured the facility, which was impressive. The large cheese graters were just as I imagined, loud and big, and the aroma created from them was fantastic. The smell of fresh grated Romano or Parmesan is a smell that is unmatched by any other cheeses in the world, and a large scale grating operation like theirs creates aromas that make their way through your nostrils, into your brain, and chisel a permanent etching in your memory. After we finished the grand tour, and had tried several new cheeses, we skipped over to their sister company, which was a distribution company similar to our own. Being that we had just moved into our new facility, I was curious as to what we could adopt from their facility to make ours better.

Their facility was so large that when we pulled up my jaw dropped at how enormous it was. It seemed that it went on for miles and miles. The trucks lined up outside made our fleet of five look like nothing. It is funny because in the distribution world, many measure success by two things: square footage of warehouse and the number of trucks. When we were greeted by the vice president of the operation, that question came up. How large is your facility? How many trucks do you run? Naturally I sheepishly answered, and his remark was exactly as I would have thought. He let out a reply that in a way said, "Oh you're that small!" I didn't let it bother me though; instead I asked all kinds of questions which showed him that I was eager to grow and was hungry for something larger. The one question I asked wound up two days later becoming somewhat prophetic. I asked him, "How did you get so big?" He replied, "Well over the years, smaller mom and pop distributors would sell to the big guys, Sysco, US Foods, and such. Our customers didn't like that, so they would flock to us. Over the years, there were no more mom-and-pops left but us, and we wound up getting as big as we are because the customers still wanted to buy locally." I told him, "Boy, I wish Mauricio's Foodservice would sell out, they are our biggest competitor." He told me, "One day it will happen. As long as you hang on and continue to push forward, you will outlast the others." I thought to myself, "There is just no way Mauricio's Foodservice would sell his business, because they are much larger, much more successful, and everyone wants to do business with them." I sent all the pictures I took to Randy and just said how awesome it would be to be as big as these guys.

Two days later, while Cristy and I were at the airport about to board the plane to come home, I noted a call on my phone from one of our larger customers. I picked up and answered; it was the customer calling. He said, "You're never going to believe this, are you sitting down?"

I said, "Yes I am, what happened?"

"Mauricio's Foodservice (the local New Orleans food supplier) is selling their business to Wholesale Giant, (a national company). You are going to be getting all of Mauricio's Foodservice's business."

"What?! No way! How did you hear this?"

The customer told me that he heard about the sale from the owner of Mauricio's Foodservice and that this customer wanted to do business locally and therefore would be giving Perrone and Sons their business henceforth. I hung up the phone and the first person I called was my dad. For him this was music to his ears. I called Randy next and told him of the news. I said, "Here we go! We need to jump on this as soon as I get back." He was ecstatic, I told him to call John and get him prepped. That flight back was one of the best flights of my life. I couldn't believe that two days earlier I wished they would sell and now it was becoming a reality. It was so good that I had to ask Cristy if this might be a dream or not: growing a family and growing a business!

The next couple of weeks Randy and I worked on the list of items that we would have to source, price, and compile. This type of work was fun for Randy and me. We had done a smaller conversion before when we took over distribution for a customer, sourcing items, work pricing and minimums, and then executing on the ordering and fulfillment. This, however, was so large of a job that it took us hours and hours of overtime to get it done in the proposed timeframe. We had to present the program to our new customers, the owners of the company, and in order to do that we had to have all the items sourced and priced. While this was going on, the customer wanted to see if it would work out with the national distributor which bought us a little time to get the information gathered for the presentation. In the meantime we were calling our inside contacts to see how the national company was doing. Much to our delight, they were messing up left and right. The beautiful part of the whole thing was that Mauricio's Foodservice hadn't transitioned yet out of their current warehouse into the warehouse of the national distributor called Wholesale Giant. Randy and I would peek out of our computer comas to look at each other and grin when we would hear the horror stories of the alleged delivery blunders by Wholesale Giant. We were finally finished with our compiling, but when we set up an appointment we were told that they were in a holding pattern. The customer who would be buying from us wanted to let Mauricio's Foodservice move out of its facility to see if things would get better with Wholesale Giant's facility. We looked at it as a blessing in disguise, giving us more time to get our warehouse arranged and organized. Our food dealings were put on ice for a while. If only the ice wouldn't melt in the meanwhile.

Chapter 29

Isaac Pays a Visit

A week or so later, we were faced with yet another hurdle. Hurricane Isaac of 2012 had its sights on New Orleans and indeed resulted in 41 deaths and over two billion dollars in damage. It appeared that the hurricane would hit very close to the Hurricane Katrina anniversary, August 29th. Our family business had just moved into our new facility and we were trying to get organized and then this happened. "Just our luck," we all thought. We quickly realized that our new facility was set up for generator power, but we had one big problem: we had no generator. At this point we couldn't afford to buy a generator, so, we were on the hunt for a used generator. The type of generator we needed was not a size that was just lying around waiting for someone to rent. This started a whole new set of problems. We had several hundred thousand dollars in merchandise in our coolers, and no generator. I called my father-in-law to see what type of connections he had and if he could locate one for us.

He said, "I got one, but this thing is really old and I am not sure it will run. This was used by the US military in Vietnam."

I quickly said, "I'm on my way now to see it." I told my dad and brothers that I may have found the solution to our generator problem and headed off with Randy.

We pulled up to my father-in-law's place and frantically rushed to see it. When I say this thing was old, it was old, and in rough shape. It even had a bullet hole through the gas tank.

He said, "It's old, but I think we can get it to work. Just hook a hose up to the fuel line and use an external tank. If you want it, I can put it on the trailer, and you can take it with you."

I looked at Randy and raised my eyebrow and looked back at my father-in-law and said, "Well, it's better than what I have now, so all we need to do is get it working."

It took us a bit to load it, especially because the crane he had wouldn't work, and we had to wait for a friend of his to run one over to us. We finally got it loaded and strapped down. I shook his hand as he wished me luck, and I headed off. As I drove back to New Orleans from the bayou area, I could see dark clouds forming. All of a sudden, I started to have the feeling I have every time a storm comes close to us. The feeling is unique to the situation. Suddenly everyday issues and tasks are put off and survival duties take over. The thing about living in a hurricane zone is that everyone gets that way. All of a sudden you start noticing that the cars on the road look different. Traffic patterns are thrown off, and everyone starts to get supplies and starts to either evacuate or hunker down.

I felt like I was triumphant on my mission to save our business. We had the generator in tow, and all of our problems were going to be solved. As I pulled up, the wind was starting to pick up a bit. The sounds of the trees seemed to become amplified. Adrenaline was certainly starting to take over with super human senses operating. As soon as my dad and brother John looked at the generator they let out a laugh. I said, "Well what do you have in place of this?" We are so close-knit that we poke fun at each other knowing that it's all in good fun. None of them had a plan so we started to get the generator in place and called a friend of Dad's, an electrician, who knew a thing or two about diesel engines. The reaction was just about the same with everyone who laid eyes on the old beast. Dad's friend gave me a list of things to buy in order to get it started. Randy and I set off to get the parts. In the meantime the electrician had three electrical cables hooked up just to the coolers as he said the generator wasn't large enough to power the whole building. We started working to get it started, and it seemed like it took forever. We were priming hoses, pushing in pins, pulling out rods, moving dials. It was truly a challenge to get this thing working. I had never seen so many dials and levers in my life. All the new age equipment was all automatic and digital. We had to worry about the hertz frequency, the kilowatt output, this and that. It just seemed so over my head. My main focus was to help where I could and get out of the way when not needed.

Dad's friend said in his unmistakable Australian accent, "Okay, mates, let her rip, let's see what she's got."

Crank and a clunk, puff and a woof, and she started humming. It was great to get this ole girl up and back in service. By the sound of it, I don't think this generator had been run since the Vietnam War. The smell of the exhaust and the sound of the diesel engine all smelled and sounded like victory. I went over to the electrician and just watched him as he was measuring the output with his voltmeter. I could tell on his face that it wasn't coming out right.

I asked, "How's it going?"

He replied, "Well the hertz isn't running at sixty and it appears the dial that controls that is broken."

I just remember being deflated when I heard that and said back to him, "Can it be fixed?"

"I am going to try my best to get this old machine working the way we need it to," he said to me with a look on his face telling me that he was doing everything he could. He tried for an hour or so to get it working right, but no luck. He had to switch gears himself and get his family ready for the hurricane. He said that he was going to be staying in town, so, if we lost power, we could call him and he would come out when the storm passed to see if he could get it working. We parted ways and switched gears to finishing up the preparations at the warehouse so we could start preparations at my parents' house. Just like Katrina, we chose my parents' house because it is a well-built house with a generator and plenty of space for all our families. As we closed down the doors of the warehouse, I looked around and just said a silent prayer that everything would hold up during the storm. We all jumped in the car and headed for shelter. As an old saying goes, "Pray if you will, then row as hard as you can to get to the other side."

Chapter 30

An Excuse to Party: Hurricanes

"Life isn't about waiting for the storm to pass...It's about learning to dance in the rain." Vivian Greene

As hurricanes usually bring out the party for New Orleanians, it was time for us to enact the hurricane rituals. It is always a weird feeling when almost an entire city evacuates and all that is left to do is to ensure survival or pass time, whichever the storm dictates. As kids, we passed time by walking to the Lake Pontchartrain levee to see how high the water was, or playing board games, or just sitting around and talking about past hurricanes. Walking to the levee was always my favorite. The families on our block would evacuate, leaving boarded-up homes in their wake. Walking down the street, hearing a car pass down the main street every so often, feeling the wind blow through the streets and around your body, the smell of salt water in the air, and listening to the leaves sway this way and that always stimulates the senses and the mind. Hurricanes have an essence, a voice, and a personality. We even give them names! They tease, and threaten, and sometimes destroy and kill, but not always, which is why they are to be respected but not trusted. I usually would get to the levee and just watch the waves being pushed by the wind and be amazed by the power of Mother Nature. Hurricanes are often just Mother Nature's way of cleaning house, if she doesn't tear the house down in the process.

This time was no different in that we were older, and the demands of our mom making us stay inside as kids had given way to her suggestions to stay indoors which we categorically rejected. For this hurricane we had everyone in the family together except for Mara. She chose to evacuate to Birmingham, her hometown, to take the opportunity to hang out with her friends there. I didn't mind because there would be no one to tell Randy that he couldn't go with me or

John to the levee. The storm started to build overnight. It brought back memories of Katrina, though not as bad. The whistling of the house, though, was eerily similar to Katrina. It seemed as though Katrina had created more opportunities for the wind to whistle, reminding us that this new storm, Isaac, was lurking out there ready to take whatever could not withstand it. Cristy was definitely made nervous by the sounds, and I would calm her by saying Katrina was worse. This helped, but it was still something she would rather not go through again, if at all possible. None of us got much sleep that night and by the time we awoke, the storm was starting to wind down. At some point overnight we lost power, but with the generator we couldn't tell because electrical things still worked, especially the AC. What a big difference that generator made during Isaac compared with Katrina. A hurricane with or without a generator is like a car with or without wheels; we were lucky for our "wheels."

I remember seeing Randy texting back and forth with Mara. Randy  seemed upset that she had gone back to Birmingham and was partying while he was nervous about the business. I know it took a toll on him because he just wasn't into any of our conversations and was very short-tempered. I wondered what he could be telling her so feverishly. Thankfully the weather was dying down to tropical-force strength, so, Dad, Chad, John, Randy and I chose to set off to check out our properties. This took Randy's mind off of what Mara was doing in Alabama. We went to Randy and Chad's houses first in the Lakeview neighborhood of New Orleans. Typically water collects in this neighborhood quicker than others in the city, and as soon as we got to the neighborhood we could tell it was going to be a task trying to get to their houses. At one point the water looked so deep that our dad got out of the car to wade through the water and see how deep it got. I took a picture of him because he was giving us the signal to come through, but the water was up to his knees. We tried another route. We were able to get to Chad's house, and everything looked to be okay other than the power being out. We weren't able to get to Randy's so we headed to my house. Power was out and my fence was knocked down, but other than that everything appeared to be fine.

Our next stop was the warehouse. On the way to the warehouse there were several power poles snapped in half, and one set was blocking the street, so we had to go off the road a bit to get under the power lines. We finally made it there and went inside to see that there was no power. You could hear the roof flexing and hitting against the rafters. The wind certainly did some damage because you could see water on the floor. We checked on the freezer and the coolers and they appeared to be holding their temperatures pretty efficiently. We called the electrician and let him know that power was out and we needed to try to get the generator going. He said he would be able to meet us later that afternoon. We surveyed a bit more then headed back home. There was a pretty decent amount of damage throughout the city, but all in all, it seemed that this storm was going to be about electricity, or lack thereof.

Later that evening we met the electrician who worked tirelessly trying to get the generator to produce the proper power. He was concerned that the altering hertz frequency would damage the new equipment. After several hours trying, he said that there was no way it was going to work. The temperature was doing okay, so we left the warehouse to call it a day. At this point we figured the power would be back on in a day or so, and we should be good with the temperature.

The second day came without power and the temperature was starting to rise close to the danger zone. After calling Entergy, the utility company, about a hundred times, we finally got an estimated date of electric service restoration, which was projected to be in four days. This wasn't going to be good. We were all back on the phones trying to find a generator. We figured that it was going to be really difficult being that the storm knocked out power to almost all of New Orleans, and generator demands were going to be high. We finally found a generator in Baton Rouge that could be delivered the next day. The price on the generator was almost double what we were being quoted locally, but at this point we needed to get power started so we could save our product. Randy and I would frequently check the temperature, seeing it creep and creep closer to the danger zone. Check after check, hour after hour, our nerves were starting to get the best of us. The next day when we arrived, it was hovering right below the danger zone. We were really nervous that we were going to have to throw away our entire inventory of product, and the bad thing was that we had not continued our product insurance because the building was high off the ground and we figured we wouldn't need it for this season.

Just as we were making another check, John burst in the cooler and said, "The generator is here!" We all let out sighs of relief. I called the electrician as quickly as I could and told him to come as soon as he could. He got there in minutes. We were hauling cables for him to the electrical panel, splicing wires, and whatever else he needed so that we could get up and running quickly. We were racing against time and before long we had the coolers back up and running. We all let out a sigh of relief when we saw cooler and freezer fans turn over. The temperature was dropping quickly and it seemed we were in the clear. The whole ordeal felt like it was out of a suspense movie.

Throughout the whole generator ordeal, Stanley's, a customer of ours, was having an issue of their own. The owner of Stanley's couldn't get in touch with Wholesale Giant, a national supplier, and the stores were getting wiped out of product. He asked us how quickly we could get going, and as eager as we were, we told him that we could be up and running by tomorrow. He started making phone calls to local suppliers, had them contact us, and before long we were starting to get product rolling into our warehouse to help them. It was our intent to show them that we could be a true partner, and we were doing it. We had drivers that were getting cabin fever eager to get back to work. Within a day we had a crew in the warehouse. We were set for the next day to start making deliveries, and our competition was still trying to convince their employees to show up for work.

The next day all the trucks but one were on the street. We got a phone call from a local seafood purveyor who was frantic. He said, "I have my shrimp at Mauricio's, and he isn't going to refill his generators because they have already moved out their product. Can you help me out? I need some freezer space and I heard you had yours up and running." Being as busy as we were, this was the last thing we needed, but I couldn't tell this man no. I could hear how desperate he was, so I told my dad that I was taking the last truck to Mauricio's Food Service to pick up this man's shrimp. When I got there the owner greeted me with a hug and tears in his eyes. He said to me, "I will never forget this, thank you so much for helping me." I hugged him back and just told him that we needed to get his product to the freezer as quickly as we could. This was my first time ever in Mauricio's Foodservice's warehouse, so I had a unique opportunity to see how they had it set up. One thing I remember was seeing how large the freezer was. It was enormous. It was much larger than ours. Men in the food business are predisposed to comparing the size of their warehouse, delivery fleet, refrigerators, freezers and now generators.

While we were getting loaded the owner of Mauricio's walked in. It was the first time I came face to face with him and all he could say once I greeted him was, "That's the biggest truck you came with?"

"Well, all of our bigger trucks are delivering to our customers but I couldn't let this man's livelihood go down the tubes because you wanted to let your freezer defrost."

Once we were finished transporting the shrimp back to our freezer, I got back into the mode of getting our business back on track. I called many of our customers to let them know we were back up and running, and then I called some of the key employees who worked for Stanley's, our customer who had called me in the airport, to see how everything was going. The nightmare stories were coming in left and right. Stores didn't get orders that they placed with Wholesale Giant; there were orders that were filled completely wrong, and some of the orders had damaged product, but the drivers just kept on going and didn't address any of the issues with the stores.

Randy and I knew that we had our opportunity to take this business over by the mere fact that we understood how to make deliveries to grocery stores, and this other large food service company didn't have a clue how to do it. I started making calls to the director of the deli and said, "We are ready to make that presentation. I am hearing from stores that it's a nightmare. Now is the time to make it happen." He agreed with me and we set up our time to make the presentation. My older brother John and our dad usually did not join Randy and me at meetings with this customer, but this time we all went as a team. We wanted to show them that we were a force united through family that would do whatever it took to gain their business and their trust. We showed them that we would be true partners. The meeting went well. Randy and I always had a way to break tension with laughter, and this group was not immune to this type of behavior. Before we knew it, the tensions were gone; they gave us a handshake, and we were leaving there on cloud nine. We struck a deal with them that would double our business overnight. We set the timeline to transition for the middle of

October, the week after Cristy and I were expecting Julien. We certainly had our work cut out for us: delivering food at the business and a baby at home.

Within days we were starting to gear up with new hires and new trucks, and we started ordering product. The hiring process alone was a difficult task. The employees who were transferred from Mauricio's Food Service to Wholesale Giant were starting to be let go. It seemed that everyday someone was being told to leave, and the word got out that we were hiring several of those employees already.

We were getting closer and closer to the transition date, which meant Cristy and I were closer and closer to our due date. We all worked tirelessly making sure that everything was in order before the due date so that, when the baby came, Randy and John would have everything they needed to keep going while I would be out for a couple of days. Fortunately for the business, unfortunately for my poor wife, we were over our due date. I went with Cristy to her doctor's appointment and her doctor gave us an induction date of October the 18th, which happened to be on a Friday, and we were to start the business's transition that following Monday. I was excited because this would give me a couple of days to help before we made the transition. As the days kept getting closer, it appeared that Julien had no intention to grace us with his presence too soon.

Chapter 31

Oh Baby!

I suppose all inductions go like ours. We were scheduled to check into the hospital at 8:30 p.m. the day before the induction date. So that afternoon I left work at a reasonable time, went home, and packed our bags. Cristy had done a lot of the baby supply packing, so I just had my clothes and camera to pack. As we left our apartment, we looked at the crib, and then just looked at each other with some bit of fear in our eyes. We didn't say much at this point. We chose to stop for dinner at a cafeteria style restaurant called Babyface's Buffet, perfect for the occasion. It was going to be our last meal together without another human being who relied on us. We sat at the table and just talked about how much our lives were going to change. We were excited to have this addition but nervous at the same time. As in all new parent experiences, the fear of the unknown is a powerful emotion, and with our situation we knew that in twenty-four hours, whether we were ready or not, we were going to be parents. Babies don't come with instruction manuals, gauges, dials, or on-off switches; furthermore, there is a no return policy. Yikes!

We finished eating dinner and went to the hospital. The nurse instructed Cristy to get into her gown, so while she was doing that, I chose to go by the crib used for newborn babies after birth and took a picture of it. I said, "I can't believe that in less than twenty-four hours we will have a baby who will be in this." She looked at me with a nervous smile and finished getting ready. I was so tired at that point because I had gotten to work at 4:00 a.m. to tie up loose ends. I told her that I would try to get some sleep on the recliner chair and that she should try as well. The nurse came in and gave her some medication to get the process started and told her that it would be a while before she would give

Pitocin, which is the drug that jump-starts labor, so she should have a chance to get some sleep. I gave her a kiss, sat in my chair, and started to doze off.

Three hours later I could hear the nurse enter the room. She asked Cristy in a whisper if she was feeling contractions or was in pain. Cristy said that she was but didn't want to be one of those nurse-patients who gave trouble to the other nurses while she was a patient. The nurse tried to make her feel comfortable and told her that she didn't have to worry about that, but that she should tell them when she was having pain so that they could order her an epidural. After some back and forth between Cristy and me about the epidural, she decided that it was time to get it. The nurse ordered the epidural and shortly thereafter the doctor gave it to her. They asked me to leave while they gave it which made me nervous. I stepped out of the room and went to the waiting room and watched the clock. The minute hand seemed to be held back by the force of gravity, because the seconds seemed like minutes, and the minutes seemed like hours. Finally the nurse came to the waiting room and informed me that I could return.

When I walked into the room, Cristy was pain-free and in a good mood. I was relieved to see this and when the doctors and nurses left the room I sat back in my chair and tried to get some sleep. This was close to midnight, so I was pretty confident that I would be able to get some sleep before daybreak. I dozed off again, and in three hours I was awakened by a muffled Cristy.

She called my name in a panic and said, "Rusty! Rusty, wake up, I am scared."

I shot up from my reclining chair and looked at her. She was wearing an oxygen mask and I could see the fear in her face. I was shocked to see this because up until that point I had not heard a single thing.

I said, "What is going on?"

In a quick and demanding voice she said, "The baby's heart is dropping, and they want to put me on oxygen to keep the baby's heart rate up."

I jumped out of the chair and said, "Well I am up now, and there is no way I am going back to sleep."

I pulled my chair right next to her, grabbed her hand and sat next to her. I told her to keep calm, so as not to stress the baby. After this point, I noticed every beep, ding, and chirp from the monitors. When the nurse came to check on progress, I asked her what all the noises meant. This was one of the worst things

I could have done, because then I knew when the heart rate dropped for the baby. I would hear the heartbeat and then all of a sudden it would stop. Every time this happened my heart would pound through my chest, and every time I would start to get out of my chair to rush to the nurse's station to tell them, but then the heartbeat would come back. I would get a sense of relief and sit back in my chair, only to repeat the process over and over again. This was quite stressful and it made us very nervous. I tried to hide it though, because the last thing I wanted was to make Cristy more nervous than she already was. If she saw me getting nervous, she would know that something was wrong because I rarely get nervous about things.

The sun started to come out and I was a little more comfortable because Cristy's doctor was about to arrive at the hospital. In this situation when I was concerned about life, a doctor's skills and knowledge provided a safety net for my worries. She finally arrived and walked to Cristy's bedside calmly, comforting both of us when we saw she wasn't worried about the situation. She checked to see how Cristy was progressing, which wasn't much, and then told us what was happening. She said that it seemed the umbilical cord is either wrapped around the baby's neck or that the way Cristy was lying was slowing blood flow through the umbilical cord. She wanted Cristy to move and see what would happen to the heart rate. When she turned to one side, it seemed to make the situation worse, so she asked her to lie on her other side. This seemed to make the situation a little better. With an epidural the drugs can be influenced by gravity, so by lying on one side, it numbed her really well on that side, but not on the other. In addition there were several times throughout the day that she needed to increase the dose of the epidural. This made one of her legs completely paralyzed. She couldn't move it or feel anything on that leg. I would help her move her leg when she wanted to adjust herself. It was weird to see that she had no control over that limb. By this time we were starting to get some visitors who were comforting to have after a night filled with worry. I checked on work several times and everything seemed to be going well. My brothers and dad were going to come to the hospital at the very last moment before the baby was born so that they could keep working on the transition.

Cristy's doctor visited every hour, with slow progress between visits. Finally on one of the visits she said, "I think we are ready to have a baby."
Those words made my heart start racing. I suddenly felt the urge to have to go to

the bathroom, which happened to me every time I got nervous about something. When we were on the swim team it would be every time before my race. I knew with this urge that this was go time, no turning back now. This was a moment that I had to be a man and witness my wife go through something in which I had no way to help her, other than hold her hand. This was hard because I am the type of person who wants to help others if at all possible. I grabbed her hand and her doctor looked over at me and said, "Sweetheart, that isn't going to help her. If you want to help her, grab her legs and pull up when she has to push." I immediately jumped to the task and looked at Cristy with support and encouragement. "This is it, you can do this," I said to her. "Just let me know what you need me to do, and I will do it." The room was transformed, the huge lights were illuminated, nurses swarming in the room getting ready to do their parts, and the doctor was gowned and ready to go.

  The doctor started to coach Cristy on when to start pushing. With each push we would encourage her and cheer her on like we were at a sporting event. Each push brought us that much closer to parenthood. As we were getting closer, I asked the doctor to let me know when a good time would be to start filming video. I had the video camera set so that it would catch Cristy and me and the baby in view when the doctor lifted him up. She told me that she would let me know, and we went back to our pushing and cheering routine. Shortly after that she told me, "Um, you may want to get that camera ready," and before she could finish I had it rolling. I could see Julien start to make his grand entrance. "One more push and you two are going to be parents," the doctor said. We looked at each other during that pause and didn't say anything, because the looks on our faces said it all. The doctor commanded the last push and Cristy started pushing. All of a sudden Julien was there, and I could see the umbilical cord wrapped around his neck with his little hand holding it so that it wasn't choking him. That moment was the best moment in my life. He started to cry and the doctor put him right on Cristy's chest. We looked at each other with tears in our eyes. I held onto his little hand and rubbed it while I gazed over him. It was the most beautiful thing I had ever experienced in my life. The nurse handed me the scissors to cut the umbilical cord. I cut it, and they took him to the crib to start their tests and cleansing process. I hugged Cristy and gave her the biggest kiss I could and thanked her for such a wonderful gift. After they had finished their tests they gave Julien, who was all wrapped up, to Cristy. We had the nurses take some pictures of Cristy, Julien and me, and then the nurses and doctor all got in for a group picture. We were so excited and eager to let our family know that we successfully delivered new life to the world. Life doesn't get any better than this! There is pain when we enter this world and pain when we leave; hopefully what we do in between makes all that pain worthwhile.

After Cristy fed the baby, it was time to see all of our family in the waiting room. When a baby is born at this particular hospital, they play a nursery rhyme across the hospital, so every time my family heard one they wondered if it was ours, getting their hopes up each time. I walked out with the biggest smile on my face. When I saw everyone sitting there waiting, they all popped up with smiles and tears and I said, "We have a new baby boy in the family!" Everyone was so happy to hear that the delivery went well and I led them to the room. I took pictures of everyone holding Julien. I particularly

enjoyed watching my parents and Cristy's parents hold him because I could just see the joy and love in their eyes; however, the person I enjoyed seeing the most holding Julien was Randy. I could see and feel that he was really moved by holding a new life created by his twin and Cristy. I could sense the thoughts racing through his mind. I made a point to get a picture of Randy and me while he held Julien. After the family had their turns holding Julien, I passed around the cigars to the men. I had one special cigar for Randy though, because this was the first time I would reveal who the Parrain would be. I made sure I gave his cigar to him last, and written on his cigar was the phrase, "Parrain or Godfather". He looked at it and nearly cried when he noticed it. He said, "I think he can call me Parrain." He was so happy to be Julien's Parrain.

It was time for the nurses to take Julien to the nursery to do their tests and monitor him for a while. This gave Cristy and me time to get something to eat, and while we were eating all of our families chose to let us have our time alone, and they all went their separate ways home. The first moment we had alone was so special; we looked at each other with joy and happiness and reminded each other how much we were in love with Julien and each other. Later that evening the nurses brought Julien back so that he could nurse. I was nervous about this process because yet again I had no way to help with nursing

Julien. A lactation specialist came in and she was really good at teaching Cristy how to do it. I paid attention very closely to her, because I knew that Cristy would probably not remember all the details still coming off of medicine and the natural high of birthing a child. Julien was having trouble at first with feeding and the stress I felt before he would latch was really new to me. The father instinct in me to feed my child was pushing through all other emotions, and when he finally would latch on, I experienced a flood of emotional relief and happiness. That night we didn't get much sleep, which is nothing new to parents of a newborn, but it was new to us. After one of the midnight or later feedings, I held him in my arms while he slept. I watched him the whole time sleeping peacefully. I just couldn't believe that I had a baby boy.

The next day was about the same, feeding Julien every three hours, changing diapers constantly, and trying to get organized to check out of the hospital. After one of his morning feedings, Cristy wanted to take a shower, so I held Julien in my arms and he dozed off. I looked down at him and for the first time in my life realized that I could cry tears of joy. While my eyes were filled with tears it was like trying to see underwater in a swimming pool, when I got a text from Randy.

"How are Julien and Cristy?" he said.

I replied, "They are doing well, Julien is sleeping on me." I snapped a picture of me holding Julien.

He replied to me, "Oh does he look like us :)"

I said, "Yeah, weird to look at him and see us as babies on home videos."

"Yeah, I have the picture of us two, and he doesn't look like that just yet but I can see it coming. So weird. Yesterday was a very emotional day for me, very happy!" Randy said to me.

"I bet, I am still emotional. It's truly an amazing experience that I haven't really had time to process. He's amazing!" I replied.

He said, "He sure is amazing! For the brief moments when I held him I put myself in your shoes and could imagine how happy I am going to be when I have my own one day; it's so mind blowing."

I replied, "Yup, it hits you when you hear that cry for the first time."

"Yeah I can only imagine, and I am overflowing with happy emotions, and it's not even mine. It's just the thought that his genetics are of yours and mine and he looks so much like us. Makes me want to have a boy first to see how strikingly similar they are to each other."

I said, "I guarantee you're sensing my own thoughts. I bet they would look alike."

He replied, "I know I am (sensing your feeling) too. It's too weird to even describe to Mara all of the emotions I am feeling. Crazy."

I snapped another picture of Julien and sent it to him.

He said, "Just absolutely crazy!! Chokes me up every time I see a picture."

I told him that I get choked up every time I look or think about him.

Randy said, "Yup, I bet that's where a lot of mine is coming from too. You take our (three) birthdates and add one more 6 and you get 18 (all together)."

Our birthday is March the 6th, so by adding the number 6 for him and 6 for me equals 12, and adding another 6 equals 18, and Julien was born on the 18th of October. He was showing me that the three of us are connected by the number 6. For anyone confused here I caution this has more to do with twins and their mind set than it does math or numbers; although, musicians and mathematicians have a lot in common.

I said to him, "Without a doubt. These emotions are too strong for them not to transfer (to you). That's a pretty cool thought about our birthdays."

To know exactly what he was talking about could have only been understood by twin minds. We always had that gift being twins. We ended our conversation not having to say much more; we were feeling and talking to each other through our minds. Not only was having Julien in my arms filling me with emotions, but the thought that the connection I was creating with Julien was being created in Randy at the same time was very powerful. I just couldn't hold it together any longer and cried with joy. This was a moment in my life that I will never forget, and a moment that only other twins may understand. Tears can soothe a troubled soul but can also mirror and reflect the brightest light of our happiest moments.

We made it through the first two nights, but now came the impending discharge from the hospital. In the hospital I was so comfortable knowing that at any moment if we needed medical assistance or even medical advice, all we had to do was call the nearest nurse. Now we were on our own. Of course we had the help of our parents for which we were grateful, but medically if something were to happen, I knew that we were not as close as I would comfortably want to be. Looking at this new life, I wanted to protect him and make sure that he would be safe. I can remember being a boy when we got our first dog. I would watch Odie sleep and make sure he was still breathing, and with Julien I was the same way. Pets have forever taught us humans how to love and parent.

     We took pictures with some of the nurses that helped us and I walked to the car to get the car seat. When I got back Cristy held Julien in her arms as she was wheeled to the parking garage in a wheelchair, and I had everything else in tow. Once we ever so gently and carefully buckled Julien into his car seat, I put him in the car and drove off. I have always been a fast driver, but for once in my life, the cars were honking and passing around me the same way I used to do. I remember looking at every car on the road as a potential hazard to life. "Hey, buddy, there's a baby on board here," I would think.

     We videoed the ride home and Cristy videoed me carrying Julien into the house. It was a special moment for both of us. The house was quiet, especially since Randy was watching our dog, Maximus. He is a big fluffy white German shepherd who is very attached to me and is very protective of me. I was sure to bring home the blanket that they wrapped Julien in right when he was born so that I could let Maximus smell it and get acquainted with Julien's smell before he came home. We asked Randy to watch Maximus one more night so that we could get settled and become comfortable being home with a new baby, which he had no problem doing.

     The next day I went to get Maximus and I was very nervous that he wouldn't like the fact that we added a member to our family. I wanted to make sure that he had zero energy left to jump on Julien or accidentally bump him in any way. He was only a year and a half old so he had a lot of energy. I took him to our usual park and threw the Frisbee as hard and as far as I could. It worked. When I finally brought him home, Julien was in his little swing sleeping, and Maximus walked up to him, gave him a sniff, and then plopped down on the tile floor from exhaustion. My plan worked. One less stress for the day. Unfortunately I only had the weekend to enjoy Julien because come Monday we were starting a new venture at work, the distribution of products for another company, Stanley's, which would turn out to be an undertaking that almost put us out of business.

Chapter 32

Close to Being Far Away

In my early years of learning the business, I found out quickly that there is such a thing as having too much business, especially when you aren't fully prepared for it. We thought that we had prepared enough, but there was no way that we would have been able to foresee what was involved with doubling the family business overnight.

On the day Julien was born, our dad had sent out an email to the partners of the business, saying we have double the amount in accounts payable than we do in the bank. Things were starting to get scary. The first day back to work was the day from hell. The orders were pouring in and we were struggling just to keep up with entering the orders in the system. Once we had completed putting the orders in the system, the next hurdle was to pull the orders. In the past, we normally had a lot of product but we knew where the entire product was just from repetition. But since we had all new products in a new warehouse without the muscle memory of locations, pulling a single order took over an hour for one person. That day we had over fifty orders to pull. To top it off, we had hired new people to help handle the influx of business, but the new people were unfamiliar with the product and our systems. That night we didn't get out of the warehouse until 11:00 p.m., which made it a nineteen-hour day for John, Randy, and me because we got there at 4:00 a.m. The bad thing was we weren't finished pulling orders that needed to go out early the next morning. By the time I got home, Julien was sleeping already, and I had just enough time to take a shower and try to get some sleep before either Julien woke up and needed to eat, or my alarm clock went off at 3:30 the next morning.

The next day seemed worse than the day before. We didn't get the trucks which normally would go out at 8:00 a.m. until mid-day. It was as if we were not able to catch up from the day before, and we were being bombarded again with more orders that needed to go out the following day. All of a sudden I started getting calls from the Stanley Company looking for orders that we obviously misplaced, calls about damaged product, late trucks, miss-picks, just about any other possible problem. Usually when it came to adversity, Randy and I could tackle it and be confident we would succeed, but this time we both were in doubt. Usually I was the leader when it came to business, but with Julien interrupting my sleep and my energy, Randy picked up the slack and came through. He was creating ordering procedures to be put in place to help us wrangle this bucking bronco.

After two more horrendous days like the first two we had devised a plan that would help us gain control of the situation. Orders which we could execute without waiting on new equipment would be filled. On that Friday, knowing the plan to streamline and get better organized, I called Amy at the Stanley Company and told her that next week she would not be calling me because we would have this thing under control. She was doubtful but wanted to believe my words, either because she thought I was confident, or because she was hoping I was right for Stanley's sake.

That Saturday we got a piece of equipment that would print labels for each item being ordered, which would prevent pulling the wrong item and also prevent giving away extra product that had not been invoiced. The label printer would also allow us to print a shelf tag so we could identify the products easier on the shelves. We also started implementing a location code that would help us find the product on the shelves and would help us to locate a product when filing an order. Then we implemented a checklist of orders that arrived in our email to make sure that we picked every order and every order made it on the truck. No more lost orders. When Monday came, we were in much better shape than the previous week; at least we made it appear that way on the outside. Internally we were still shell-shocked trying to tame the beast. For each problem that would arise, we would quickly develop a plan to solve it and prevent that problem from happening again. We were building good business practices without even knowing it.

We were so busy that I didn't have the luxury to be home with my newborn. Cristy sent me pictures of Julien dressed in a Halloween onesie, and it broke my heart that I was missing his first Halloween. John as well missed his first Halloween with his daughter because of the amount of work. I didn't have much time to think about it, though; we were busy recording locations for items and putting out fires as they arose.

For the grocery business, October through January is the busiest time of the year, and we had taken on this new business in our busiest time. While we were trying to handle the warehouse and problems of logistics, our dad was trying to handle the payables and receivables end, which was looking pretty grim. He came back to the coolers where Randy and I were stacking product and gave us some scary news. "I just want to let you know that never in my life have I ever been in a situation like the one we are in now," he nervously said to us. "Our accounts payables are higher than our receivables, with just about nothing in the bank to pay it. I am scared about this situation; I just don't know what to do. I have never been here before and I can't take it. I have to go home." He walked out of the cooler and I looked over at Randy.

"This isn't good, Randy. I don't know what we have done. This isn't what I had in mind when we tried to enlarge this business."

"I know, Russ, this isn't good," he said to me.

We had been through storms before, Randy and I, but this time I was affecting innocent family members who had not created the problem. No matter how hard we physically worked, the financial situation was not going to change overnight. To make things worse when we were in the freezer one Saturday getting ahead, one of the fire sprinkler pipes got hit and jettisoned water all over the place, and because this happened in the freezer, water instantly froze to the ground. We all ran to shut the water off and on the way back I saw John lying on the floor. He ran into the freezer to help and he slipped and fell. Instead of making progress with locating items in the freezer, we were smashing the ice on the floor with mauls for the remainder of the day. Things just seemed like they couldn't get better, no matter how much effort we put into trying to improve the situation. In a favorite episode of *I Love Lucy*, Lucy can't keep up wrapping chocolates on an assembly line that begins running faster and faster so that she tries eating the product just to keep up. This was a Lucy-on-the-chocolate-assembly-line situation, but without the humor.

It was up to me to make this better; at least I felt that way since I was the one who really pushed to bid on this business. I called the main contact at the Stanley Company and told him things were not looking pretty. Fortunately, he was able to work a more favorable pricing structure, and we were slowly able to raise some prices to help the situation. It took a month or two before the situation started to level itself out. My dad would send weekly updates on the payables and receivables and with each email I looked for any sign of hope. Throughout the entire holiday season there was not a glimmer of hope until the end. We were so consumed by the business that I don't even remember what we did for that holiday season. All I know is that the only thing I could think about was how I couldn't let the family business go under on my watch, and I knew Randy was there to make sure of that as well.

One thing I do remember was that for this particular Christmas everyone in our family was together, which hadn't happened in the last few years. As the family grew so did our obligations to split the holidays with in-laws. New Year's Eve we were going to go to my parents' chalet in Pine Mountain, Georgia, to try and relax and spend time with Cristy, Julien, and my parents. I was finally able to relax some after three months of chaos. At this point it seemed that somehow we weathered another big storm and that what was left was the cleanup. Life to this point had continued to throw curve balls, and the lesson to learn from each of them was obviously perseverance and resiliency. What I learned in this situation is that you don't conquer adversities on your own. I was extremely thankful for Randy, John, and some of our great employees. Without the help of the group as a whole, we would have failed. It's important to pause on the journey and smell the roses and savor the sweet taste of success, because

> *Success gently knocks, then runs away.*
> *She knocks lightly again day after day.*
> *One day she knocks but says, "May I come in?"*
> *Let her in, and thank your friends,*
> *For they're the ones who had her stay.*

By Jay Hoecker

Unfortunately not every tough challenge can be accompanied by help. Unlike this storm, the next one coming would have me feeling alone in my attempts to cope with adversity. Business trials and tribulations were nothing compared with what lay ahead. The Future doesn't share her secrets: She loves us too much to do that.

Chapter 33

Breaking News and a Breaking Heart

One Friday morning I was sitting in my office when an unusual convergence of our dad, Randy, and John happened in my office. My twin brother sat next to my father while John stood. As I wondered why, they closed the door and were all looking at me. Randy spoke.

He said in a teary voice, "I have a brain tumor."

"Brain tumor!!??!! Is it cancer??!!?? Is it cancer??!!??"

Then Dad so calmly said, "This isn't as bad as you feel." He continued to explain the situation while Randy sat there with tears in his eyes. In that moment my life as I knew it would be rocked and tested.

I went home trying not to cry all day. I needed to tell Cristy. I needed her to tell me that everything would be okay. That moment was when it hit me; when I repeated the life-changing news. I cried myself to sleep that night and several thereafter. What was my worry? How could I know whether this would be as bad as I feared? Randy had found out that I was taking his news pretty hard and sent me a text to bring me out of a depression that was obvious:

"Hey, you know I'm going to be fine, please don't let this mess you up too much. John said you're taking this pretty hard and it's really just going to be fine. Love you, Russ! I am not worried, you shouldn't be."

"I know, Randy, it's just hard to grasp. I know you will be fine and I am praying for that. I love you too! I will be strong for you because I know that will help," I said.

"My time here isn't done and you know that, so much I still have to do. This is just a speed bump and an awaking for the whole family to be aware of our bodies." He said this while he was trying to reassure me, and maybe even himself.

One week after his diagnosis Randy came to work and dropped off his new album for his band ZamaPara called *Peace of Mind*. Peace of mind, huh? Well that is timing at its worst, if you ask me. The second I listened to it, I cried. His work, a culmination of years of trial and error, had been masterfully pieced together so that he could say to the world, "This is me, and what I am about has finally come to fruition." The music was so profound, so honest, so Randy. At first my favorite song was "War," a song written about something so fitting for what we were all about to experience. We were now at war with his tumor, hoping that we would win. Cancer presents an odd mixture of challenges: being educated while doing battle, and being at peace with yourself while being in conflict with your body. I am not sure if he wrote it with these intentions, but for me it represents Randy's battle for his life:

> *The color that leaves us when you are scared*
> *No allegiance open to the fires and the bombs of hell*
> *War is between us here*
> *Open your mouth and taste the fear*
>
> *The water is rising red from the blood we've shed*
> *Justice in the hands of the ignorant man*
> *Who are we not to see disease*
> *Please the need for these sinful deeds*
>
> *Oh my brothers and sisters what can I do today*
> *Oh my mother and father what can I say for this place*
> *All I want to do is go and run away from it all*
> *Why is it that we live this way?*
>
> *The babies they lay their heads across the fire*
> *No place to hide in fears it will not die*
> *Murder is slave to fill the grave*
> *The more we take the less we save*

The power and lust fills their desire
You think you're right but you lack what's right inside
Can't you see it's not what you need
Pride is your fight for the world to bleed

Oh my brothers and sisters what can I do today
Oh my mother and father what can I say for this place
All I want to do is go and run away from it all
Why is it that we live this way?

Every temptation lurks for justice they speak
The garden is where we all started to think
The fruit draws its seeds we eat
Amidst we fall when we have no feet

If the fall had come upon us while we are here
Left for the rest to crawl to preserve
Iniquitous man rule with your hand
The lengths on me you cannot stand

Oh my brothers and sisters what can I do today
Oh my mother and father what can I say for this place
All I want to do is go and run away from it all
Why is it that we live this way
So run, run, run away
Now run, run, run away
Oh there's no time here for you now so run away
Oh there's no place you can stand so run away
Oh now before it's too late.

"War" by Randy Perrone June 24, 2009

An intimate video of Randy playing this song can be seen here:
https://www.youtube.com/watch?v=EKXJKvBeaAk

With the stress we had encountered over the past year and predominantly over the previous three months, the headaches that Randy had been getting were blown off as just headaches from stress. They would go away with over-the-counter medicine, so he wasn't concerned at first. On the way back from a business trip in Houston that we both had attended, Randy realized that the headaches had to be more than just stress headaches. When Randy went to a doctor, one of my sister's colleagues in a leading neurological practice in Louisiana, the doctor was very skeptical he would find something in the MRI but he ordered it nonetheless. My sister went down with Dr. Grant, the lead neurosurgeon, to review the MRI and that is when the tumor was discovered. My sister then called Randy right away. Because we are twins, my family's and my concern was that I would have a tumor as well. I went to get checked by the same doctor that evaluated Randy and then I also had a MRI. When I had the MRI I felt like it was necessary for me to have a brain tumor so that Randy wasn't alone through this. I actually was a little let down knowing I didn't have a tumor. Survivor's guilt is not imaginary. Randy obviously was happy that he didn't have to further suffer with me having a similar ailment; he was always thinking about others, especially me due to our strong bond.

The weeks after this were somewhat quiet. Randy went through more testing to find the best method of eradication. There were options of radiation only, then waiting to see what the tumor would do; and there was surgery. So Dr. Grant's methods were going to be radiation first then "wait to see" what happens. Surgery was something he was willing to do, but in order to find out what the tumor was they needed to get a biopsy of it. Randy and Andrea went to MD Anderson Cancer Center in Houston to get a second opinion. There they met a neurosurgeon who has done these surgeries often and was confident that he could do this surgery with no issues. The plus side of going to MD Anderson was that the lab able to do the biopsy analysis was in the same hospital where surgery could be done. This was the deciding factor on where we were going to have the operation. Dr. Grant's hospital didn't have the ability to do the lab on site; therefore, Randy would have required additional surgeries, one to get a biopsy and one to attempt to remove the tumor.

The decision was made that we were going to go to MD Anderson to have the procedure done. Several weeks passed, and I pretty much put it in the back of my mind. I know that Randy didn't, though. This was on his mind all the time. Our family, as partners in our business, decided that what was important was to let Randy do as much or as little toward work as he chose. I am thankful that we did this because this was valuable time for him to do the things he needed to do and also the things he wanted to do before his surgery, which was to work on his music and record as many songs as he could before his surgery. An omen, if you will, to prepare himself for the potential of death, and for me to prepare myself for a life without him. Such a valuable and memorable gift he was able to give us with his voice, his words, his feelings, all wrapped up in his music.

  We had had Julien's christening four weeks before Randy was to go to Houston. This was a big deal because Randy being Julien's Parrain meant the world to me and to him. I was so happy at this point that he was able to be Julien's Parrain and that he was going to get to hold him in front of our whole family. We asked Father Billy to do Julien's christening. Father Billy, the same priest that officiated our wedding, was one of the priests who served at our church when John, Randy, and I were altar servers. We really had a great relationship with him, partially because he was tall and funny, and because he was from Ireland and had such a great accent. He was really close to our family while he was at our school and church. This was the first time for him to have had a wedding and a christening for the same couple.

  While he was doing the christening, he also delivered a sermon that was just perfect. He explained that years go by, and the buildings that each of us walk through generally will be there for generations who have yet to be born. This was important especially because it was a way to let us all know that our time is more limited than the objects around us, and that we should not only appreciate the time we do have here but also appreciate the time of those who walked the same road before us. At that moment he wasn't aware of Randy's tumor or his upcoming surgery. As we were leaving the church to go to my parents' home for a post-christening party, our dad mentioned to him Randy's situation. He was shocked, and quickly said to us, "I have the oils for anointing of the sick, and I would like to lay hands on Randy right now if that is okay." We all said yes. He pulled out his oils and asked us all to raise our hands up to Randy's head. He started Laying of Hands on Randy and his voice was so powerful and majestic in the way he prayed. This was the first time I had ever witnessed this sacrament for someone, and I felt each hair follicle on my back stand to attention as though they were laying hands as well on Randy. I started to tear up watching and hoping that this sacrament would allow God to protect Randy and heal him. I remember seeing Randy there with his eyes closed with the same hope that we all had. It was such a relief on so many accounts to have such an important figure in our lives give Randy this sacrament.

Several weeks before the surgery, my mom had a conversation with Randy at work. She told him that she thought he should go to the sperm bank and make a deposit so that when he came back home after having radiation, he would have sperm banked that had not been exposed to the radiation. This way when he married and had children, there would be untainted sperm from before his treatments. My mom, always an optimist, thought of everything when it came to her children's lives. This being a great concern for a grandmother seemed to be so thoughtful and such wise advice. This selfless act of preparedness would become a terrible nightmare. As Saint Bernard said, "The road to hell is paved with good intentions."

Randy focused a lot on himself from the time of his diagnosis to the time of his surgery. One of the most important things he did was record his music. He told me one day that he was going to the studio a lot. He said, "I am trying to record all of my music before the surgery. I want to make sure that if I am unable to play, the band and I could still work on another album." I loved this idea. Randy had written so many songs in our lifetime. Some of them I hadn't heard in over ten years and I thought it would be great to be able to record some of his older songs in a professional studio. The studio he used was engineered by a good friend of his who really believed in the music he was making. His extreme attention to detail is one of the reasons Randy's first album turned out well, in addition to Randy's great talent. The extreme attention to detail, however, limited Randy on how many songs he was able to record. The time he put into the recordings also put a strain on Randy's relationship with Mara, who had become his fiancée about a year ago. There were nights when he would be at the studio for hours. He would come to work the following day and tell me how it was going, and I would ask about his progress. He would say, "We are getting there but I don't think I will be able to record all of my songs." We hadn't really talked about the surgery all that much, and I had my mind set that I was going to go to Houston whether he wanted me to or not.

"You know, I really want you to go to Houston for my surgery."

"Randy, I was absolutely going to go," I said. "There is no way that I could be here while you were there in surgery."

"Thanks, I will feel so much better having you there."

Two days before Randy was to leave for MD Anderson Cancer Center in Houston, he came to the office about mid-day. He walked into my office and presented a legal sized envelope and said, "Here is my will. I am giving you a copy of it. Do you want to read it?"

I told him, "No I don't want to read it because we won't be needing it," and I put it in my desk.

He said, "Well, if you are not going to read it, I want to tell you two things: one I am making you my executor, and, two, I am giving you my favorite guitar."

I didn't know what to say to either, all I could feel was honored to have his guitar, an instrument representing his passion to make music. In hindsight, I should have read it, because at that point I would have been able to pick out some potential issues with his requests and could have asked him what he meant by certain things. This is a lesson that I try to pass on to anyone facing a situation similar to this. It should not be feared; it should be embraced, because after the fact when the person who wrote it is no longer there to decipher it, then it becomes difficult to figure out what each bullet point means, and difficult to also try to figure out what wasn't said. Now is all we ever have; the past has

closed its door, and the future is never at home when we get there, always anxiously rambling away just out of our reach.

That night Randy invited us over to his house to have dinner. I had just started to give Julien his bottle, and so I sent a picture to Randy saying, "Sorry we missed dinner. This baby gets upset if he doesn't eat and sleep by now." I was feeling bad about the situation, and I feared that I should have gone in case this was one of my last times with Randy. He said, "It's all right. I would like to see you tomorrow though and take Maw Maw and GG to dinner if y'all want to join us?" The next night the whole family went to get pizza for the last time as a family unit. We all sat at the biggest table available. Julien was sleeping the whole time. As we were finishing I thought to myself, "Randy didn't get a chance to hold Julien. So I told Cristy, "I wanted Randy to hold Julien."

She said, "Well if you wake him up, he is going to want a bottle."

I said, "Perfect, I will let his Parrain give it to him then."

So we woke Julien and gave him a bottle and handed Julien to Randy, who was so happy to be able to hold his godchild. This may have been one of the only times that Randy fed Julien. I saw this moment through my fear of the whole situation and quickly started to take pictures thinking these could be the last pictures we would get of Randy holding Julien. I will always look at those pictures and think back that my intuition would eventually be shown to be right, and I'll forever look at those pictures thankful that I acted to memorialize that special moment. Julien will someday see those pictures and know that he was loved by "Daddy's twin."

As I now sit here at Randy's desk I recall the day he left for Houston. Our mom, Randy, and Mara flew out the Friday before his surgery and I was left here to watch over the warehouse. Our offices were right next to each other with an adjoining door that Randy and I removed so that we could converse with each other through the working day. As I looked through this opening at his empty desk, I couldn't help but be reminded about the impending surgery. His lights were out and the front door was closed. I walked into his office and just stood there looking around. I took notice of everything in his office. The feeling in my gut was that Randy would never sit at his desk again. I kept looking around and started to cry and get nervous. I just knew in my heart that something just wasn't going to be right about this surgery and all I could do was start to prepare myself for the day he would no longer be next to me. As I was leaving work I still wore a face of worry when Joe, one of our key employees, came up to me and tried to give me some confidence in this situation. He put his arms around me and said, "Don't worry, Randy will be just fine. He will be back to work before you know it."

"I am just so nervous about this surgery, Joe," I said to him, "I just hope that it goes well. I wish we didn't have to do this."

When I left I looked at every corner of the warehouse. Randy's mark was all over it with all the work we put into this place, the two of us working in tandem along with our older brother to grow our family business.

With having a newborn at home, I wanted to stay as long as I could before I took the trip to Houston. In hindsight I wish I would have gone earlier, but yet again, how was I to be sure my gut feelings were not just my being nervous about the surgery? I was going to drive to Houston on Sunday with our friend Ben. He was the only friend who wanted to come for this surgery. Ben was always late wherever he went, and this was looking to be another such instance. He had a flat tire on his truck, which we were supposed to take to Houston, and he had a plan to fix it the morning of our departure. We were supposed to leave New Orleans at five o'clock in the morning so we could get there in enough time to be with Randy.

Randy sent me a text saying, "Don't wait for him, he will have to be on time or else the train will leave him behind."

I could tell how important it was for Randy to have me there, "Don't worry, if he isn't here on the dot, I am leaving him because I don't want to be late for your surgery."

Much to my surprise, Ben was on time and we set off in Randy's car to Houston. I was nervous during the whole ride. We listened to Randy's music almost the whole way. I remember texting Randy a screen shot of his music on Rhapsody, and told him how proud I was that it was available on such a large scale that anyone in the country could listen to it. He replied to me, "Nice!" I asked him if he would get royalties on this and he said, "Yup!" I could picture his proud face and smile just as I was so proud of his achievement. When we arrived in Houston we picked up Randy, Mara, and Mom from church. Randy didn't regularly go to church, but his concern and our mom's concern was evident through this, which again added to my concerns.

After we picked them up from church we headed back to the hospital's hotel to check in. While we were checking in, Randy saw a girl he met a day earlier. She was at MD Anderson to undergo more treatments for an aggressive cancer. I noticed that she had a prosthetic leg and asked Randy later what happened to her leg. He said that she had to have it amputated to prevent cancer from spreading through her body. Randy was always someone who could talk to people and feel their pain. He was able to bring light to a soul at the darkest time. Even with his own tough road ahead, he was able to bring this girl some type of friendship and relief.

Ben, Randy, and I put our bags in our room and hung out there for a bit. Ben showed Randy and me a new iPhone app and we were both glued to it. Ben had to step away for a bit leaving Randy and me in the room. We sat there in silence the whole time, looking at our phones, but all the while talking to each other in our minds. I kept saying to myself how nervous I was, and I could feel his calm throughout our silent talk. Ben came back in and we all decided that we wanted to go for a drive to cut the tension.

Ben, Randy, Mara, and I jumped into the car and headed to the store. It was near Easter time. I know this because when we got to the store, Randy and I spotted the marshmallow Easter bunnies we grew up loving, not to be confused with Peeps, and grabbed a bag each and started salivating over them while we walked through the store. We came across the sporting goods section and saw a football and a Frisbee and decided what we were going to do for the remainder of the evening. We put them in our basket and walked through the store to the checkout acting like kids do when they are first without their parents in a store. We got to the checkout and I hurried to buy our items before anyone else could. This was my gift to Randy, a way to take his mind off of the upcoming surgery.

As soon as we hit the car we opened our Easter eggs and ate them in front of Ben and Mara, while they watched us and just couldn't understand. What they didn't know is that this was just another thing that Randy and I had enjoyed doing ever since we were kids. We were grasping and holding on to the past and the present as best we could. When your past is slipping away, you grab anything you can hold, even if its marshmallow Easter candy.

As soon as we got back to the hotel Ben, Randy, and I were itching to get to a field by the hotel to throw the Frisbee and the football. Mara wanted to take a nap in the room, which was great in my opinion because I didn't want to share this moment with anyone other than the three of us. We headed to the field like children, giggling and cutting up the whole way through the lobby and to the field. We started to really cut up by throwing the Frisbee at each other's legs trying to hit them. It was just like it had always been with us, having a good time, not concerned about the world. Once we reached the field, we formed a triangle and started throwing to each other. While throwing the football and Frisbee in rotation, I couldn't help but keep an eye on Randy. I made sure every time I was about to throw the football to him, he was aware and looking, because the last thing I wanted to do was hit him in the head and potentially cause an issue with his surgery. Part of the fun was making sure each was on guard, because if not, he may get surprised or hit by a ball.

As the Frisbee would fly over his head and into the ditch right behind him, all I could do was watch like a mother watches her child, hoping he was being as careful as he could going down the ditch, and when he would surface again give a big sigh of relief that he had made it safely. We spent about two hours in this field, throwing the Frisbee and football back and forth, but what we were really doing was helping to keep our minds off Randy's surgery and on something that was comforting to him. My mindset was that whatever he wanted to do, we were going to do. As the sun was starting to set, we got some phone calls from our mom saying that our dad and Andrea had just arrived and that we had to start getting ready for dinner. I can almost recall saying, "Aww, Mah," when she called, not wanting to leave the park, not wanting to let this special moment go away. This was a moment when we knew that what had just happened would never be forgotten by any of us. All of our worries were back, and I knew that Randy was thinking, "Would this be the last time I am able to run, stand, walk?" and all I could think was, "Would this be the last time I see my brother have fun? How would this time together be remembered for me? Would this be the last memory of him enjoying life?"

We rushed back to the room because we knew we were running behind, and in true mother-son interaction our mom said, "You need to take a shower still? We are going to be late. Hurry up!" I jumped in the shower and took the quickest shower that I could. I didn't want to be away from Randy at all. I literally took three minutes to shower and get ready. It seemed like superman could not have changed as quickly as I did. We all met at our parents' room and were ready to go. It was our mom, dad, Andrea, Ben, Mara, Randy, Mara's sister Sara, and I who would be going to dinner. This was the support group who had all arrived in Houston for Randy's surgery.

We went to an Italian restaurant about twenty minutes from our hotel. Randy was driving his car and it seemed like he knew exactly where he was going. I thought to myself how much I must have missed in the two days we were separated that he could know where he was and I didn't. I always knew where we were whenever Randy and I went anywhere, so this was an uncomfortable feeling for me. He navigated Houston's maze of highways and got us to the restaurant. We dropped everyone off at the front, and then we went to park the car.

We walked to the restaurant, talking with our minds, twin talk. The hostess sat us at a large table. It felt good to have us all there for Randy, and I knew it gave him some peace of mind to know he wasn't alone. He sat at one end of the table and I sat toward the opposite end. Our dad of course was at the head of the table, our mom to his right, and Randy to his left. I remember looking toward Randy, watching his moves, watching what he was doing. When he ordered a beer my heart started racing.

I interrupted Randy pouring the beer and I said to him and Andrea, "Hey wait! Can he have a beer?"

Andrea told me, "Yes, he can have a beer or two according to the surgeon."

"Well that doesn't make sense to me, but hey if the surgeon said he could, then I guess he can."

As dinner went on, we talked, we laughed, we had some quiet moments, but all in all it was such a special evening. Randy was getting phone calls and texts from everyone. He was literally answering texts as he was getting a call, with people wishing him well, and I could see the sincere appreciation on his face. His smile, profound and unique, is something I will never forget, and at that moment it was shining through very brightly.

As we were finishing dinner, I started to realize that we were getting closer and closer to the surgery. My mind shut down. All I could do was stare off into space, my worries showing all over my face.

Mara's sister, Sara, said to me, "Rusty, are you okay?"

I snapped out of it for a second and said, "Yeah. Yeah. I am okay." But I was a total wreck at this point.

"Are you sure?"

"Yes, I am good, thank you."

I know Dad saw it and he started getting concerned. He didn't want to bring attention to it so that my brother wouldn't notice it and start to get nervous. I brought myself out of it for him and continued the dinner, in a somewhat solemn mood for the remainder of the dinner. We all got dessert and coffee and then the check came. Randy pulled out his wallet and said, "Daddy, I got this," and wound up paying for the whole dinner. I remember looking at him sign the paper and thought to myself, "Can we keep that copy? It has his signature on it." As we all rose from the table, I volunteered to drive but Randy seemed to object, so I said to him, "Randy, you have had some alcohol, and we are in Texas, and if you get pulled over, your surgery won't happen." He understood my concern and gave up rather easily compared to past driving situations. We piled in the car and headed back to the hotel.

As we were driving down the road, Andrea spotted a pharmacy and she demanded we detour to it so that we could get a special anti-bacterial soap. The soap is usually ordered by doctors for patients who are going into surgery within 24 hours. I don't believe he was ordered to wash with it, but my sister being a physician, and another mom figure in our lives, suggested he do this as an extra precaution. I thought to myself, "This was a smart idea, another way to ensure nothing would go wrong tomorrow." I waited in the car and I don't remember if I was in the car with just Randy or if anyone else was in the car with us, but I started again in a whirlwind of emotions. We reached the hotel and I pulled in the valet/drop off circle to let everyone out.

"Randy, stay in the car with me," I said in my mind, using my telepathy as much as I could to give Randy a hint to stay with me while I parked the car. I wanted to talk to him alone, potentially the last opportunity I would get. I just looked straight ahead not noticing who was getting out, and I heard Randy say, "I am going to ride back with Rusty to the garage." I wanted to cry, I was so happy he heard me and was going to ride back alone with me. I was in the front seat and he was directly behind me. We said nothing verbally but so much in our twin talk on the short ride to the parking garage. I parked pretty close to the entrance, and shut the car off. We opened our doors at the same time, closed them at the same time, and looked at each other. Still in silence we started to walk back to the hotel.

As we made our way out of the garage I put my arm around him and said, "Are you nervous?"

"Nah, I am not nervous. Are you?"

I gripped him tight with my arm around his shoulders and said, "Yes, I am really nervous!" and I started to cry. My tears came down like rain.

He turned to me, put his arms around me and said in a calm, cool, and collected manner, "Russ, don't worry! I am going to be fine."

I hugged him tighter and just bellowed out, "I am so scared Randy! I am so scared to lose you! I don't know how I would live without you in my life, Randy. I am so scared!"

He just hugged me, rubbing my head as a dad would do to his son, calming me down with his protective and reassuring nature. We sat there between the hotel and the parking garage and we hugged each other tight as I cried into his shoulder. My tears fell down like children's tears do when they are hurting. My memory brought me to a moment in life when Randy and I were kids and it was just us with no other worry in life. We stood there arms wrapped around each other for what seemed like an eternity. I recall seeing some people coming out of a door across the street and thought to myself, "I don't care what this looks like, I need my brother's embrace now more than I have ever needed it," and stood there crying and being consoled by my brother. It was as if I was the one getting surgery and he was calming me down and assuring me that I would be okay. There are moments in life that the brain etches into its core memory, and this one is in a spot that even old age won't be able to tarnish.

As we started to walk again, arm over shoulder, I wiped my eyes and thought that it would be so obvious that I had been crying when we got back to the room. We didn't say much after that moment, but I felt if he were to leave this earth tomorrow, then I would have had my opportunity to tell him how much I love him.

When we got back to the hotel room where everyone was, Randy and I sat on one of the beds right next to each other. There were some beers in the cooler that Randy had bought a day earlier, so we each had one. "Our last beer together" is what I said to myself, preparing for what might happen. We sat there  and everyone was talking when our sister started to take pictures of Randy and me, and I was happy that someone was getting pictures of this moment. Randy wanted to call the girl they met in the lobby a day earlier so that she didn't feel alone. She was at MD Anderson with no family, and Randy wanted to make her feel like she had family there to support her. I was jealous at that moment, thinking "Do I have to share what feels like my last moments with Randy with a stranger?" I didn't say anything because I knew that Randy wanted to have her there, which did create a special bond with her, Randy, and our family. She quickly accepted the invitation and came to our room and enjoyed a beer with our family. She was so courageous in her journey and I think that Randy really fed off of her courage given his own plight. She made him feel some comfort that he wasn't fighting cancer alone. We found out some time later that she had lost her battle with cancer. I can only hope that she was surrounded by family.

I didn't want the night to end, but we all had to get up early the next morning, and the last thing I wanted was to jeopardize Randy's surgery by staying up late.   Everyone kissed goodnight, and Ben, Randy, Mara and I started walking in the direction of our rooms. As we reached Ben's and my room, Randy reminded me of the time to be awake the next morning, and I reassured him that I would be up before then, walking down with him.

Going to sleep was the hardest thing to do knowing that early in the morning we would be walking to the hospital with Randy. I just couldn't help thinking that tomorrow could be the last time he walked on this Earth. I couldn't help thinking that the longer I was awake, the longer it would be until we had to face this scary reality. Our room was quiet. No words were spoken before bed, thoughts and worries racing through my mind. I had my sister send the pictures she took in the room and looked at Randy's smile while his arms were around my shoulder, and thought this is the type of picture that you see after someone has died and you remember the smile as if he were still here. It was painfully prophetic, and all I could think about was Randy and what he may have been thinking at this moment. As nervous as I was, I wondered how he could sleep. Well he wasn't sleeping, in fact he wrote to the world one last message and posted it on Facebook:

> *"So tonight I lay my head down and tomorrow starts a new day for me. I have been absolutely blessed and humbled by everyone praying for me, thinking about me, and wishing the best for me and my family. It's incredible to see such a great force of positivity and spirit asking for me, just some person who happens to be living and breathing*

amongst everyone else.

My sweet lovely fiancé, has been a trooper since day one but especially since the discovery of what I have. I can only imagine what life is like in her shoes. They say it's not just the person who has the certain health issue, but the family too. I am glad it's me. I wouldn't want to be in their shoes wondering, worrying, and praying for their loved one to get better. I am glad to be taking this bullet instead of them, my lover, my twin brother, my family, and my friends.

Tomorrow is definitely not my end, I have so much more to live for and do. Trust me when I say that, I believe our destiny is in the hands of our own outlook, spirits, and thoughts of how it's supposed to be; and tomorrow is not the end of me and where my thoughts and desire take me. It's the beginning of a new outlook, a new life, a new appreciation of life, an understanding that it could always be worse. I am so grateful that it is me who has what I have and not anyone else who I love and care for so much. It's a new beginning for me and my family and a huge appreciation for how short and fragile our lives are. When you go to sleep tonight, make sure you tell your family that you love them, your kids, your friends, even new strangers turned friends on how much they mean to you. Tomorrow is never guaranteed, today is what we live for and I am excited every day I get another with the ones I love and the passions I have, the gifts I have been given, and the challenges I am able to take.

Thank you to my support team who is here in Houston with me and who are at home and around the country who are praying for me. I am really humbled by all of this. I can't believe I have deserved all of this love and prayer, but somewhere I must be doing something right; and for this I am truly humbled. I wish I could hug every single one of you and show my appreciation and love.

Stay tuned for more to come from this guy, it's the beginning of a new life and I promise I will give back all that has been given to me in the last two months. My fight may not be over tomorrow, but it all starts then and I can't wait to see what comes!!

Rusty, I know you would rather take this and put it in your body. I am so thankful that it's me who has it and not you. I kiss the ground for that in thanks. I wish I could take every illness and put it in my body so no one else would have to suffer, but life isn't that way...I feel your pain, literally (we can feel each other's pain like no other human can explain). I'm sorry you're hurting through this, but I will be okay and I'm very happy it's me and not you.

Stay positive saying don't worry about a thing 'cause every little thing is gonna be alright."

I didn't read this post until Randy had already gone to surgery and as soon as I did the tears flowed like a river as I realized what a beautiful picture of himself his words painted.

My alarm was set for 4:00 a.m., but I naturally woke up beforehand. I wasn't going to wait for anyone else to wake me up or hold me back. I brushed my teeth, packed my bag, and said to Ben, "Making sure you are up, see you by my parents' room." I looked to my brother's room and started to my parents' room, the whole way my emotions were running wild. As soon as I got to my parents' room, I knocked on the door. My mom opened up and I started to cry uncontrollably. I said, "Mom I am so scared!"

My dad quickly warned, "Russ you have to hold it together; you cannot let your brother see you this way. This is going to be hard for him and we all need to be strong."

I quickly pulled myself back together for Randy. The last thing I wanted was to give him a reason to worry. My emotions had to take a back seat to help my brother make it through this. One by one the support group got there. Lastly Randy and Mara walked up and it was time.

The walk to the operating room waiting area was a quiet one. Everyone took turns walking with Randy, holding him tight. I don't recall much of this walk other than how nervous I was and how I needed to curtail my emotions. "I cannot let him see me worried," I said to myself; "this is important for me to stay strong for Randy." It was finally my turn to put my arms around Randy. We walked as we did the night before, except this time there were no moments of just him and me alone. Last night would be the last time for that. We walked through the maze of hallways all the way to the surgery waiting room. Everything was in slow motion as we made our way closer. The roller coaster was approaching the apex of the climb and we realized there was no turning back. We had weathered many storms together and now this one. Oh, that Rodgers and Hammerstein could be right when they wrote,

> *When you walk through a storm*
> *Hold your head up high*
> *And don't be afraid of the dark*
> *At the end of the storm*
> *Is a golden sky*
> *And the sweet silver song of a lark...*
> *("You'll Never Walk Alone")*

Chapter 34

Surgery

Randy and I walked up to the nursing station to check in. He was his normal self, making conversation with the nurses and making them laugh. When we finished we all sat in silence, waiting for that moment they would call his name, and that would be the no-turning-back moment. They finally called his name, and with tears everyone gave him a hug and a kiss. I gave him my hugs and tried my hardest to hold back my tears. This was extremely difficult to do, because at this point I was very emotional. As he walked off to the pre-op surgery center I sat back and told myself that I needed one more hug from him. I raced up out of my chair and ran down the hall, calling out his name, "Randy! Randy! I need one more hug."

He said to me in his cool voice, "Ha ha, Russ, don't worry; everything will be okay."

That was the last time I saw Randy on his feet and dressed in his usual attire of shorts, sandals, and shirt. Walking the other way was such a hard thing for me, fearing in my heart that this would probably be the last time I saw him this way.

At this point we were texting back and forth letting people know that they could visit him before they called him for his surgery. I wanted to go last so that I wasn't worried about anyone waiting on me. Finally I got the text to come. I rushed to see him, his jovial self in full hospital garb and in such a positive mood. At this point his peace was made that whatever happened from this point would be in the hands of God. We talked briefly, and I hugged him one last time. Right before I left the room I snapped my last picture with my brother, as emotional as that was, I held back the tears so he didn't see me in poor shape. As

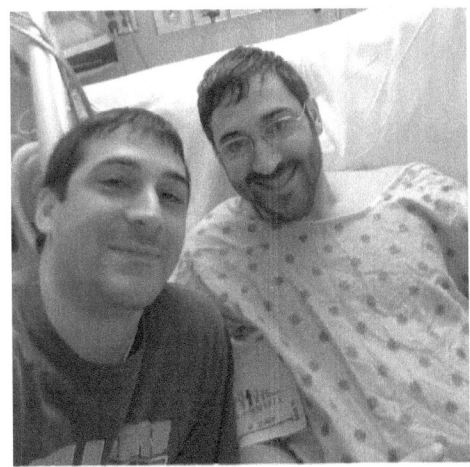

soon as I got back I got desperate to talk to him, to communicate how much he meant to me, how much I loved him, how scared I was about this surgery.

I sent a text to him, "I love you, Randy!!!! Please tell them you have a twin out here so be extra careful." I sent him the photo of us we had just taken and said, "Show them this!"

Then he said, "I love you too!!!! Everything is going to be just fine, trust your older brother."

"I do trust you."

"Good. I'll see you when I get out brother!"

"I will be counting the seconds until then. I love you."

He said, "Me too! Kinda, haha, if I can. Love you too buddy!!!"

The surgery started around 8 a.m. and the anxiety started. This was the worst anxiety I had ever felt in my life. All I could do was keep reading his last post on Facebook and cry. Everyone wanted to get something to eat, but I couldn't stomach any food. I refused the offer of anything to eat. I waited in that waiting room until they returned and when they did, my dad asked me if I wanted to walk back to the hotel room for something. I went with him and that is when I felt so uncomfortable being so far away from Randy that I told Dad I wanted to go back, and that would be the last time I was willing to leave the waiting room until his surgery was completed. We were supposed to get updates every two hours. Waiting for these updates was painful; waiting for one of them to deliver bad news, telling us that something terrible happened in surgery or that he was gone. This was my fear; knowing that my brother's life was literally in the hands of another human being. That is the most uncomfortable thing you can imagine, a loved one at the mercy of the talents of an individual. Wow.

Between meetings, I was reminded what it was like to be so nervous that I would have to pee. It wasn't like there was any fluid to pee, just drips. The same used to happen to Randy and me before our swimming events and other high anxiety times, such as at the birth of Julien. Each time the nurse would come in the room I would think, "Is this us? No that is someone else". Finally they called our name. I popped up like a buoy in the water that was being held down and finally released. I was always the first one up, the first one in the room, and the first one to ask a question. "How is he? How is the surgery? When are we going to know something about the tumor?" Each time the meeting was finished I knew I had just enough time to go to the bathroom and let my worries dribble from my bladder. Then it was back to waiting, listening to his music, talking to my sister, Andrea, about the surgery and how scared I was, crying on her shoulder, and just feeling more vulnerable than I have ever been. I cared not about what people saw in me, a weak man, just as I don't care right now writing about it. My emotions for him then and now are both sincere and powerful, and that is just what people will have to accept.

With each update from the nurses came more anxiety. The surgery was supposed to take six hours and we were at that mark. The first meeting they told us that they were working their way toward the tumor. Two long hours had passed and that was all we had, still getting to the tumor. "Okay, take your time, don't damage anything," I was thinking. In the second update they had finally reached the tumor and had taken the biopsy, but there were no results yet. So we went back to our seats and waited for the next update. Seeming like a day had passed, we got called again for our third update.

"They had to get another biopsy so it is taking a little longer than normal," said the nurse.

"Taking longer than normal?" I thought to myself, "Here it is. This is going to be a problem." Would my fears be right?

Another two hours went by before they updated us. The tumor needed to be removed. They started removing it and should be finished shortly. The doctor would come see us once they closed him up. This provided a little relief, then, knowing that soon they would be out of his brain, and any potential for a mistake would no longer be an issue.

Finally I heard our name called. This was the moment we would get to talk to the doctor. We were led to the same room where Mom and I had prayed that morning. We all sat down. As soon as the doctor saw me I made a comment to him, "Look pretty close to your patient, don't I, doctor?" He looked at me, took a double take, and said, "I was about to say, you recovered rather quickly."

This I felt broke the ice. He sat down and I sat right next to him. He started to explain the surgery.

He said, "The surgery took a little longer than expected. There was some bleeding that we had to control as we were making our way to the tumor. There were some veins that we had to squeeze our way through…"

I started to think to myself, "Why are you telling us about these particular veins, did something go wrong?" I said to the doctor, "You didn't hit the veins or anything, did you?"

He replied, "No, we made it past the veins and made it to the tumor. We started to remove the tumor and sent it to the lab. We waited about fifteen minutes and had to send another biopsy. This turned out to be a parenchymal pineal tumor that we had to remove. As we were removing it, we couldn't tell how close we were to the hypothalamus so we left about half of it in there. It was bleeding a bit, but we were able to stop the bleeding and we closed him up."

I felt some relief that at least they were out of there, which left the next hurdle of finding out if there would be chemo and radiation. We were anxious to see Randy.

I asked the doctor, "Can we go back to see him now?"

He said, "They are almost done and about to send him to recovery, you will get to see him shortly. The nurse will call you back."

I was so excited to finally be able to see Randy. The day had been very long, and to see him awake was going to be such a relief. As the doctor was leaving he mentioned to us that they were going to send Randy to a regular room after his recovery period. I looked to Andrea immediately and thought that going to a regular room and not the ICU didn't seem right. So Andrea and I decided that we would stay with him overnight, and each would take turns being awake watching Randy as the other slept. We got up and went back to the waiting room to be called to see him.

The nurse came out and said that he was ready to start having visitors, but warned that he would be sleepy and groggy due to the anesthesia. I immediately thought to myself that I wanted to go last so that he would have had some time to become more aware and possibly wake up by the time I saw him. I don't recall who went first, but two visitors were allowed at a time. The first two went and I waited and waited to hear from them how he was doing. When they came back I asked, "Was he awake?" They told me that he wasn't awake but was moving around. It seemed he could hear them but wasn't waking up.

The second two went, and again I waited for their return. Upon their return I asked the question again, "Did he wake up?" Again they said that no he wasn't awake. The next pair went, and I knew that Andrea and I were next. The anticipation was getting to me; I wanted to see him in the worst way. It seemed that everyone was taking so long, but at the same time I kept telling myself, the longer they take the more likely he will be awake for me. The third pair came back and again they said he wasn't awake but was moving around and making some sounds. It was finally my turn to go see him. Andrea and I walked back. I was so very nervous.

"What will he look like? I hope that he doesn't have any nerve damage."

We finally arrived at the room. Andrea and I walked in and at first I was a little shocked. His face was so swollen all I could feel was so much pain from seeing him look the way he did. Andrea said something while I was looking at him. He moved his head around a bit, but didn't wake up.

I finally said his name. "Randy...Randy," and his eyes popped open so fast and he looked directly at me. I said to him, "You look great. How do you feel?"

"Beat up. How are you doing?"

In a moment when he was in so much pain, he was concerned about me; this stunned me. I said confidently, determined that he wouldn't hear through my lie, "I am doing good." I added, "I love you."

"I love y---" he went back to sleep.
I wanted to hear it so badly, I asked Andrea what he said and she said, He tried to say I love you too but fell back asleep. Let's go and let him rest."

She was right; I didn't want to take any energy away from his healing. We left the room and I was happy to have been able to talk to Randy. I realized that of everyone who went to see him, I was the person who saw him awake and talked to him. I didn't know it then, but this would be the last words he would say to anyone, and it was to me that he said them, which meant the world to me, "I love you too...."

I called Bo back from a missed call earlier. I was happy to talk to Bo as I hadn't talked to him in over two years. I answered the phone happy to be talking to someone who was close to Randy. He started off saying how he wished he had been a better friend to Randy and me and that he was finally finished dealing with his own demons and wanted to get back into our lives. I was so happy to hear this as I had worried about his health and his habits. The whole time we talked, I vacillated back and forth between confidence and anxiety about the situation. I remember talking myself out of being nervous, telling Bo about how Randy woke up for me and talked, and how excited I was that the surgery was over. It was impossible not to be nervous. I would say something to him exposing my concern and he would ask if everything went well. Then I would bring myself back to being confident in the situation. While I was talking to him, my phone was ringing and ringing. Someone was trying to call me but I didn't care. I was finally talking to my friend, and he was spilling out his sorrows to me. It felt great to finally be back in touch and to have my friend back after all of these years. It rang again. I didn't even look. I kept talking but was of two minds at this point: anxious and relieved. Up and down, up and down. I don't even recall how long that conversation lasted, but it seemed like forever. I saw my mom wave me down from the hallway and so I ended the conversation.

  I went back to the table and they were all eating and talking to each other. I didn't really feel like eating as I was starting to get nervous again. My dad said to me, "Russ, you need to get something to eat. Why don't you get some chicken noodle soup? It is really good." So I reluctantly got up to get some soup. I put the broth in a bowl and headed back to the table. I started slowly eating the broth. My anxiety was just getting worse and worse. I could feel something just wasn't right. The center of my chest was getting heavy and my heart was starting to beat really quickly. I was having feelings that I knew weren't good ones. All of a sudden Dad looked at me and said, "Russ, why do you have such a worried look on your face. Didn't you hear the doctor? He said everything went as well as could be expected."

  "I won't be fine until I know Randy is walking out of this hospital."

  I wanted to cry. I was experiencing such anxiety and pains in my chest. It was getting worse and worse and Dad could see it. My heart was racing a thousand beats per second it seemed. The sweat was starting to bead on my forehead.

Dad looked at me and said, "Do you want to go back to the hospital room to see Randy?"

"Yes!" I gasped. I was waiting for someone to understand my anxiety and that I wanted to go back, and go back fast. Everyone at the table started to get up.

Andrea said, "I am going to go back to the hotel room, get showered, and I will be back to the hospital room to relieve you so you can shower for the night."

At this point I wasn't thinking about anything but getting back to the hospital room. I don't believe I said anything at all and started off to the hospital, so, with my dad and Ben in tow, we headed back to the hospital recovery room. I couldn't hear anything, and I don't recall saying anything either. I just had to get back to the recovery room. I kept going faster and faster. Faster and faster I rushed to Randy.

Dad had said to me trying to calm me down, "Russ, the doctor said he will be fine. He may not even need radiation or chemo."

"I am not worried about later," I said to my dad as I sprinted toward the recovery room, "I am worried about now!"

My heart was beating out of my chest. I just knew there was something wrong and I needed to get to Randy. Faster! I kept telling myself. I need to get there faster! I started to break away from my dad and Ben.

When I finally got back to the recovery area, I looked over at his room. He was in room 10. The lights were off. I asked the nurse, "Did they move Randall Perrone yet?"

The nurse looked at me confused, so I said with purpose, "The patient in room 10! Did they move him to his room yet?"

She quickly said, "Hold on, I'll be right back."

"What the heck is going on here?!" The power of my heart was thrusting through my voice, "Where is my brother?"

Then a doctor came up to me and confirmed what my feelings were at dinner, "We had an issue."

"What!!" I said frantically. "I knew it! I knew it!"

I started pacing feverishly back and forth in utter anxiety with an uncontrollable feeling of disaster. As I was saying this my dad finally caught up with us and reached me in the recovery area. I will never forget the look he had on his face. A look as though he had just woken up and was confused as to where he was. He said in a voice of defeat, "What happened?"

"I knew it! I knew it! I knew there was a problem."

The doctor chimed in, "He became unresponsive and we sent him to get a CAT scan."

"Yes," I am saying to myself, "Well?"

"When we were doing the scan he went into cardiac arrest," the doctor said. "His heart stopped for 5 minutes."

"That's what that feeling was," I said to myself as my heart jumped into high gear. My blood pressure flew through the roof quicker than an exploding tank of gas.

I called my sister, Andrea, in a desperate panic, "Randy had a problem, please come quick!"

"Where are you?" I can hear in her voice the sound of desperation as I tried to explain where we were. I could hear her starting to run back. "Where are you, Russ? What is going on? What happened?"

"Where is he? Where is my brother?" I said.

"He is in the ICU," said the doctor.

"He is in ICU; he had a heart attack, Andrea!"

"Where is the ICU?" I demanded.

"It's two floors up," he said.

"Let's get the elevator and go up!"

We got in the elevator and frantically pushed the button. I don't even remember the floor we were on, only that it was two floors up. The doors to the elevator started to close and then it jammed halfway open. I put my hand between them and with an adrenaline surge I pushed the elevator doors open and in desperation and determination said, "Can we take the stairs? We need to get to him NOW!"

"Yes, take these stairs," the doctor said.

We rushed to the stairs. We got to the ICU and I looked at a room about thirty feet away from us and saw a room of doctors, nurses, and techs swarming like you see in the movies. They were moving so fast around this patient. I knew right away that the patient in that room was Randy. They wouldn't let us in. At this point Andrea and our mom made it to the ICU, and they saw what I was seeing. We all couldn't believe it. Andrea went to the doctors to try and find out what was happening. My heart was pounding so hard I felt I could be next. We went to the waiting room and we started praying. All I could see was the staff flying into action.

"Please, please, God, don't let this happen" I said to myself. "I need my brother; I cannot make it without my Randy."

Andrea came back and said that she couldn't get any answers as to what was going on other than what the doctor had already told us. At this point I don't recall what my family was doing; I sat down in a chair. This was my moment to use whatever twin powers I had to help Randy, so I started calming myself down.

"If I calmed myself down, I could calm Randy down and his heart would be okay," I said to myself. So I took deep breaths in and deep breaths out, I was straining my mind like the time I strained to tell him not to steal the bike. I was doing everything I could to communicate with Randy and calm him down. I tried my hardest in hopes that I would communicate with Randy:

"Randy, calm down. Randy, calm down. We are here, calm down. Slow down your heart. Be calm, let them help you."

I knew our special way of communication could get to him. I started to feel a calm come over me. I felt like maybe he was listening to me because my anxiety started to wane. As I was feeling this I heard people around me say the nurses were starting to slow down in the room.

"Hey they are slowing down," said Sara.

"They are not moving so fast. I think that he is calming down," said Ben.

I spoke to them in a whispering, calm voice:

"He is good. He is good. We are good. He is good."

The sudden ease of tension was Randy talking to me and sharing some relief from his distress. At this point I felt that we had dodged a big bullet, and he needed me there to keep helping.

As Andrea left the area to talk to the doctors, and things started to calm down a bit, I called my brother John.

"Hello," he answered in a sleepy voice, I don't remember the exact time but it felt late.

I said calmly and slowly, "John."

"Yes," he said back.

"Get on your knees and pray for our brother,"

"What?"

"He needs us now more than ever."

He livened up quickly and said, "What happened?"

"Please get on your knees and pray for Randy." I continued, "We had an issue; he is okay now, but I need you to pray. Get to Dayna, and get here as fast as you can. He needs us!"

I called Cristy and let her know that Randy had an issue and was in ICU. Cristy with ICU nursing experience shined through right away. She started asking questions. "What happened? Did they do this? Did they do that?" she asked. After this point my memory is clouded. I don't recall my conversation with her other than to say, "I need you here. Bring Julien, call your mom and sisters and let them know what is going on." She packed our son, Julien, and started to Houston. I said to her before I got off the phone, "Please drive as safely as you can. I cannot afford to lose you or Julien."

My parents had called all of our family and some close friends. In an instant our aunts and uncles were on their way. Our dad and mom's friends, Lefty and his wife, called Dad when he learned that Randy was in a coma and asked if my dad needed him to come. Dad, not wanting to inconvenience Lefty, told him no. On the third call my dad said yes. They jumped on a plane that night. Not able to get a room they camped out in the waiting room for the duration. At a point in time Dad, who never takes sedatives, asked Lefty if he had anything for anxiety. He just so happened to have something for anxiety and happily obliged. Friends like that are hard to come by, and here he was offering help to my father who was on the ropes.

We later found out that the half of the tumor remaining started to swell and bleed. It had grown so much that it started to block the cerebrospinal fluid canal in the brain and spinal cord. The pressure built up so much that it started to push down on the brain stem and that is when his heart stopped beating. When they did a ventriculostomy to drain the skull, the fluid shot across the room because it was under so much pressure.

That first night in the meeting room was the worst night of my life. The hospital rules were that the ICU waiting room was to be vacated at a certain time. I believe it was 10:00 p.m., but cannot recall completely. They saw the desperation on our faces; they knew that if they forced us to leave we could become patients ourselves in the ICU, given our passion about the situation. They brought us to a small meeting room. A room we found out later was used for breaking bad news to families. We prayed the rosary over and over. It seemed we prayed it over a dozen times. I remember my mom played a recording of an Irish priest leading the rosary to some soft music. There was no opportunity for sleep. This was serious! Randy was in the ICU room and we couldn't go in there. They needed to work, work, and work as hard as they could to save my brother. And we needed to work as hard as we could to ask God to save Randy. It was a two-front battle to save him.

"Get in there and do something," I was thinking. "What could I do? Was there any way I could help." I pleaded:

"Please, please, please help me, God! Help my brother get out of this bad situation. I promise I will be your servant for the remainder of my life if you bring him back to me. Bring him back to us!"

The commitment was evident. We were determined to do our job. We were ready to do whatever it took. All we needed was a miracle from God. I thought:

"My sister! My sister is my savior. She knows what is going on. Andi, as we called her, what do you think? What can you do? Big sister, please help! Don't let this happen. DO SOMETHING!"

We prayed through the entire night. The hours blended into each other. At times we could go into the room, and then there was another test to be done, another scan of Randy's brain, so we would have to leave the room again. Eventually that evening Dayna and John arrived. Relief!! We needed more people who love Randy to pray for him unendingly. SAVE HIM! Their faces said it all. How did this happen?

The sense of urgency seemed to subside and we were allowed inside the room to be with Randy. I remember looking at him and just feeling this pain that I couldn't explain. It would come in waves as I sat there weeping over my twin. Straining was the only thing I could do to counteract the pain I was feeling. One of the nurses came in and said she was going to look at his pupils quickly and asked if we wanted to stay or step out. I wanted to stay. They took out the flashlight, pointed it at his eyes and opened them. Nothing happened. I looked at his eyes and knew just by looking at them that Randy was gone. He was no longer there. His body was hanging on but his mind and soul were no longer in his body. Looking back, the calming feeling I got in the ICU waiting room was his body releasing his soul. I had to ask Andrea just to be sure. "The pupils are supposed to close aren't they?"

She looked at me and I could tell by her face that the answer was yes and that she knew as well that this didn't look good at all. We knew in our minds that his angels had come for him. It would take some time for our hearts to follow.

The next test they would do would be to turn off the oxygen machine and see if his brain would trigger his lungs to breathe on their own. They warned us, "You will hear some beeping, don't be alarmed." They turned it off. I looked with despair at his chest. "Did I see it move?" I said to myself as I realized: no it didn't move. "Come on! Move for God's sake." But nothing. They turned it back on and did the next test. They pulled up the breathing tube and I asked, "What does that do?" The nurse said to me, "Well, it is an uncomfortable feeling in the lungs, if he coughs then we know there is some progress and that his brain is recovering from the trauma." I looked at his body, "Please cough," I said to myself. They pulled the tube up and there was no cough.

I had to start preparing myself. The night was long, very long, and dark, and even though I had my family there, it was very lonely. I kept playing over and over Randy's last words to me, or anyone for that matter. "I love you." I would feel the pain come over me again and again. We stayed by his side all night praying and hoping for a miracle.

We were all huddled in the room the following morning when a nice lady walked into the room. She was so quiet and concerned about not making too much of a fuss when entering the room. Her name was Dr. Theresa and she was the ICU doctor. She was there to assess Randy and see if there had been any progress over the night. Her ability to show that she truly was concerned about Randy and our family was very apparent; I could sense that she came from a family much like ours. I was asking her all kinds of questions, and her answers were straightforward. She would make visits throughout the day, and the more visits she made the more attached she became to our family. There was a moment that she started to cry and apologized for becoming emotional in front of us. We quickly told her that we were honored that she was able to show us empathy, which is sometimes unusual for many doctors. She would do tests on Randy, and my eyes would be fixated on him. I could tell there was no progress.

Andrea's previous colleague from New Orleans named Dr. Prescott happened to have transferred to MD Anderson after finding out his wife had breast cancer. He came to the ICU to speak with us. As a neuro-oncologist he was very knowledgeable about the situation and having spoken to my sister and having looked at the charts, I was very trusting of his judgment. He and Dr. Theresa would converse outside the room, and the whole time I was trying to horn in on the conversation, looking for any sign of hope from either of their faces, but all I got was despair. I got up to go to the waiting room to cool down a little bit. I couldn't bear the pain any longer. As I was in the waiting room I caught a glimpse of Dr. Prescott. When I approached him, he was very sympathetic in his manner to me.

"Doctor. I am Randy's twin brother. I need to know how bad this is. I want you to shoot it to me straight, don't sugarcoat it for me. How bad is this? What is the likelihood that he can come out of this?"

He sighed and you could see his body just slump as he told me with his foreign accent, "Randy has serious brain damage. He was without oxygen for twenty-one minutes. Three minutes is the point where brain cells start to die. He is not responding to any of our tests which is consistent with serious brain damage."

I asked him, "If you had to give me a percentage for his coming out of this, what would you guesstimate?"

"I would say that there is close to zero percent chance that Randy will come out of this."

I knew what he was telling me was the truth. I thanked him and calmly went to the bathroom. I could feel myself starting to get weak, and my eyes were starting to get puffy. A strong pain fell upon my chest and I lost control of my emotions in the bathroom. I looked in the mirror at myself and saw him.

"Why Randy, why did this happen? Why are you leaving me? You cannot leave me now! I need you in my life. Julien needs you, Mom and Dad need you, and your family cannot live without you."

I cried uncontrollably in that bathroom for several minutes then pulled myself together. I knew now that my time was limited with Randy, at least with his physical body.

Later into the night I was exhausted but I couldn't pull myself away from Randy to get any sleep. My mom wanted me to try and get some rest and told me that she would be by his side while I was resting. When I went to the waiting room, each time when I would doze off, I would get an electrocution feeling in my head and body. I couldn't sleep without being jolted back to life. It was as if each time I closed my eyes I was being transported to Randy's body. I finally was able to get a couple of minutes of sleep that felt like hours and immediately felt guilty about it and vowed that I wouldn't sleep again; I would spend as much time with Randy as I could, staying next to him, holding his hand, caressing his head, and hugging his lifeless body.

I got up and went to his room, feeling guilty that I had been away, even though a short period. At this point there weren't many people in the room but my mom was in there by his side kneeling and holding his hand. A mother brokenhearted is what I saw. I pulled up a chair right next to his bed, got in the chair and held his hand. I looked at him, his breath being controlled and tubes down his throat. I could see a tear running down his cheek. I got a napkin and wiped it from his eyes. I knew these were tears for me and my family. I got back in my chair, held his hand and lay with him for the night. A thought ran through my mind, and I started to prepare myself for the moment that my brother would actually die. I said that to myself over and over again in disbelief. Randy is going to die. I couldn't believe that I was here, holding his lifeless hand, wishing for another outcome, but realizing his death was near.

The hours passed slowly, Mom and Dad never really leaving his side. I looked at my mom kneeling next to him saying the rosary. I told her how sorry I was that she would look at me and see Randy and hurt for the rest of her life. I started to cry for her. The strong pain in my chest came back and all I could do was tense up. I could feel every tense moment rush blood to my brain. I felt as though my head would explode with my muscles tensing to withstand this pain. It was a pain I had never felt before, one I will never forget, and hopefully one that I will never experience again. My dad at this point was praying his Rosary and was getting really emotional:

"Touch the cloak of Jesus and come back to us. Please touch the cloak of Jesus and come back to us. Jesus, please bring him back to us."

Up until this point I had only seen my dad choke up once, at his father's funeral. To see him in this state was demoralizing. It hurt my heart seeing him like this. I couldn't imagine the hurt that my mom and dad were feeling. Even though my hurt was something they wouldn't know, their hurt is a feeling I couldn't understand and hope to never have in my future.

I wanted to be with Randy all the time, but I didn't want to be selfish for any of my other family members, even though in my mind I felt they would have understood why, so, I gave up my seat for one of my siblings. The sun pushed away the night and we faced the challenge of watching my brother lie in the bed with no life. A new day was here, another day had passed since my brother was awake, another day passed since I ate anything, and another day had passed since I was able to get sleep. The machines were keeping him here, but I knew he was not coming back.

I took this day as my day to say goodbye to Randy. The mental shift from being hopeful that Randy would come out of this nightmare was creeping into the spiritual preparedness that we take when the inevitable death of a loved one faces us. I was wearing the same shirt I had worn the day of the surgery. It was an LSU football shirt, and I wore it for Randy. We were always debating whether professional football, the Saints, or college football, the Tigers, were better than the other. I would always have my argument as to why professional football was more exciting than college, but for Randy I wore the LSU Tigers shirt as a good luck omen. As I looked at Randy's lifeless body, he was still in his surgery garb. I am not sure why it took me as long as it did to do this, but I felt that for him to leave this world in hospital clothing that he would not have wanted to wear outside the hospital would not be appropriate for him. I took off my shirt and laid it on his chest. I couldn't get it on him physically because of all the wires and tubes, but at least when I looked at him, he was in familiar clothing, clothing I knew he would be proud to be wearing. After I put it on his chest, I hugged up close to him and just rested my head against his, holding him as tight as I could.

I remember feeling his beard with my fingers as I rubbed his face. The feeling reminded me of our constant flip-flopping preferences regarding facial hair. I had a flashback to a better time in life. The time was a few months before I was to get married. Randy had facial hair, and I didn't. At one point four years earlier I had shaved my beard, and from that point to the surgery he would always say that I was doing our twin-ship an injustice by not having a beard. We would always go back and forth joking about this, with my telling him he was a disgrace to our "twin-ship" and vice versa. That is how we were, joking and always trying to keep one step ahead of the other.

For my wedding I told him, "Since it is my wedding, I want you to shave."

He reluctantly said, "I will shave for your wedding, but for my wedding you will have to grow out your beard again."

"Deal," I said.

I was shaken back to reality as I was touching his beard and decided that I would grow my beard out, and I would do so for two reasons: The first is that my feeling of my own beard, and the look of my own beard, would allow me to constantly feel and see Randy. The second reason I would grow it out would be for him, knowing that my promise to him would never be able to be fulfilled after he took his last breath, so this would be my way to honor our deal. As I now sit here and write, I put my hands to my face and feel my beard, yearning to once again be able to feel Randy's. This again is my own way to have that special bond with Randy that no one else can, so why should I not do so since others don't have that luxury.

As Randy lay in the hospital room my thoughts ran wild. When I would caress his head, I would whisper in his ear my thoughts. I would have conversations with him, bringing up our childhood. For my whole life I lived with two regrets when it came to Randy. There were two instances when I failed to stand up for him and help him and these instances had been eating at me for my whole life. I didn't want to have these go unmentioned to him and never apologize for these. Deep inside I knew that he wouldn't have wanted me to hold on to them, and my only way to cleanse it was to tell him how sorry I was. I put my head in his pillow, right next to his ear and I whispered so no one else in the room could hear.

"Randy, I have to tell you how sorry I am for the two times I watched you in danger and I stood there afraid to do the right thing. That time that we were by the clubhouse behind Mom and Dad's house, and an older boy, for whatever reason, didn't like you. You stood your ground and he hit you in the face. I was so shocked to see this but couldn't do anything to help you. I was too afraid that if I did, I would get hit too. The other time was when we were at a YMCA dance, and you were dancing and some boys didn't like that you were dancing so they pushed you into the fence. There were two of them in your face, and I looked then like a coward, not able to do anything for you out of fear for my own safety. Well, Randy, I tell you, I have always regretted those two moments and have made it a lifelong goal that I would never ever let you down again, and, Randy, I tell you now, I will never let anything or anyone try to hurt you again."

    After I confessed and apologized, a weight lifted off my shoulders. I looked at his face and noticed a tear on his cheek. I knew that he heard me, and he cried in his soul, so hard that it made it through his lifeless body. I felt his sorrow was more for me than for himself that a moment in our lives, which he most likely had forgotten, had eaten away at me up until that point. I lay there on his pillow, and I spoke to him, I spoke to his soul, letting him know that his journey here on Earth was not to be over, and that I would be his instrument for continuing his mission, a mission to spread his music and his generosity to the human race. I told him that I would make sure Julien knew who his Parrain was, he would go through life knowing you without ever remembering your awesome being.

    The minutes turned into hours and I got up to let someone else have time with Randy. I made my way to the bathroom and then to the waiting room. I sat there for a moment and quickly gathered myself and went back to the room. I saw that most of the visitors had gone to lunch, and only Mom was in the room. She was kneeling at his side, praying as hard as she could, trying to ask Jesus for a miracle to bring back her baby. I was so selfish in wanting to be with him, and seeing that no one was at his other side, I pulled up my chair and grabbed his hand. I lay my head on his stomach, looking up at his face and I put his warm hand on my face. I could feel his pulse on my cheek and I just lay there taking his energy from his body and carrying it to mine. I lay there for an hour or so, thinking that in just a short moment I would no longer be able to do this. There were already talks about the next steps, and I wanted nothing to do with those talks; I just wanted to be with Randy and feel his spirit and warmth.

    My mom took a picture of me lying like this, and I could hear her talking to someone walking into the room. I blocked out who it was. All I could hear was a sigh and someone starting to cry. I could hear whomever it was say, "Seeing this just breaks my heart," then hugging my mom. It was one of her friends, and I was happy that someone was there to be able to comfort my mom while I was taking my time with Randy.

Dad came in and walked by me to put his hand on my head, and gave me a kiss, and then gave Randy a kiss on his head. I could hear him weeping, and it just made me cry to hear that. His heart ached so much that his tears carried the blood of his soul down to the earth and I could feel the quake from those powerful emotions. So much so that it made my heart break for him and for our entire family. I just couldn't be selfish enough for myself any longer and I got up to give him and my brother, John, who had just entered the room, a hug. I feared that in John's mind while looking at me with Randy that he would feel left out. Throughout our life, Randy and I had made it our goal to never make him feel like he wasn't equal. When I hugged him, he grabbed me so tight and started to cry. I knew that when we were hugging he was holding me tight feeling Randy through me. By this point our sisters were also present and then our core family were all at Randy's bedside. We group hugged and all looked at Randy and wept, all in our own way wishing that time would just stand still so that we wouldn't be one less in our core family.

As we were holding each other, we could hear Dr. Theresa coming to our room. We turned to her and she saw us and started to get emotional. When she was able to gather herself she told us that Dr. McNulty was finally coming to speak with us about what happened. This would be the first time the surgeon would address the family and explain what happened since Randy's surgery. We as a family were definitely upset over the length of time that had passed without hearing from him, but we understood at the same time that he was devastated by this and couldn't face us without becoming emotional, and felt that wouldn't be fair for us. We were all led to a board room. We waited there until the surgeon finally came in. You could see on his face that this talk was the last thing he thought he would be doing, and this meeting was not going to be easy. He sat down and started to explain the surgery again.

He said, "The surgery was going well, and there was some bleeding. I stopped the bleeding long enough to feel it was safe to close him up. Apparently what happened in recovery was that the tumor started to swell from the surgery and also started to bleed. By looking at the CT scans taken as he coded, you could see there was a total blockage of the canal in which cerebrospinal fluid flows from the brain to the spinal cord, which created pressure on the brain. This was enough to push on the brain stem, which caused his heart to stop while he was getting his CT scan. They tried to do CPR and twenty-one minutes after his heart stopped they were able to get a rhythm."

I remember thinking, "Twenty-one minutes? Why were we told five minutes by an ICU doctor? With five minutes of no oxygen there is hope, but twenty-one minutes is too long. We were given a false hope."

He continued on, "After looking at all the tests, it appears that there is nothing we can do. Randy is completely brain dead, he will no longer be able to live without machinery."

I was already expecting to hear this from the doctor because I had talked to Dr. Prescott the day prior when he had given me the same outlook. To the rest of my family, this was the boat of hope sailing off without them.

My mom requested frantically of Dr. McNulty, "Well can't we do more tests; I just can't abandon him without doing more tests."

He said, "Yes, we can do as many tests as you want, but there is one test that will confirm for you what we have already told you. This test will measure brain activity. There will be about fifty probes placed around his head to try and get any sign of activity. We would like to have one person try to stimulate Randy while we do this."

Right after he said this, someone, I don't remember who, said, "Rusty. If he is going to respond to anyone, it will be his twin brother." Mara looked over at me and then to the doctor and asked if she could be there too. He said that it would be okay, and I looked at her and said it would be okay as well. I told her, "I want to make sure that we stimulate him enough to get a reading without a shadow of a doubt." Dr. McNulty started to talk again, "If this test doesn't prove to be fruitful, then my recommendation is to remove the life support. At this point his quality of life isn't going to get any better." As he said this, the entire room erupted in shouts and crying. He excused himself and looked at my parents and myself and apologized that he couldn't have prevented this situation. We shook his hand, knowing that any more grief to him would be detrimental to his desire to keep trying to heal people, and returned to focus on our family. We all held someone else as we walked out of the meeting room in pairs. I could see my dad practically having to be carried out of the room, he was so broken.

It was time for the last test, and the nurse asked everyone to leave the room. I asked her if I could stay as I would be the one to try and get some type of reaction from him. She obliged and I watched her put the probes on Randy's head. One by one, she placed them and all I could think was that I hoped we would have a miracle and get some activity. It seemed like the probes would just keep coming. There were so many she placed. Once she was done she asked for Dr. Theresa and another nurse to come in and then directed me to start talking to him. I looked out of the room for Mara to come in, and as soon as she came in we started to talk to Randy.

"Randy, this is Rusty; it's time to come back to us, Randy. You have to get up now; there is no reason for you to be lying there."

Growing up we would always be called over the intercom by our mom, and we would just hate hearing it when we were in a deep sleep. This is the same tone that I used with Randy. I knew that if I could bring up those feelings of not wanting to move or get up, that maybe the probes would register some frustration. I looked at the screen each time, with nothing happening. I would get louder and louder and more insistent.

"Randy, it's time to get up. Let's go, we have to get out of here, Randy! You have to get up. No more of this foolishness; it is time to get out of that bed! Come on, Randy! Get up, we are here now to watch you get up! Randy! Randy!"

Nothing was happening on the screen. Mara started to talk to him, and as she talked I looked with hope that I would see some type of activity. There was just no activity at all. My hopes in the beginning turned into despair which led to hopelessness. This was it. This was real and there was nothing we could do other than the obvious. The song by A Great Big World called "Say Something" was released several months after his death, and I realized that the song had a meaning about us trying to get him to come back to life.

Say something, I'm giving up on you
I'll be the one, if you want me to
Anywhere, I would've followed you
Say something, I'm giving up on you

The doctors put their arms around me, gave me a hug, and said how sorry they were and as they were leaving the room, one of them instructed me to bring back our loved ones. The social worker came to us with a lady from the hospital and I could see that she brought a blanket with her. It was a blue knit blanket and as she offered it to my mother, she told her that with each stitch in this blanket a prayer was said to help the suffering from not suffering any longer. My mom took the blanket, held it tight, and draped it over Randy. I remember seeing the lady as if she were an angel coming from the clouds. I don't remember when she left, but that blanket was another comforting device for me and for my family.

My dad had asked for a priest to come and lay hands on Randy for the second time. The priest came in and walked up to my side of the bed. I was huddled by Randy's head, caressing him and touching his face as the priest started to put his hands on his forehead. He started to pray and asked that Jesus protect Randy in his passage through to him. He asked Jesus to greet him with open arms. As I heard this I felt the presence of the Spirit and was thankful for any help that we could give Randy in his passage. Once the priest was finished he stayed with us for a bit and wanted to know about Randy. As he was asking my parents about him, I would listen to the answers and draw memories from them as they were spoken, not saying a word, but just lying there touching Randy's cheek. It seemed visitors were coming from all over the hospital.

There was a chaplain who came in and asked if it was okay if he sang a song for Randy. We all encouraged this kind act, and he started to sing "How Great Thou Art." The way he sang it was so peaceful and beautiful, it gave me chills and I started to tear up and held Randy tighter. I remember looking at this man, who had never met Randy before, and was amazed that he cared enough to sing for a soul who was about to depart the Earth in front of people he had never met. As he was singing, the friend Randy had made in the hospital, Kayla, came down to see Randy. We stood up and greeted her with hugs. She looked at him and was speechless at first. She looked at me and was dumbfounded by what had happened. She was with us for a few moments before she had to get back to her own treatments in the hospital. My mom hugged her and told her that she will forever be in our hearts and prayers, and that if she ever needed anyone to talk to or be there for her, that we would be her family.

Chapter 35

Edge of the World

As in the title of one of Randy's songs, he was now on *the edge of the world*, and we all knew it in our minds if not our hearts. Dr. Theresa came in and asked us if we were okay to start turning down the oxygen rate. She told us that if we didn't start soon that Randy would eventually run into issues with his heart. She informed us that the medicines they were giving him to keep him stable were starting to affect other functions and that they were counteracting those symptoms with more medicine. She said eventually he could have another heart attack, and that would be traumatic for us to see. We asked if we could each have a moment with Randy and if there was going to be enough time. She nodded and gave Mom a hug and told her to take whatever time she needed to say her goodbyes. Everyone moved out of the room and we started one at a time. I remember going last, waiting for my last moment alone with Randy. When it was my turn I pulled out something that I wrote for him while he was in surgery, but modified while waiting for my turn with him. I pulled the chair next to him in bed. I read it to him:

> *"You never know how much you love someone until his life is literally in the hands of God and all you can think about is whether God has a plan to keep him with us or to take him to do His work.*
>
> *The hardest part is waiting, because my mind starts wondering whether or not the big hug and the words of love are the last that I will ever get to give to you. It's so scary to think of it like that. People can say until they are blue in the face that you shouldn't worry about that or think like that, but when my DNA, a person whom I have known to be there with me my entire life, is in the situation you are, thinking*

about how much my life would be empty without you, it shatters my soul and heart. It's as if I can only breathe if you inhale and I exhale. Only you can quite understand the feeling that I have at this moment, a moment that in our life path will always be burned into my mind and memory. My only regret is that I have not been stronger emotionally for you through this tough time in your life. The only reason I feel this way is because only you can feel my emotions: happy, sad, excited and scared shitless. I pray that you should never have to feel the same way I do because this hurts me to my core. Listening to your music, hearing your voice makes it hard but I can't stop. I feel helpless and the only way that I find can help is through persistent thought of you. The pain of that is my suffering, sacrifice, and agony in my garden of life. I would gladly take all this pain and a thousand times more just to have you returned to me.

So God, I know you're listening, I beg of your mercy and your healing touch to bring my twin brother back to me and his family who love him oh so much. His time on earth shouldn't be over."

After I read my letter to him, I told him that I would make sure that everything here is taken care of. I would be his arm on Earth to get things that he wanted done. I would make sure his music was spread throughout the world. I made a vow not to alienate our brother John and to include him in my life the way we had included each other. I told him how much I loved him and that I looked to the day that we could be together again. I got up and went to get everyone. Dr. Theresa came back in and looked at all of us for approval to start the process. Our family looked at each other and each gave a slow and reluctant nod to start.

She was not happy to have to do what she was about to do but realized, like we all did, that there was no other way. She told us that she was going to turn off the sounds of the machines so that the beeping wouldn't bother us as critical alerts would pop up. She started with bringing the oxygen down, then began to slow his breaths on the machine. She kept it at this setting for a bit, and then came back in and adjusted it some more after asking us for approval. After several adjustments, she warned us that the next adjustment would be the last. I knew this would be it; it was the point of no return, the moment that Randy would leave me for the rest of my life. I was no longer an ordinary twin, losing my other half.

Dr. Theresa warned everyone in the room of the appearance of someone that is about to die, and tried to comfort us. I didn't want to see Randy without life. When Ben lost his father, he wanted to go back and see him and when he returned he told me how he regretted seeing his father deceased, with no color and no warmth. He said he can never get that image out of his head. I didn't want to see and remember Randy like that. Dad had started praying his rosary and asked God to take Randy before he finished his rosary. As I had my lips on his forehead, I could see his lips out of the corner of my eye start to turn blue. I quickly closed my eyes and waited for the moment I would hear Dr. Theresa say he had left us. Dad was granted one of the two requests, and that was for God to take him before he finished his rosary. There was no flinch, no pain. He just drifted, peacefully, into eternity. Dad told Mom that he wanted to be buried with this rosary when his own time came.

When she let us know that he was gone, the whole room erupted in crying, and I quickly moved away from Randy, making sure I didn't look at him. My sisters and brother quickly grabbed me in the corner and we all hugged and cried together. As I was hugging them I had a glance at Randy and saw his pale face, and I quickly looked back down and said to my brother and sisters, "I want to leave the room so I don't see him without life and color. Can we all go to the waiting room?" We hugged there for a moment longer and then we moved toward the door of the room.

Everyone moved to the waiting room except for my Aunt Jane. If she wasn't my hero before this she became mine afterwards. When we were babies she helped my mom take care of Randy and me. She told me she helped care for us evenly but may have spent more time with Randy. She stayed in the hospital room after Randy died because she wanted to give Randy his last bath, a gift I could never repay. The thought that Randy was looked after by family for the special practice of cleaning a body after death was a relief. I could not handle the thought that Randy might be just another patient the hospital staff had to prep for transport, and my aunt prevented this with her readiness to offer this service; Randy was not just another routine, he was special to my aunt and he was my twin. She later told me that she had a special time to talk to Randy. Telling him how she had been able to give him a bath as a baby, and now she was bathing him to see Jesus. She told the nurses about his life and how much they would have loved Randy. She knew that Randy wouldn't want anyone to be uncomfortable around him, so she was his voice to break the discomfort of cleaning a deceased person. As she was finished she gave him a little tap on his butt, the same way that she did when he was little. Such a special moment, for such a special person.

When we returned to the waiting room I sat down and was overtaken by a feeling I had never felt before. I could feel my brother passing through me. The extreme happiness I felt was one of the last moments that we would share our emotions. It was a moment I never wanted to forget. My mom and dad hugged me by my legs and they knew what was happening. I didn't want this to end, but it started to fade and at that moment I was able to get up and start comforting others who were in the waiting room with us.

When we all settled down a bit after Randy passed away, Mom came up to me and said, "Do you want to be the first to let everyone know Randy is gone. Do you want to post on Facebook?" I said yes and left the room. I found a spot in the hallway near the ICU and sat down. I remember the view outside the window: the day was pretty, not that many clouds, clear and sunny, what seemed like a perfect day for Randy to depart. I started writing my letter. I wrote,

> "Well my friends and family, today is the saddest day of my life. A day that growing up I dreaded and never wanted to come. My brother, the person I shared a womb with, a person who when I looked at him I was looking at myself, has passed away to be with God. This will be a lifelong challenge for me and my family. All of us are so saddened by his leaving us, but in time we will learn how to cope, but never get over, and he will NEVER BE FORGOTTEN!!!!
>
> We can ask, why so early for such a good person? See he helped as many people as he could in life but that wasn't good enough. The problem is that only one person at a time could be helped here on earth, now as an Angel he can help many many people.
>
> He is in peace now and I can vouch for that. The troubles of the world, his illness, and his stresses are no longer going to take his energy away from doing good and helping people.
>
> Randy you will be missed by so many people. I am going to miss having my best friend around all the time. This is going to be my

lifetime struggle but I know I have you with me to guide me through it. Your godchild, Julien, will know you through our stories about you. Everything all makes sense now. Julien was your son too; when he was born you felt all of my happiness and surge of emotions. I will never forget that, ever. It is something only you and I will be able to share and remember. He will always remind me of you, and that will make him loved more than any other child has EVER been loved. I am so relieved that you are at peace, even though it hurts me to the core. I love you more than anyone else could imagine, which was no secret to you.

Godspeed my loving brother and I look forward to the day that we will be reunited in heaven!

A couple of years later my dad was flipping through his lyric book and saw a poem that Randy wrote several years earlier, but as we noticed the poem, it explained what we were going through.

The wind blows the rain
In each direction changed
I'm back in my car
I've got to go home
The clocks are running fast
This thing we made called time
Has got me down
Why do I have to leave?
Right here is where I live to be

The lights are off
No longer in my eyes
It's the end of the world
Inside this room goodbye
You and I go our separate ways
I can feel the life
Leaving my presence of sight
Don't go without ever knowing
That we have created a moment
Frozen in time

Russell Perrone ⚜ 240

By Randy Perrone

    Did Randy know something we didn't know? How could he have been so prophetic in his writings so long ago? Was he waiting for us to see this after his death to wonder if his purpose on this land was to be an Angel with limited time to help people?

Chapter 36

After Good-bye

After leaving the ICU we went back to the hotel. We reached the hotel lobby and there we all were, in disbelief of what just happened, when all of a sudden my dad noticed the piano player was playing "Somewhere Over The Rainbow" which happened to be one of Randy's favorite songs. The follicles along my spine stood to attention and my mom said to me and my family, "This just feels like the ending of a movie."

Everything was so surreal. It was as if we were in a dream and none of this was really happening. For the remainder of the day we were together as a family. The group of friends had retreated to their rooms, to going to the pool, to moving on with life, and it was just us again. Our true family core, left behind to wonder, "What happened here? Did this really happen?" I can remember my sister Dayna saying to us, "This happens to other families, not our family. This just cannot be real." I remember thinking:

"My brother is dead. I cannot believe that Randy is gone. Is this real? Well this *is* real, and now we will have one less member of our large close family."

The remainder of the day we huddled in the room, talking about memories of Randy intertwined with spells of crying and emotions of disbelief. I can remember all I wanted to do was be with my family, even when the group of friends wanted to go to the swimming pool, all I could think of was being there with my family. Cristy's sisters came from New Orleans just to bring Julien back, and at that point I was so numb that Randy's passing wasn't even registering with me. My mind was frozen in time, a time when I can still hear Randy's voice so clearly in my head. "Don't worry Russ. Trust your older brother." It was as though I could hear his voice and was comforted hearing it, not knowing how permanent this would be. Death is permanent, and numbness is not.

I remember wanting to go to Randy's suitcase and smell his shirts. Anything that reminded me of him, I was starting to want to hoard. Hoarding is a symptom of loss but a cure for nothing. There were things that were not with me, things that were important, like his watch. I knew that his fiancée had his watch so I knew at least it was in semi-safe keeping. I held on tight to the football that we were playing with the evening before his surgery. I recalled having such a grip on it, protecting it like I would protect Julien. "This was the last football we threw together," I said to myself. "I won't let this out of my sight." After a long night of lying around in the hotel room, I retreated to another room with my sisters and brother and we fell asleep. That night, I had a dream of Randy and it had nothing to do with what just happened. Our lives were as they had been: normal, healthy, and full of life; and then he disappeared. I couldn't decide if this were a true nightmare, the terrible dream that I would have in my sleep of him leaving, or the reality that awaited me when I awoke. I woke up not sure where I was. I looked around in a trance and realized that I wasn't home, I was in a hotel room sharing a bed with one of my sisters, and then it all came back to me. I just lost it. I couldn't compose myself; my tears were falling like rain. As soon as John and Dayna, who were sharing a bed, heard me crying, they hurried and piled in the bed comforting me. We lay there and all cried trying to comfort each other. I know that they felt my pain. I could tell how each one of them grabbed me to try to say, "Don't worry Russ, we are all here for you." That lasted a while, and when we had composed our emotions we decided to go to our parents' room and be with them. I had never felt so together at this point yet so broken; one of our own was not here any longer.

That next morning we got in touch with all the people that came to Houston to set a time to get breakfast at the restaurant in the hotel. We all went down together and sat at a big table. There were about 30 of us filling a wing of the restaurant. Everyone was conversing with each other, some tearful, some joyous. This was our suffering, not theirs. At this point I still couldn't eat. It had been four days now since I had last eaten, and food at this point was something I felt guilty about desiring. Randy could no longer enjoy food, there was no way I was going to either. Everyone was concerned about me; at this point I am sure the ten pounds that I lost that week had already come off. My face was scruffy, and my emotions worn on my shoulders. All I wanted to do was stare into space and hold our football. My thoughts were everywhere and everyone could see that. The only person I really wanted to talk to at this moment was my Aunt Jane and only because of what she had done for Randy after he passed.

We finished breakfast and everyone was getting up. My friends huddled by me and we were talking. I was still holding the football and I wanted to extend the olive branch to his fiancée and let her hold it. I told her it meant a lot to me and I would like her to hold it for a while. As soon as she took it she started flinging the football in the air, as if this didn't mean anything to me or as if to say, "I don't care if this was special with Randy and you, this is just another football." I said to myself, "Please don't drop the football! I can't believe you are just throwing it like this is some toy." Sure enough she dropped the football and I quickly reached for it as if it were a baby falling to the ground. I grabbed it and she said, "I'll be more careful with it," and I gave it back to her. The conversations were happening around me and all I could think about was getting the football back. This obviously didn't mean anything to her, which is okay, but I wanted it back. When you're sliding down a slippery slope, you cling to anything in reach.

As the conversations transitioned into getting ready to depart Houston, we started to move away, but all the while my eye was on the football. She had no intention of giving it back to me, and I had to ask, "May I have my football back?" She said to me that she wanted to keep it. I said no, explaining that the football meant a lot to me, so she reluctantly gave it back to me. This was the start of what became a tension between Mara and me. She had every right to want to hold on to Randy's things; however, I felt that my relationship with Randy gave me the same right if not more, at least for certain things. I noticed she was wearing his watch and I didn't say anything to her. I said to myself, "At least I know where it is, and it won't be lost."

We went back to the hotel room to figure out driving arrangements. I would ride in Randy's car with Mara, Ben, and Sara. I don't quite remember who was going with my parents, but I wasn't about to go home in any car other than Randy's. As we were packing up, I felt the need to take care of unfinished Randy business. I wanted to go and thank the doctors for helping our family, for being so caring of Randy and us when they didn't have to be. Mara said to me she wanted to drive Randy's car home. I was reluctant to do this but I wanted to keep the peace so I acknowledged her request and said, "We can switch up half way, but before we leave I have some unfinished business. I will only be a half hour or so." Ben asked if I wanted him to come with me, and I told him, "This is a job only I can do," and immediately morphed Randy's mind with mine. I felt this was Randy speaking to me to thank the people who made his transition to the afterlife as easy as it could be for him and for his family.

I took the elevators to the floor that had a skywalk to the hospital. This was the same skywalk that we as a group walked with Randy to his surgery. Instead of going to the surgery center and tracing my steps there, I went straight to the ICU. I got there and looked at where Randy had been. The room was empty: no more bed, no more activity, and no more Randy. I spoke to the nurse at the nursing station and asked to see Dr. McNulty or Dr. Theresa. They told me that Dr. McNulty wasn't there but Dr. Theresa was. I asked if I could see her. I waited there for her to come. All the while I looked at the room in disbelief. I just couldn't believe it. This just didn't seem real.

I finally heard footsteps down the hall and turned to see it was Dr. Theresa and the social worker. I started to cry and gave her a hug. I thanked her again, and we sat in the waiting room so they could talk to me.

"I want to thank you so much for so much love that you showed my family and Randy. I am also here on his behalf thanking you for him. He would have wanted me to do that. Dr. Theresa, you were just so comforting to us and I cannot thank you enough."

She proceeded to talk and started to cry herself. She told me that she couldn't help but feel like she was taking care of her family. She came from a similar background, and for her to see us in that shape had struck a chord in her heart. She asked if I was okay and if I needed to talk to anyone else. I told her I was okay and requested for one last time to see the room where I spent what seemed like a lifetime with Randy on his deathbed. She didn't hesitate and said, "Go right ahead, and take as much time as you need." I went into the room and just stood there stunned. I looked at the very spot where Randy had been and couldn't keep myself together. With the room being empty, and Randy nowhere to be found, the reality started to sink in. My eyes could see what my heart didn't want to believe. I spent some time there and retreated from the room. I went to Dr. Theresa again and gave her a big hug. Her hugs were so warming to me. This someone I had just met had a piece of my heart and a piece of Randy's heart. We shared our goodbyes and I made it out of the ICU. I walked the same hall I walked almost 24 hours prior. The same surreal feeling of being in a movie that my mom had experienced, I now was feeling. It was the closing scene of the movie, the closing scene of a life, and the start of being Twinless. I walked into the distance as the main character does and the credits start; however, my movie wasn't over. It was just beginning. As I imagined Randy singing his song, "As I Lay Thee Down to Sleep," I assumed my heart was as broken as it could get, and could not have imagined what lay ahead.

Chapter 37

Willful Intentions and a Will Full of Tension

I hopped in the car and noticed that Ben was wearing Randy's watch, a watch that I saw Randy wear for sixteen years. I asked Ben why he had the watch on and he told me that Mara forgot it on the sink counter and as he was leaving he grabbed it. He told her that he had it and she almost forgot it. All I could think about was, "How could she have forgotten something so important? What if Ben didn't see it and it was left behind. Randy's watch would have been lost forever, and it would have been my fault for not speaking up about safekeeping his possessions." We started driving in the car. I could tell Mara was already loopy by the way she was driving. She only made it about an hour until she wanted me to drive, so I was happy with my self-control and for not getting emotional about her driving Randy's car, as I had preferred to do, or for leaving his watch in the hotel.

As we were getting closer to home, Mara asked if she could have an hour just by herself at Randy's house. Of course I didn't object but was hoping to be able to be in the house that Randy and I had remodeled. We wound up going into the house, and as soon as I walked in I could feel a presence there. Mara said she felt it too, and this was the perfect moment to give her some guidance:

"Look, when you feel the special presence, you want to be sober so that you can recognize that it is Randy you feel."

"Thank you Rusty. That sounded exactly like something Randy would tell me."

We walked in to see that Tim, Sara's husband, and Mara's mom were there and it was clear that she just wanted to be with her family, understandably.

That evening my friends came to my parents' house. A group of people were talking when Sara grabbed Mara unexpectedly, and said something to her. About a minute later Mara tapped me on my shoulder and asked if she could talk with me. She began asking me questions, some that made me uncomfortable during my grieving process. Most of them were not about my brother as much as they were about what my brother would be leaving her. Questions about house, car, mortgage, life insurance, and personal objects may have eventually been pertinent, but they were certainly ill-timed within a day of Randy's death. I felt Randy standing next to me and I could sense his unhappy feelings through mine.

I maintained my calm the entire time she and the group of friends were there, not letting anyone think that I was any different than before she burdened me with those questions. As soon as she left and just my immediate family were present, I walked up to my dad and his friend Lefty.

"Dad, we are going to have a problem." I said to him.

My dad at this point was in shambles and he replied to me puzzled, "What do you mean we are going to have a problem?"

I looked at Lefty and at Dad. "You wouldn't believe the conversation I had with Mara."

I proceeded to tell them everything she asked me, and Dad was just in disbelief that she would be asking after-death financial questions so soon after Randy died. He didn't want to believe it so he shrugged it off. He had also had some drinks, understandably so in the current situation, so I knew that he wasn't quite ready to take on a fight.

"Rusty, that is terrible," said Lefty. "Remember when we were in Houston and we were all leaving the hospital after Randy died. I told you about my experience in estate law and that if you needed anything, anything at all, I would help you as best I could even though I haven't practiced in fifteen years. Rusty I have to tell you, I have a feeling you will have to work hard to make sure that you and Mara agree on a life without Randy and how to act and what to do to keep each other happy."

"What do we do?" I asked.

I was completely clueless how last testaments and wills worked. Lefty was my biggest hope at this point to be able to navigate through these trying waters that lay ahead. There seemed to be an issue over Randy's will and his intentions. What were Randy's willful intentions, and would his will be full of tension? Lefty and I talked.

"I don't know anything about my powers as the executor. I have no clue what I am supposed to do and how I am supposed to make sure that everything is done according to Randy's intentions."

"Do you have the will? I can look it over to see what it looks like; maybe I can give you some pointers."

I didn't have a copy of it, so he suggested that we talk to my dad's cousin to review it when I could get it. It was my mission now to both grieve for Randy and protect his intentions as best as I could. Only I could do this for my brother. No one knew him like I did. I kept this all to myself, not really talking to anyone about it even within my family. I was going to make sure I did the best for my brother. I had promised him.

With me bringing my concerns to my dad, he was concerned also that he wouldn't be able to get one possession of Randy's, so he asked Mara for a cigar box that he had given Randy, and to his surprise she obliged. Upon taking it home he rummaged through it and came across a half used cigar neatly wrapped in a zip lock bag. Dad lost it. I came over that evening and the first thing he did was bring me the cigar box.

"Russ, I want you to take this," he said to me. "I cannot look at this without falling apart. I want you to have it."

"Dad, I don't want to take the cigar box, but if you cannot handle it I will hold it for you until you are ready."

"I don't think I will ever be able to have it. All I ask of you is to please keep the partially used Cigar. Don't ever throw it away."

I took the cigar box, and to this day still have the half smoked cigar that Randy left for better times and that, like Randy's life, was snuffed out long before it was finished. In fact, there are several cigars that Randy had, and I haven't touched them and won't touch them until there is a special occasion that Randy would have wanted to celebrate.

We were scheduled to go to the funeral home to start the preparation for Randy's funeral. My parents and siblings along with Mara and her mom and sister were going to be there. We parked and all of us walked in, and Mara was walking next to me holding me by my arm. I remember being apprehensive, but I wasn't going to push her away because of my previous encounter with her; I wanted to keep this as peaceful as possible. The funeral directors started going over the types of caskets and what Randy would wear and all I could do was sit there not saying much. My parents would ask me questions of what I wanted, and all I could do was softly say what I thought would be good. The question of what he would be wearing came up and I wanted to give him one of my suits. Mara said that she would love to see him in one of his without a tie and I obliged to the suit but told her that I wanted to see him in a tie. Given all of the people who were going to come see Randy, I wanted him to look professional and good-looking. The funeral director asked if we wanted to go see the tomb in which he would be buried. It was a welcomed interruption to the awkward silence in the room. Mara gravitated to my side as we headed off.

That evening my sister, Dayna, called me to come take a look at some videos she wanted to play at the wake. I knew that Randy had done a music video when the new warehouse was empty but I hadn't had a chance to see it. I wasn't aware that she was working on this video until I got there, so needless to say it was really special to see it. The song he played was called "Solais Sioroi". I was not sure which language that was, but what I found on the internet indicated it was from the Irish Gaelic, and the title means eternal light. The setting of the video was in front of our walk-in coolers. Randy noted how great the acoustics were when we were almost finished building the coolers. The coolers being so large, playing inside them would have produced too much reverberation, so Randy and the other musicians sat in front of the opening to them, using several carpets, some Christmas lights, and candles, and started playing. As I watched the video, I quickly regretted not being there for this. He mentioned it to me but at the time I was busy with renovating my apartment in the evenings. The song was uncannily perfect for the funeral. These lyrics in particular,

"*Mother that cries when death hits the dirt, yielding the flood that comes from the hurt. Lay thee down and the questions are birthed, for why no sound when he absent the earth.*"

Randy Perrone in the Song

"*Solais Sioroi*"

The video can be seen at this link:
https://vimeo.com/61012943

She started editing the video and I added some suggestions with fades and transitions. It was a unique experience to be able to help Dayna edit this song. It wasn't Randy's full band who participated; in fact, there was only one regular band member there, who was playing the bongos, and there was also a guest cello player. The ensemble was so perfect for that song, and I could just imagine Randy putting it together in his mind as he wanted it to sound, look, and feel. One of the coolest parts was at the end of the song when a train can be heard coming to a stop in the background, which may seem like it was inserted after the fact, but in reality the timing just happened to be perfect. Randy's true happy personality came out after the train's screeching stopped when he simply said, "I like it," with the biggest smile on his face. You could tell that at that moment he wanted nothing other than to be in his music.

We finished the video and then Chad, Dayna's husband, started to show me some videos that a friend dropped off to add to the collection for the wake. These videos were taken when we were in high school. To see how young we were then was just heart-rending. If I knew then that I was going to lose my brother ten years from that point, I would have lived my life differently. I guess we all would do some things differently if we could see the future. Sometime we just have to try to forgive ourselves for what we were not. As Lilly Tomlin once said,

"Forgiveness means giving up all hope of a different past."

We got to the funeral home early so that we could help set up and see the arrangements that we ordered for Randy. I was reluctant to go into the room right away. When I saw him lying there, I flashed back to the first time I had ever seen a deceased person in a casket, my grandfather Papa Joe. I will never forget that time because, when I looked at Papa Joe, my thirteen-year-old mind couldn't comprehend why he looked so different. I feared Randy not looking like himself, but I was happy to see that they were able to keep him looking like himself for the most part. I touched his hands and noticed how cold his body was; I knelt down and talked to him while my sisters and brother stood by me.

"I can't believe this is happening, Randy, I just cannot believe you are no longer alive. Please wake me up from this bad dream."

I finished talking to him and praying for him and walked around to see all of the arrangements that people had sent. The room was full of so many flowers, some in the shape of crosses, some in the shape of hearts, and there was one that my Aunt Sandra and Uncle Ralph sent that was in the shape of a guitar. That one was my favorite. When we were finished looking at the arrangements, we went to see the TV that was playing videos of Randy, including his music video. There were also TV's that had picture slideshows and poster boards with old photographs on them. It was truly heartwarming to see all of the memorabilia and flowers that others had provided for Randy.

  The funeral director approached us and told us to stand next to Randy as visitors were starting to come. I made a point to hug everyone who walked into the room. After a while I noticed that the line was starting to creep out of the room, and then suddenly the funeral director came up to us:

  "The family will have to walk down the line, because the cars are continuously coming, and if you don't, we will not be able to end the wake on schedule."

  I asked the funeral director if this were the largest wake he had seen and he told me, "This is already shaping up to be the second-largest wake in the funeral home's 150 year long history. The largest was a baseball player for LSU that suddenly collapsed of a heart attack." (The baseball player was Wally Pontiff, Jr. His mom attended "adoration chapel" at our church the hour directly before my dad, every Wednesday morning for the last eight years.) "Either way you look at it, it is obvious that Randy was loved by many." The funeral director continued, "People were parking over a mile away to attend, and that was just amazing to see." Seeing that many people made me feel really good for Randy that so many wanted to pay their respects. It made me realize how important it is to families who have lost loved ones that we pay respects to them. As I was walking down the line, I noticed that it wrapped around the hallway and out of the building, and I just couldn't walk any further because people were grabbing me and hugging me. I remember not crying throughout the wake, I held myself together so that everyone walking up to see Randy would have a shoulder to cry on. The one thing I recall and am amazed at is the fact I remembered every single person's name. I am usually terrible with names, but for whatever reason they were coming out of my mouth with confidence, and I attribute that to Randy. I saw school teachers, friends from the past, even people who were "enemies" of Randy and mine growing up. It was truly heartwarming to see this kind of turnout.

I lost track of my family, because they were all scattered trying to greet everyone at the event. Before the wake was over, Mara and her group of friends wanted to go to a bar, and all I could remember was that I just wanted to stay with Randy until the end and I wanted to be with my family. The wake lasted a record length according to the funeral director, and he gave each of my family members a big hug, and you could see how upset he was that Randy was gone, a person he had never met. Even in his death Randy was still touching people.

After the wake was over, my family went to eat at a restaurant, and all we could talk about was how impressed and humbled we were that so many people came to see Randy and our family. Tomorrow would be very difficult. There was a funny moment in the night, one that had Randy's doing written all over it. Randy never really liked taking showers, so it just so happened that earlier in the day New Orleans had issued a boil water advisory, which meant that people couldn't take a shower before they came. It was his way to mark his event.

The next day was the funeral at our parish church, which was a moment I dreaded and there was nothing I could do to stop it. We arrived early and already the number of cars was stunning. A line formed to visit the family. We gathered around Randy to greet all of the visitors. I hugged more people in those two days than I had hugged in an entire lifetime. The number of people present was humbling. A true testament to Randy's and my family's ability to show our love to all was that we had so many people come to show their love and support during this hard time.

The mass started and after the gospel, the pastor said that we could come up and say something about Randy. The eulogies started, first my dad, then my mom, followed by my sisters. It was time for my brother and me to go up together as my sisters had. We walked up to the altar to start our eulogies, and when my brother finished, I motioned for Mara to come do her eulogy. When she was finished I stood in front of the podium. Looking at the full church, over 800 people, I was in awe. This was the church that we had attended almost my whole life. We went to school here, we served as altar servers here, and now I was in the same place about to speak about my brother and his life. Again I felt the surge of Randy passing through me and wanted to thank the congregation for attending. I said over the microphone, "I just cannot be more thankful for all the support Randy has received. Please look around you, look how many people are here." The congregation started to look around and you could hear chatter. In true Randy fashion I said, "This is humbling and as Randy would do…" I stepped aside, put my hands together in a praying form, took a bow, and then said, "Thank you." The entire congregation broke out in applause. This was Randy through me I thought. I started my eulogy.

"Can you imagine someone who throughout life has been right by your side, someone who could understand your thoughts without you even speaking, and someone you never imagined life without? Randy was a person with built-in friendly competitiveness in sports, in school, in being mischievous (which I am positive most of you know we were), and most important of all, he was a good person. That has been the story of my life for the last 29 years and 358 days. Randall William Perrone was known for his mischievousness as a young man, for his love of his music, for his mission of helping others, but most importantly of all to me, he was my twin.

Some of my fondest memories are of a time when we were younger and always up to no good. For most of you here, you either have heard our stories or you were part of them. To tell them all would take days, and believe me I will repeat them all over time, so to pick one or two of them is extremely hard. With so many stories I have put titles to them, some of you might recognize like: candy grab when we were five, doughnuts in UNO's parking lot (and no, I am not talking about eating), doing a fantastic display of the words "Merry Christmas" on the roof of my parents' house, the great escape and capture, deck change, operation switch class, grunge road, Turnbull fireworks show, handcuffing Jared to the street sign, Sheraton parking garage, smoke bomb in the attic, tooth paste on attic floor, operation diaper hide, a river runs through it, bathroom window suction, R&R as Santa or Easter Bunny, club house part 1,2,3, and 4, operation skip swimming, BB gun misfire, saga of the motion detector, and the list goes on. Since some of you might not know these I will share some of my favorite episodes.

In High School, if you were on crutches or hurt, you were allowed a friend to accompany you to the front of the lunch line. Well Randy and I had a spark of imagination to use a friend's crutches so we both could get in front of the lunch line. Later that day one of the lunch ladies inquired to my mom, "Boy those twins sure help each other so much. By the way how is Randy's leg?"

My mom not knowing what was going on said, "What do you mean? What's wrong with Randy's leg?" The lunch lady said, "Randy was on crutches and Rusty was helping him get his lunch." My mom quickly realized that we had duped the lunch lady.

Another story told many times involved our lighting fireworks out of the upstairs den window and throwing them out. Randy so eloquently stated, "Oh we would be in so much trouble if Mom and Dad found out about this." Just as he finished, we heard my oldest sister's voice say, "You're right and they will find out about this." Needless to say my parents weren't too happy. Since I can go on forever and we don't have much time, I will leave you with a prayer, sort of. My last story took place at the resource center at Brother Martin High School, a gathering place where we could talk quietly while doing homework, a place we visited every day. One day when the disciplinarian was walking toward our table, Randy told our friends there to follow his lead. As the disciplinarian was passing Randy started saying, "Our Father who art in heaven," which was followed by a quick remark from the disciplinarian, "Oh, Perrone, I know you're not praying; now be quiet and do your homework!"

With all the mischievousness, there is also a part of his life in which dedication trumped trying to get into trouble. Randy was truly dedicated to his music, which started when he was sixteen years old, in a friend's apartment Uptown. Our friend pulled out a guitar and played "Stairway to Heaven." Once he saw this, he was hooked and asked that friend to teach him to play. He was so devoted to playing that he quickly surpassed the talents of his teacher and started to advance by

crafting beautiful words and melodies to create his own songs. I never knew that what he was doing was creating a way for us all to know him through his music. I can recall his very first time playing in front of people at the Neutral Ground Coffee house. He was very nervous, so I was there to make sure he was comforted by the fact that he was heard with love and open ears. His passions for music led me to sacrifice my closet and turn it into a sound room so we could record him playing his own music. My uncle later noticed his commitment to music and allowed us to build, with our own hands, a music studio so that he could pursue his dream of being heard by the masses. Since then he went on to record an EP (extended play CD) and an album. I have listened to it over and over, always blowing me away. See Randy was so passionate about his music that we rarely saw him not holding his guitar at his house. His mission to be heard by the masses now will continue with my help.

Randy was also known for having a kind heart. He strived to help people wherever he could. Once in Chicago we couldn't finish eating our pizza, so he put the pizza in two boxes and gave it to some homeless people standing nearby. Another one of his many kindhearted gestures happened recently at MD Anderson where he noticed a younger woman who was undergoing cancer treatments. She was all by herself through her ordeal and Randy reached out to her and invited her to our family's hotel room to enjoy our last beers together before his surgery. Because of this she will always be in our minds, and we will continue to extend an olive branch to her as he did. His very last words were spoken to me after his surgery. I was visiting with him in the post anesthesia area and asked how he was doing. The very next thing out of his mouth was, "How are you doing?" Even in pain he was concerned about others. Randy was and still is my inspiration to be a better person. I just can't imagine a kinder human on this earth.

Randy was known to most of my family as Randyroo, or Randy, or Friend as we did when we played as kids, or "You" when our dad couldn't tell us apart but was mad. To me he was known as my twin, a lifelong companion who, no matter what, would always be there for me. We would be there for each other in good times and in bad, in sickness and in health, and death would be the only force to part us. This sounds pretty similar to a marriage; however, the difference here is in marriage two people choose to be together to make those promises to each other, but my relationship with my brother was chosen by God, executed by my parents, and celebrated through the love and friendship between Randy and me. I was told growing up that twins have a special bond, which is true. We lived this bond.

There were many times that I could literally feel Randy's emotions, especially when he was in BIG trouble. The most recent time other than his death was when my son, Julien Bartholomew Perrone, was born. Randy couldn't stop texting me, telling me how he was speechless and couldn't stop feeling like he was the happiest man on earth. He was convinced that Julien was a part of him, considering we share the same DNA. Almost all brand new fathers experience by themselves the joy and the rush of strong emotions once their first born child arrives in this world. I had the rare and unique experience to share my emotions with Randy, so much so he was crying at his house while I was crying at the hospital in joy. I remember our conversation and it reminds me of our special connection.

When eating in the hospital cafeteria, the evening that Randy's course took a turn for the worse, I was overcome with a surge of worry and emotional pain. I felt Randy's distress, a feeling I had never felt before and one that will live with me until I lay my head down for the last time.

In Randy's own words,

"Today the sun sees me: tomorrow it may not but that doesn't mean it's not there. I may be gone flying so high, with the wings that we all try to make. The clouds will open and close behind me; up through it all I will make it through. I won't forget all of those who have helped me become who it is I long to be. If I'm gone tomorrow, then will you remember me? Have I done enough to leave? Please don't forget me when I go, because I will always be here. Up in the trees looking down on the ground that you all walk on so you don't fall off the edge of the world, confused and lost in this ride of life, in that we all will die, we all will, will die."

Randy, my brother, I feared this day my entire life. As a child, as a teenager, and as an adult I used to fear living my life without you and every time it would bring me to tears. Never in a million years did I expect those fears to come true before we reached thirty. Our birthday in two days will be the first birthday in my life that I can't hug you and wish you happy birthday, but I know and I feel that you will be there with me in your spirit. Live in our hearts, live in our minds, and most of all live in our actions, my sweet brother. May your heart and soul be at peace while you rest. I love you."

After my eulogy John, Mara and I went back to our seats. The priest was starting the closing words and allowed my family one last visitation with Randy before they were to close the coffin. We all went up together as a family and just looked with tears in our eyes at my brother just lying there lifeless. We held each other tight, touching Randy on his face, holding his hand; just all soaking up the last time we would be able to touch his body. We started back to the pew and the priest was about to close the casket when I just couldn't take it and ran back to him to give him one more kiss. I remember one of my tears landing on his cheek as I gave him a kiss on his forehead. My brother John quickly came up to me to hug me and he pulled me back to my seat. I will never forget the moment that they closed the casket and I realized that I would never see his face again here on earth. The congregation all stood up as the priest did, and the final prayer was said. They sang "On Angels' Wings," which was always my favorite song for a funeral when we were altar servers, and now it was being sung for Randy. I didn't want to talk or look at anyone while we followed the pall bearers down the aisle. I could hear sniffles and crying while we made it out of the church. We went straight to our limo and watched as the church seemed to endlessly flow with people through the exit doors. Again I just couldn't believe how many people came to my brother's funeral. While we were on our way to the funeral home, we just spoke about Randy. I didn't talk much. All I could do was soak in what everyone was saying and give an occasional smirk or nod to what was being said.

Randy's Jazz Funeral with horse-drawn hearse. 3-4-2013

We pulled up to the funeral home and saw two big all-white horses attached to the horse-drawn hearse. I was so mesmerized by this sight and thought to myself how perfect a way for Randy to be led to his tomb. The second line band was waiting there for us to arrive, tuning up their instruments. The leader was dressed in a tuxedo with tails, a top hat, and a baton, waiting to start the procession. For most who aren't familiar with our many unique traditions in New Orleans, the tradition of a Jazz Funeral or Second Line draws its roots back to the African influences on the city. Traditionally the music played isn't jazz but New Orleans style music played by a brass band. The beginning of the procession, called the First Line, starts off with somber music and it is played the entire way from the church or a starting point to the tomb. Once the body is entombed, the tempo picks up for the Second Line which takes place from the tomb to either someone's house or back to the starting point. This tradition was almost exclusive to African Americans or musicians until about 1960, but growing up Randy and I always viewed this as a unique New Orleans tradition.

We got out of the limo and walked to where the horse-drawn hearse was. The automobile hearse that was carrying Randy pulled up next to the horses and they moved Randy to the horse-drawn hearse that would take him along this final stretch to the tomb. We all watched, holding each other's arms, crying and speechless. As the band was ready, I remember looking around and saw people crowded behind us, there were even some people who were visiting the cemetery. I was so proud to be able to show our history and traditions to others. We started off and walked about a mile to the tomb site. All I could feel

was pride that we were giving Randy this type of a burial. When we reached the tomb, the band stopped and the pallbearers moved Randy to the tomb. The priest started to say some prayers and allowed a moment of silence before we were to start heading back. We as a family decided that we wouldn't follow the second line back but instead would get in the limo by the tomb and head back to my parents' house for a post funeral gathering. As everyone followed the band back to the funeral home, it left Randy there with no one. I got out of the limo and went one last time to touch the casket. I sat there for several minutes and collected a sunflower and a bird of paradise flower, both of which were Randy's favorite flowers. Unbeknownst to me, one of Randy's past band members saw this and snapped a picture of me standing there with him. He later sent it to me and I was so happy to see that.

Inside I know how much I cared for Randy and never wanted to leave his side, and now I have a picture to remind me forever that I never wanted to leave his side all the way to the end. Aristotle said, *"Love is composed of a single soul inhabiting two bodies."* Was he talking only about lovers, or might he have also been thinking of twins?

A couple of days later, on Saturday, we had a second line take place in the French Quarter honoring Randy. It was an opportunity for those that couldn't participate in the funeral because of work to pay their respects to Randy. We started the second line in front of the building that once housed our family business on Decatur Street. It was such a fantastic tribute to Randy, drawing about a hundred people. The street was closed off for us and we walked to a park right outside the French Quarter. How better to honor a musician than with music! Everyone had a good time celebrating Randy's life, just as Randy had enjoyed celebrating life itself.

Chapter 38

Trouble Following Grief

After the funeral and the second line took place, my mom, dad, and John sat down to go over financials of the funeral and also other matters, one of which included a life insurance policy that the business had taken on Randy. When my brothers and I joined the business and became partners, our dad had the foresight to take out life insurance policies for the three of us, naming the business as beneficiary. This was designed to allow the business to buy out and provide for our spouses and children in the event of an untimely death without strapping the business for much-needed cash. Since Randy was not married, there was no one to support, and considering that our business was in big financial trouble this was a much-needed boost. Although it helped out, I would have in a heartbeat taken my brother to still be here to work through the hardships than accept the money.

There was also another policy where Dad was named the beneficiary. He decided then that he didn't want Randy's "blood money," but instead he was going to use it to build a Perrone tomb, so that Randy's entire family could spend eternity with him after each of us had taken our last breath. Randy and I always talked about having a Perrone tomb, and now his gift to our dad was going to be a way that we could afford to do it. We called the funeral home and set up a meeting to go see plots and designs. We picked out a design that holds four caskets with room at the bottom to store the remains of previously deceased members. I made it clear that Randy's remains weren't to be moved and that I wanted to be put right next to him when I die. Naturally my mom and dad obliged me and grabbed my hand as I cried. We looked at potential plots in the cemetery. We finally came upon a plot that was all the way to the back, and had a patch of grass in front. We were also told we could plant some trees behind the tomb, as long as the root systems weren't invasive to damage the tomb. We went back to the parlor, drew up the paperwork, decided on the design and were done.

As we were driving away, my dad told us that he had money remaining from Randy's insurance and he wasn't sure what he was going to do with it. What happened next was one of the best decisions I think he ever made:

"I know what I want to do with the remaining money. I want to start a college fund for each of Randy's nieces and nephews in his name. This way when they grow up, and are ready for college, they will have a gift from their uncle who most of them will never remember."

I cried silently in the back seat when I heard this and all I could say to Dad was how happy I was to hear this. What a great story to tell my children when they were ready to go to college that their uncle gave them this opportunity. Our dad even thought about Randy's unborn nieces and nephews and pledged that he would match the fund for any new child born so that every niece and nephew would get this opportunity from Randy. I always knew it was our dad who gave Randy and my siblings our good will, but this was a moment when I looked out the window to the heavens and thanked God for such a great gift He provided me and my siblings, that of being children of such great parents. So here it was, Randy still taking care of other people. Randy, with his death, saving his family business, allowing a tomb to be built for his family, and providing college education for all of his nieces and nephews.

A couple of days later, Max wanted to meet at Randy's house to go over the will with me. Because I had not read it since it had been written, I thought it was appropriate for him to explain everything. I knew that I was the executor of the will, but I wasn't sure what that meant, what my role was, or what were the details of Randy's wishes. The notarized copy was at my office, and I was staying away from the warehouse so I didn't have to deal with the emotional reality of Randy's not being there. Max and I went to the back porch to read the copy he had and discuss everything. Ben was there and so was Mara. We were going over everything when Mara wanted to go inside for a break. That is when my world started to crumble because it was at that point that Max hit me with a curve ball.

Max said, "Randy didn't state anything about Mara having any inheritance of the business shares. When I mentioned it to Randy, he said to me, 'Don't worry about it. It's taken care of'. I wasn't sure what he meant by that."

Then I said to Max, "Well, we have a buy-sell agreement that states that only a blood lineage of my parents can own the business. That is what he meant by 'It's taken care of.'"

Max answered, "Yes, but the residual clause states that any immovable or movable property not otherwise mentioned will be split between you and Mara equally."

At this point two things were suddenly clear to me: (1) longstanding legal descriptions of the family business' organization clearly state that ownership of shares in the business are restricted to individuals who are lineal descendants of my parents; (2) there was ambiguity in the will regarding "immovable or movable property not otherwise mentioned." Wishing that Randy were present to help sort out his intentions would not help me. I was left with the pain of grieving the loss of my twin brother and also bringing clarity to his last intentions and wishes. We finally ended our visit and I headed to my parents' house.

Before I left the house I made a point to get Randy's wallet from Mara and also I was able to get Randy's watch. I traded one of his Lyric books for the watch. Dealing with Randy's important things representing our memories of him was awkward, painful, and sometimes came with conflict.

I met my dad at his house, and he brought business documents with him. You could tell in his eyes that he wasn't ready for this work, just having been dealt the biggest blow a man could receive in his life, the death of his child. The buy-sell agreement did state that only a direct lineage from my parents could own the shares, but in a subsequent statement it clearly said that in the event that the shares are given, through death or any other measure, the company would be forced to buy the shares, and the recipient would be forced to sell the shares back to the company. After all that we had been through, working sixteen-hour days trying to get into our warehouse, and then sixteen-hour days trying to not let the undertaking with the Stanley Co. put us out of business, we were facing yet another challenge in our business history. We were determined to make sure everything was done to maintain our legacy. Family discussions followed in which there was a consensus that we all wanted to honor Randy's intentions, some of which were not clear. We all wanted Mara to have anything Randy had designated to be hers, and we all needed to protect and preserve the family business according to the legal documents under which it was established, of which Randy was a part, and with which Randy was familiar.

That evening Lefty, my dad's friend who was in Houston when Randy passed away, came over and I took him up on his offer that he made in Houston to help if I needed it. I looked at this situation as similar to what my great-grandfather went through during the Great Depression. I remembered the story of my great-grandfather telling the bookkeeper to find the door and never come back.

As Lefty and our family proceeded to evaluate all these matters under the stress of grieving Randy's death, many meetings during upcoming days and lost hours of sleep during the nights brought us to the point of several meetings with Mara and her lawyers together with our lawyers. The important issues relating to differences of opinion in interpreting the will involved our family business and Randy's banked sperm. Randy had both a legal legacy and a biological one, and I had both of these as my companions on a journey I never wanted to make.

Chapter 39

From Legal Recordings to Musical Ones

A few days later I wanted to get in touch with Randy's band. I made a promise to Randy that I would make sure his music was spread around the world, and the way to start this was to sit in front of the band and talk to them. I had always been involved with Randy and his music until I got married. At that point I started a family, and while I started to focus on my family, Randy had several band members leave, and new ones added. So I called Andy, who was his first band member and who played the drums, to set up my meeting. We were going to meet at Dixon and Mike's house. Dixon played the bass, and Mike played lead guitar. I had met Mike and Dixon before at a couple of gigs, but I hadn't met Jake, the newest member, who played hand percussions. I sat down in front of the entire band.

"I want to say how sorry I am that Randy is no longer with you. I want to offer you something. Considering we were twins, I may be able to sound like him with practice, and may be able to fill in for Randy on vocals. But, the thing is, I want everyone to be on board fully or I won't do it. I want to make sure that everyone is okay with it and not think that I am coming in to take over. What I will do is leave the table so you can discuss it, and I will come back and you can give me the decision. Remember if just one person says no, I will be on the sidelines, helping, but not the way that I am proposing."

Their faces looked like I hit them with a curve ball. I didn't think any of them would consider it. I got up from the table, went inside and waited. Then Andy came inside to get me and we sat down at the table. Dixon said, "Of course we want you to do it." I got up and hugged each one of them. I told them at any point they did not like what they were seeing and hearing, then anyone of them could just say the word and I would step back. We sat there and discussed several issues and topics and then set a date each week to get together to practice. It was going to be Mondays or Tuesdays of every week. We went inside and Andy pulled out a CD of Randy singing which I had recorded in my closet. This was the very CD Randy and I dropped off to Andy right after Hurricane Katrina. This was special because that was the first time we met Andy, and he chose to join the band from Randy's music that I recorded. Listening to those songs was a time warp, bringing me back to bittersweet memories of Randy and me spending countless hours throughout the late night recording his early songs. It was so special to be there and listen with the band. I hadn't really been given musical talent, like what God gifted to Randy, but I did bring my didgeridoo to show the band that I could play something. The didgeridoo is a hard instrument to play because of the amount of air needed on a continuous basis to maintain the sound. I was determined several months prior to Randy's death to learn how to circle breathe, and Randy was so proud that I was able to do it. He even said in his humble way, "I cannot even do that; see you do have some musical talent." It made me feel good to remember his words as I was demonstrating for the band. Andy said in a joking manner, "Now you need to learn how to play guitar."

  I thought to myself, "Gee I have tried and tried to play guitar, I don't want to let Randy down if I try and fail again." I told him that I would think about it. We finished up the evening with hugs and words of peace and love and went our ways. On the way home I told myself, "I am going to learn how to play guitar, and I will do it for Randy. This will keep me focused so I don't fail, doing it for Randy." I knew how proud he would be if I could.

  One day not long after the first meeting with the band, I chose to pick up Randy's favorite guitar and try to learn to play it. I messed around with some of the chords that Randy initially taught me when we were teenagers, but I was having a difficult time doing it. I called up my cousin Evan. Randy had taken Evan under his wings and taught him guitar. They would play together whenever they had a moment free. He answered the phone and I asked him if he would come over and teach me to play the guitar. He just so happened to be at the cemetery so I said that I would come to him. I grabbed Randy's guitar and headed out to the tomb. We sat across from Randy as Evan taught me some of Randy's songs.

We started on a song called "Destination" which was a song he wrote years ago after a road trip we took with a bunch of friends to Florida. It was our first trip without our parents. We stocked the car with plenty of beer and we headed out on the three-hour drive to Florida. We had so much fun on the way there that we adopted the slogan, "May your ride exceed the destination." The song being the main theme of the book, I leave it to Randy to describe how exactly he thought it would be written:

Driving down this highway
Where are we going
No one knows but
We go there the same way
And passing hundreds of people
Like time passing life by
It just goes, it never stops, no

And Life is a journey
Sometimes we walk through hell
But That's just life, you've got to
Take it as it comes
And day by day live your life to its full
Because you never know when your ride will end

For all we know this journey could be your last
And what would you have to show for it
Can you look back and say that
You lived your life until it's full and not let life live you
When you ride, make it better than the destination

I once knew a man that told me to live your life in a dream
And dream your life away while you sleep
And take them as far as your feet can carry the beat
And make them as real as anything

Do you ever find yourself asking the question?
Why you were put here
What's your reasons
And many people go through life and never find that answer
Seems as though they are just alive to die

For all we know this journey could be your last
And what would you have to show for it
Can you look back and say that you lived your life to it's full
And not let life live you down
So when you ride, make it better
Make it better than you have ever had it before
Better than that destination.

"Destination" by Randy Perrone

An intimate video of Randy playing this song can be seen here: https://www.youtube.com/watch?v=zdUSgBWlI0g

It was difficult to try to get my fingers to do what I wanted them to do. Muscle memory is an interesting thing, and when you learn to play guitar, you have to build this muscle memory in order to make the guitar sound good. We practiced for several hours until the sun was going down. I took some videos because I was determined not to let time go by between Evan and me getting together again without practicing. It was my therapy to sit down while Julien was sleeping and just practice the chords. Before I knew it I was starting to jump from chord to chord and I was actually making the guitar play the song. This success left me craving more. I texted Evan a video of me playing the song, and he wrote back how impressed he was. I felt so special to have Evan, who had been taught by Randy, teaching me. In my mind it seemed that Randy was teaching me how to play guitar.

Then as I thought that I came up with the challenge of watching one of Randy's videos on YouTube to see if I could learn another of his songs just by looking at his moves. I pulled up one of my favorite songs of his, called "War." This song was a hard song to play because it involved fingerpicking as opposed to strumming. To fingerpick is difficult because as you hold down one of the strings, your finger must pick only that string for it to make the desired sound. I worked on this song for a while, because I knew that if I could get this one down, I wouldn't have much trouble on some of the easier songs. It took me several days to get that song down. I would switch back to "Destination" when I got discouraged, because playing that song gave me the confidence to keep going. I was experiencing the truth that this guitar journey may well exceed its own destination. I wanted to make sure that the next time I was going to play with Evan he would know that I had been practicing between lessons.

At this point I was starting to really see a place for me in music. We were going to start practicing with the band on Mondays or Tuesdays and I was getting excited to show them how much I had progressed on the guitar. Still a long way from being able to play and sing at the same time. I was getting the hang of it. The first practice with the band was awkward. They were all happy to have me there, each person giving me a big hug when I got there, and then we sat down for a bit to talk about what we wanted to do. My goal was to sing the songs that the band had just released on the *Peace of Mind* album. This was the first time that I had ever really attempted to sing with a band, much less use a microphone that would amplify my imperfections. The whole band could tell that I was nervous about it, that I was holding back my vocals so as to not embarrass myself.

Andy pulled me aside and gave me some encouragement.

"Don't worry about what it sounds like. Feel the power within your belly and push it out as hard as you can."

I took his advice and just let go of my inhibitions. It felt amazing to get that power from within to push through my vocal chords, through my mouth, and into a microphone. I knew then why Randy loved playing and singing music so much. It was a release of energy, good and bad, in a way that others could sit back and enjoy.

When we finished the first practice, we talked about how much we all missed Randy and how proud he would be that we were getting together to keep the music alive. It felt good and bad at the same time. I was happy to be part of the band; I just wished that I would have had the drive to do this while Randy was alive. That would have made his world so much brighter, as he always tried to convince me to join him. He would always say, "Everyone remembers twins. Could you imagine if we were to be on stage together? It would give us an advantage over others just by the fact that we look alike." Where is that forgiveness of self when we most need it?

As I jumped in Randy's car and headed home it started to rain. I cried the whole way home, one of the hardest cries I had had since he had passed away. I remember the pain hurt so much that I screamed to the top of my lungs, I screamed so hard that I actually lost my voice for a couple of days. I sat outside my house, rain coming down on the car, and just stared off into space. My mind was going a million miles a second, wishing that I was with him, and wishing that this was all just a bad dream. I walked inside and climbed in bed with Cristy. She could tell right away that I had been crying. She pulled me close to her, put her arms around me, and tried to tell me that everything was going to be all right. I couldn't control myself. My body shook, my eyes poured, and I was holding my breath trying to keep it all inside.

At that point she was starting to get concerned about me, so I pulled myself together and let her know that I was all right. She asked me if band practice pulled that out of me. I told her no, but in reality it was being with the band members and singing Randy's music that etched in stone the harsh reality:

"I am here with the band because Randy isn't."

The combination of his absence and the issues I was having with Mara and Randy's will were taking a toll. I knew then that the tipping point of my emotions would be when I had to confront Mara about the will.

Chapter 40

Decency and Deportment in the Digital Age, or Not

It came time to have a meeting with Mara about the will and see whether we were going to have some potential issues with the business. We tried to discuss Randy's will and his intentions regarding the business and other matters. There was tension and some heat. Mara apparently didn't take to the conversation all too well so she asked us to leave, and our communication with each other became strained. The fallout from this would be far worse than I had imagined. We were living in the new digital age with all its wonders and warts. All over Facebook, my friends were posting on my page and my mom's page things that should have been between Mara and us:

"Honor the will…evil has shown its ugly face, and we hope Randy can see this…your family are grave robbers."

All of this was written publicly so that all of our friends and family could read. These are people Randy and I considered close friends, close enough to be family, who were publicly bashing a friend who had just lost his brother and a mother who had just lost her son. My mom started to fire back wherever she could. It truly got ugly between our family and my so called "friends."

That evening I called Ben and Max's mom trying to plead my case as best I could without disclosing too many facts regarding the will that I was advised not to disclose. I kept pleading with her to understand that I had Randy's interests at heart and that she should not make judgments from one side of the story. I told her, "You know me very well, and you know that I would do anything for Randy. You have to just trust me." She and Ben begged for me to tell them everything, but all I could say to them is that they had to trust me.

That evening I had trouble going to sleep. I wanted so badly to dream about Randy and have him tell me that I was doing the right thing. That night I didn't sleep long enough to dream of Randy. I woke up and went to work and left early to go to the cemetery to visit with Randy. This had been my daily routine since Randy's death, but now I was scared that someone would find me there and try to harm me.

On the way my mom called me and told me that I needed to call Aunt Jane about something she experienced last night. I called her right away and what she told me was chilling and a relief at the same time.

"Hi, Aunt Jane," I said to her when she answered.

"Hey Russ, how are you doing?"

As I started to talk I was choking up and tears were running down my face, "I am not doing so well, Aunt Jane. I really wish that I was with Randy right now."

"Rusty," she said to me in a calming voice, "I am not sure what is going on but I feel like I have to tell you what happened to me last night. I usually don't have any trouble sleeping, and when I sleep I stay asleep all night. Last night I woke up in the middle of the night and my room was pitch-black as normal. I felt a presence in the room and I instantly knew that it was Randy. I felt him hold my hand and he said to me, "Aunt Jane, make sure Rusty is okay." Rusty, when I tell you that I thought about you all morning, I mean all morning I thought about you. I didn't want to tell your mom about it because I wasn't sure how she would take it, but I knew that Randy needed me to find out if you are okay."

I cried for a bit and was finally able to talk to her, "Aunt Jane, you don't know how much that means to me right now. My whole world seems to be crashing down on me and all I want to do is be with Randy. I cannot take any more stress, Aunt Jane."

She interrupted me, "Russ, let me tell you, son, you are a strong person and I am not sure what is going on outside of just the loss of Randy but I have to put this into perspective for you. How much worse can it get? You've already lost the most important person in your life. Whatever you feel is coming down on you cannot be worse than that."

"You're right," I said. "You are absolutely right. It means so much to me to hear you say that to me, and to know that when Randy couldn't get to me, he was able to get to you."

I felt much better after talking to her and went to visit with Randy like I had done since he was gone. I even kept a gun by my side, however, just in case someone would want to do harm to me. At this point I wasn't sure what people could do in a situation like this. I looked up at the sky above Randy's tomb and soaked in what nature had to offer me. I felt so alone, more alone than I had ever felt in my life, but shelter from my storms at this point had to wait because what was needed of me was to be strong and finish this obligation for Randy. There are angels of light and angels of darkness, and my job would be to not get crushed between them. If fact on another visit to the cemetery, while I was playing the guitar at Randy's tomb, I felt someone was behind me. I turned around and my heart skipped a beat seeing our childhood friend, Zane, standing there. It was a relief to see a friend I could trust and talk with about all that had happened since Randy's death. He said for some reason he knew he needed to go to the cemetery that day. In this instance the angel of light overpowered the angel of darkness.

Chapter 41

Desperate for Order

My mom, being a caring person, found an organization called Twinless Twins. They were formed in 1987 to be a support group for twins who had lost their twin. I thought this was a great idea, feeling that there wasn't anyone who really understood what I was experiencing. The feelings I was having had to be similar to others who had lost a twin, and here would be an opportunity to find people with similar situations. I joined their Facebook page and looked around on the page for a day or two. I saw people of all types and all situations posting stories. Some twins had lost their twin through suicide; this didn't appeal to me, not my situation. There were other twins who lost their twin at birth, obviously not my situation either. After searching I started to find twins who had similar situations to my own. I felt brave enough to post on the page. I mentioned that I had just lost my brother and that I wasn't sure how to operate. The number of people who opened their hearts to me was amazing. I finally felt like I was able to tell someone how I felt and know that they truly understood my feelings.

I received several private messages from twinless twins who were part of the organization. A twin named John messaged me and told me that I could call him anytime if I needed to talk. I saved his number and on one of my daily visits to the cemetery I called John. I talked to him for a couple of hours. He was older than me by thirty years. He lost his brother about fifteen years ago. I felt he understood, but I didn't really have a deep connection to his situation, as he was fortunate enough to have had a longer life with his twin. I feel he picked this up from my conversation and invited me to go to Houston in a month to a regional meeting with other twinless twins of all backgrounds.

I was reluctant to go until one day I got a reply to my post from a woman named Jessie. She told me that she had lost her sister a year and a half ago. I knew that she would be a person who would understand me much better. I messaged her and we started to talk and share our stories. Wow, I thought to myself, her situation is so close to mine that it is just uncanny. I mentioned to her about the meeting and asked if she planned to go. She was reluctant to go and I told her I was reluctant too, but would go if she went. She agreed to go and I felt a sense of relief. Finally I was going to get to talk to someone who was on the same path, just a little ahead of mine.

It just so happened that the day after the fallout from our meeting with Mara, Cristy and I set off to Houston for the Twinless Twins meeting. Everything that happened the day before was weighing me down. The fallout from meeting with Mara about Randy's will had happened almost the way I feared it would. I felt completely alone other than my family being there for me. Everyone who I used to call my friend, was no longer a friend, and seemed against me. They just didn't understand when I told them to trust me; no one did, and it was extremely difficult to be in a position like this so close to Randy's passing. My phone rang several times from my ex-friends trying to talk to me about my meeting with Mara and about the will. All I could do was ignore the calls to prevent me from saying anything that would complicate the issues.

As we were driving I received a call from Dixon, one of Randy's band members, and I thought to myself, "Not them too." All my support structures seemed to be failing and falling apart, and I was worried that this one would too. I answered the phone cautiously and the first thing he said to me was, "Rusty, how are you doing?" This was out of the ordinary from the calls I had been receiving from my "friends."

"Good?" I said with hesitation.

He began to tell me how he had been contacted by Mara, and that she was saying I was trying to get everything that I could from Randy and not let anyone have what Randy wanted them to have.

I told him, "Dixon, I cannot say much about the whole ordeal, but all I can say is, trust me. You know that Randy would have meetings with the band, and would say, 'If y'all ever made it big, the only person I would have manage the band would be Rusty, ' because Randy trusted me more than he could trust himself to do it right and with good intentions at the forefront."

Dixon with no hesitation said to me, "Brother, I do trust you and we trust you. Whatever lies and misconceptions they are spreading, you don't have to worry about us believing them. We are with you. I know that when you can tell us what is going on you will, and I know that if you are doing something as drastic as what they say, you are doing it for our best interests."

To hear this was so relieving to me. It truly was a weight off of my shoulders and added some motivation to keep on the path of protecting Randy's interest and intentions at all costs. We spoke for a couple of minutes more and I told him I was on my way to Houston to go to a Twinless Twins meeting to help get some much-needed therapy. He was happy to hear that. When we got off the phone, I looked over at Cristy and said, "Now that is how a true person of character should handle a situation like this. I wish people who have been my friends for so much longer would have gone about it like this." We didn't say much after this and just pondered the whole situation.

On getting closer to Houston, I wanted to call Dr. Theresa to see if I could visit with her and the staff. I called her cell phone and she answered. I told her that we were coming to Houston for a meeting and I wanted to stop by and say hello. She said she would be there, which was a relief to hear. Everything seemed like it was falling into place. I would visit the hospital before our cocktail gathering with the Twinless Twins group. As we approached Houston, I looked at the horizon and skyline as if watching a movie, in slow motion with dark clouds over it. Coming back was going to be difficult, but I was determined to conquer this task. I needed to get some closure to this whole ordeal. I wanted to trace my footsteps back, an opening of the wound so to speak, so that my brain could record the area permanently which would solidify this event and make it real. Up until this point the only way to explain the last three months had been:

"One day I went to sleep and everything was normal and great, then I woke up the next day and my twin brother was gone, my friends hated me, and I felt like my world had fallen apart."

Once we got settled in a hotel in Houston I called Snow, a close friend of mine from high school who was living in Houston. We arranged to meet the evening we arrived in Houston for dinner. I so much needed some good friends that would not judge me, who could hear the whole story without fear of it getting back to Mara or the others. I picked the same restaurant where we took Randy the night before his surgery. Again I wanted to retrace my steps.

When we arrived at the restaurant, it was close to the same time we had met the night before Randy went to surgery. We unfortunately didn't sit at the same table, but I had it in view. Cristy and Snow's wife started talking and I started to explain to Snow everything that had happened since Randy's passing. Up until this point, every time I would talk about this, to either my family or my attorney, I would get all worked up, serious, and stressed. This time however it was different. As I was explaining it to him, it all even seemed somewhat ridiculous. Oscar Wilde once said,

"If you want to tell people the truth, make them laugh, otherwise they'll kill you."

I started laughing uncontrollably when describing event after event to him. All he could do was laugh as well. We always had a great relationship where we would make each other laugh, and this was not different from any of those previous moments; however, this seemed funny because what I had gone through the last couple of months could not have been concocted even for TV or a movie. It was so far-fetched and unreal that all I could say to him was, "I mean, can you believe this is really happening?" It was the first time I had laughed since Randy passed away. The first time I had a smile. It was the first time that I felt comfortable to be alive. At this point talking to Snow was in a way like talking to Randy; laughing about our hardships as we always had in the past. He was my connection to my brother, and I really was thankful for that.

Robert Frost said, *"If we couldn't laugh, we would all go insane."*

I believe that Randy was preventing me from going insane with this uncontrollable laughter about the doom and gloom looming over my head. The remainder of the dinner was great. We all spoke of stories of the past. We laughed a lot, and one thing that I can say confidently is that laughter is balm for a broken heart. Without laughter, life can to be just too harsh. This night proved to be a great healing experience for me. The opportunity to be with a friend who really cared about me was a taste of being with Randy, my twin, who cared more about me than he cared about himself.

The next day the Twinless Twin cocktail gathering started at 4:00 p.m., so we had time to lie around and relax. I wanted to go to MD Anderson, and I told Cristy that I wanted to go alone. We agreed that when we finished lunch she would start getting ready for the evening and then I would go back to MD Anderson. We ate lunch and then I walked Cristy back to the room, gave her a kiss and she said to me, "Good luck, I love you. I wish I could go with you but I know you need to do this on your own." I hugged and kissed her and told her that I had to do this for my healing. I left her in the room and started off to the hospital.

The surroundings started to become familiar to me. I saw the Walgreens where we had stopped for antibacterial soap, and then I came upon the hotel. I was finally here. The amount of energy I could feel from this place was so great that my mind felt like it was no longer in control of my body. I parked my car and walked out of the garage the same way I had done with Randy, leaving a space for Randy as if he were walking right there next to me. I stopped at the point we hugged for what seemed like hours. I looked around, looked at the ground where his feet would have been, and just felt the wind blowing through my being, feeling Randy's presence all around me. I then walked to the lobby and looked around. At each spot I stopped, I scanned the area in a trance-like state, creating the scene again, replaying each step and each moment. I next went to the field where we played the night before Randy's surgery. I walked to the area I went to first and looked in the area Randy went to first. I could see Randy running and throwing the Frisbee and football to me. In my imagination, I recalled everything that happened in that field. I started walking to the area where we played, and remembered looking down the ditch and just thinking how steep it was. Every time Randy ran down this ditch to get the overthrown Frisbee or football I would get nervous, seeing how steep it was. I just remember wondering to myself why I would have let him go down there before his surgery. I guess it doesn't matter now, but nonetheless, my trance state brought back those worries.

I sat down in the spot I remember Randy being and picked up some twigs by me. All I could do was just sit there and think. I lay back on the ground and looked up into the sky. The sky had clouds where the sunlight had not been peeking through. When the sun did shine down on the field and lit it up, I knew this was Randy speaking to me, letting me know that he was still with me. I savored the moment for some time. I broke up a twig and put it in my pocket to bring back home with me. Several years after Randy's death we stumbled upon one of his songs he recorded and I feel it was meant for me in this moment, beneath the trees.

> *I feel lost but I know my place,*
> *To the strangers that we are to the lives we chase,*
> *Meet me at the house in the trees,*
> *That's where you will find me*
> *Waiting for the breeze.*
>
> *From the song "Tree House" by Randy Perrone*

I got up from lying in the field, put the twigs in my pocket, and went to the hotel lobby. Walking the same path we did the night before his surgery, looking at the flowers along the pathway and seeing Randy's hand waving over and through them, I hit the lobby and saw the piano that the musician was playing the day Randy left us, and could hear the music as if she were playing it now. I made my way to the elevators and went to the second floor. As I exited the elevators I saw the table where we sat when I knew something was terribly wrong. The flashbacks were starting to melt into reality; it was as if I was transported back in time to the moment of each significant event that night. Walking now to the bridge, I stopped at the hand sanitizer. I stretched out my hand and the machine dispensed a dollop. I rubbed my hands together, and in what seemed like slow motion, lifted them to my nose. As soon as the smell creeped in passing all my receptors, the hairs in my nose stood to attention. I could feel the electricity-like sensations starting in my olfactory sensory neurons and moving like an electrical shock to my mind. Each inhalation further melted my conscious state to my trance state. Every smell was painful, but I found myself continuing to smell and get these shocks as I walked across the sky bridge toward the hospital. As I was winding my way through the halls, I would every so often smell my hands which would open the wound. I wanted this to be real, I wanted to get a grasp of what exactly happened so that I could face this reality and try to make some type of sense out of everything.

I made it to the hallway that lead to the ICU. I looked down at the spot I sat when I wrote to the world that we had lost Randy. The window I looked out had almost the same view, sunny with clouds. I could almost imagine that time stood still until this moment, that Randy had just left us and everything in between was a dream that hadn't happened. I saw the nurse's station. As I was approaching, I saw the room where Randy had been. This was a hard moment for me. I was quickly greeted by the nurse. "Can I help you, sir?"

I told her that I was here to see Dr. Theresa and that she was expecting me. She picked up the phone with hesitation, then I heard her saying to Dr. Theresa, "Dr. Theresa, someone is here to see you…. Yes, I will let him know." She hung up and told me to wait in the waiting room for her.

I didn't want to go to the waiting room as there were families in there. All I could think was that I didn't want to impose on these families who were uncertain what the outcome of their loved one would be. I knew what my outcome was already, so we wouldn't have had much to talk about, and if we did, I would bring them more fear of what could be in their future. So I stood in the hallway, the very spot where I called my brother John and told him to hurry to Houston. I waited for what seemed like forever, contemplating just leaving for fear of what this may look like. As I was thinking to myself about leaving, I heard a door close and the sound of someone walking in my direction. I turned around and it was Dr. Theresa, with her big smile on her face. She was happy to see me. She told me that we could go to a private room so we could talk, and also mentioned that she had the same social worker who was with us throughout the ordeal coming to talk with me as well.

I followed her to the same room where we were allowed to stay the first night Randy went to the ICU. As we sat there I could see where my mother, father, and I knelt for hours praying the rosary, hoping for a miracle to bring Randy back to us. Shortly after we got there the social worker came in and shut the door. The first words out of her mouth were, "How are you holding up?" Her care was unwavering from the time she was with us those two days in the ICU. I told her that I wasn't doing well at all. She asked me, "It's okay that you are here, but I want to know why you are here? What will this visit do to help you with losing your twin brother?"

I told her that I needed to revisit everything so that I could really understand what happened and to accept that Randy truly did leave us and this was the place it happened. The social worker started to ask questions about what had gone on since he passed away. She asked about the funeral, and I proudly described what we had done for Randy. A New Orleanian is always proud to talk about home, and describing the funeral felt normal.

They both were very supportive of how proud I was that we were able to give him such a memorable and honorable funeral. Then Dr. Theresa asked how Mara was doing. This quickly drew my attention away from the funeral and I just spewed to them what was going on. This was another moment in which I was able to talk about it without fear and I left no stone unturned. They both consoled me and were completely sympathetic to what I had gone through, losing Randy and then having to deal with Mara and Randy's will. Once the topic of Mara was over, I started to talk about the Twinless Twins meeting and how that was the reason I was in Houston. They were very supportive of this. They were so supportive that I picked up that they were concerned about my well-being, and they were concerned that I might harm myself. Throughout this whole ordeal, I think this was on every person's mind, including those in my family. And I cannot say that the thought of joining my brother through my own death had not crossed my mind. I just knew and kept with the belief that taking one's life is not the way to heaven, but the way to an eternity away from the ones you loved. I reassured them after a while that I was good in the sense that I wouldn't harm myself, but what I needed was to feel the pain of this ordeal through retracing all the events surrounding Randy's death. They understood and I could see a relieved look on their faces. They both were extremely happy that I came by to see them, and both offered their personal contact information so that if I ever needed to talk to them, I could call, day or night.

I stood up and felt a big weight fall off my shoulders. I gave them both a big hug, hugging Dr. Theresa for a bit longer than the social worker. I told her again how thankful we were as a family to have her with us, giving us the courage and confidence throughout the whole ordeal and doing it with honesty. We parted with tears in our eyes. As we left the room we passed the ICU where Randy had been and she apologized that we couldn't go in there because there was a patient there now. I quickly told her not to worry, being with them and in the same place was therapy enough for me.

Guided by self-compassion,
Walking where once we stumbled
Can give a tortured soul
The strength to carry on.

by Jay Hoecker

At this point the weight of facing this painful task was behind me. I truly felt better and received the therapy that I knew I needed. I walked away, glancing at Randy's room, and left the ICU. I was no longer in a trance, but had returned to reality. I made my way to the sky bridge and for one last time put the hand sanitizer on my hands. This time though when I smelled it, I was brought to memories of me holding my brother while he was on his death bed, and the memories of whispering in his ear how much I loved him and how I would continue his legacy here; all these thoughts flowed into my brain.

I made my way to the car, got in and called Cristy. She was concerned because I had been gone for almost four hours with no contact. She was also worried that we wouldn't make it for the cocktail gathering. I told her that I was on my way and that I felt much better after having faced my fears of returning to the hospital. I drove away and tried to get a final glance of the spot we hugged after parking Randy's car.

I made it back to the hotel in just enough time to go to the room, get freshened up, and head down for cocktails in the lobby. As we were about to leave the room Cristy asked if I was nervous. I thought to myself and quickly said, "Nah, I am not nervous; I am anxious to meet other twins in my same situation." We closed the door, headed to the elevators and went down.

The doors of the elevator opened and I saw a large group of people, mainly older than me, gathered at the bar. We walked there, met John who organized the meeting, got my name tag and ordered a drink. I looked around and hadn't seen Jessie yet, so I struck up a conversation with John. We discussed Randy and he told me about his brother David and how he lost his brother when he was much older than I am. One thing I did notice though is that the way he spoke about his twin suggested to me that he was still struggling with the loss. We were able to find some commonalities: as most twins have the same stories of friends and family calling them by the other twin's name, also similarities in the mischief they enjoyed, and in the way that he spoke of his twin as "we."

One thing all of us twins had in common was that there was never any "I" statements. It was always "we" or "us," even when there should be no reference to plural beings, we always included the other. To this day I still do that. There were so many of us there, all talking to each other as if we had known each other forever, but the reality was that not that many of us had met before now. I really felt like I was among people who could understand what it meant for me to lose Randy. I didn't have to feel out of place when someone would say, "Gosh I have no clue what you could be going through," and I would have nothing to say other than, "Thank you." I mean what do you say to someone when they are apologizing for your twin brother's death? How do you say "it's okay" or "thank you" in that the saying is contrary to the way you really feel? Being polite always takes precedence over making an awkward situation. With these twinless twins, they truly could relate, and when they said, "I am so sorry you lost your twin too," it meant so much more to me because I felt they understood the pain and the emptiness.

Cristy and I were talking at the bar when I noticed Jessie come in with her husband. There was a feeling of relief because of a higher sense of connection to her situation than I had with other twins I had met. We got our drinks and sat at a table. Cristy immediately started to talk to Keith, Jessie's husband, and I started talking to Jessie. It was great to have finally met her after talking for what seemed like several months online. She knew what was going on with Mara, but she didn't know that we had just had some real fireworks with Mara prior to coming to Houston. We talked about her brother-in-law and how he had done similar things. It was almost as if her sister's significant other felt threatened by the bond of twins and wanted to create a road block for the living. She mentioned that her sister's widower didn't let her have any of her sister Jamie's clothes, but rather was about to throw them out.

I just couldn't imagine her situation and quickly was thankful that in my situation I still had some power to do something. In Jessie's situation, her sister, Jamie, was married and had no legal will; therefore, everything went to Jamie's husband, Sol. So Jessie was literally at his mercy, and he used this power to play games with her. The more she spoke the more I was able to pull myself back together and gain confidence again in what we were doing with Randy's estate. The group made an announcement that they were about to head off to dinner and wanted a head count. Cristy and I looked at Jessie and Keith and asked them if they were going. She said no that she had to go to a softball game for Keith. She could tell right away that I was bummed. There obviously wasn't enough time to talk about our losses. She asked if we wanted to come and I quickly looked at Cristy and she made a face as if to say, "This is all for you, you do whatever you want because I am here for you." I quickly said yes we would go. I went up to John and politely declined dinner and told him that we were going to go with Jessie to a softball game. He looked at me and understood that what I needed was to be able to talk with her. He said, "I know what you need to do, and don't worry about us old farts. You need to go and heal and Jessie is the person who can help you. We will be here tomorrow for you at the meeting."

We left the hotel and drove about an hour away. The whole time Cristy and I talked about the meeting and I felt she was starting to get an idea of what I was going through. She said that Keith was very nice and that he really helped her understand what it meant to be with someone who had lost a twin. This trip was starting to make me feel whole again. I felt that I had a place in life again, and that there was hope for me to continue not only with my own life but also to continue to fight for Randy. We finally reached the ball park. We got some food and drinks and sat on a bench that overlooked the field. Jessie, Cristy, and I got into some deep conversation. It felt good to vent yet again to someone outside the current Mara situation and get an unadulterated opinion of the whole ordeal.

I asked Jessie point blank, "If you had the opportunity like I do to remove Sol from the picture, would you do it?"

She quickly answered, "Rusty, if I had the chance, I would have removed him from the picture a long time ago. You have a unique opportunity to fight for your brother, and you shouldn't let up at all. You are doing the right thing, and you also should know inside that Randy would be behind what you are doing. I know that Jamie wouldn't have approved one bit what Sol was doing, and I couldn't do anything about it other than be wittier than he was and beg him for her possessions that meant the most to me."

This was a relief to hear. I was so pumped up again to fight for what I perceived to be Randy's intentions.

After the game we talked for hours. Keith and Cristy really had a good time getting to know each other, and he was able to give her some advice on how to comfort me and also what to expect. I was listening to some of what he was saying and it seemed that he was there for Jessie in a supportive way, and I was thankful that Cristy would get to hear some of the things that he did for Jessie. For her to get an understanding of the effects of my losing my twin and what to expect gave me great comfort. I knew that Cristy would be able to help me in ways that no one else could, and the advice she was given would make our road together through this terrible situation a little easier to handle.

As I spoke to Jessie I realized that life after a twin's death is a very bumpy road. She would tell me how some days she couldn't even get out of bed, and would have to have Keith bring the kids to school and pick them up. The depression was so gripping. We shared our lows and our ways to cope with them. I told her, "One of my issues is that I don't remember the day of the week, much less the time of the year. I don't remember much of anything because of my depression. I couldn't tell you what happened last week, because I don't remember. I ask Cristy all the time what day of the week it is." To be able to explain that to Jessie and for her to completely understand showed me that I wasn't completely losing myself; moreover, because all of her major debilitating depression had subsided gave me hope that eventually mine would too. We walked to our cars, gave our goodbyes, and headed back to the hotel.

Cristy and I were in the car and were so happy to have been able to talk to them. It was as much of a healing process for Cristy as it was for me. She was really able to find hope for herself that eventually she would get her husband back, or at least close to the way he was before Randy had passed away. As John Holmes said, *"There is no exercise better for the heart than reaching down and lifting people up."* We had been lifted up.

We woke up the next day nervous and curious about attending our first ever support group, not sure what to expect. We walked into the meeting room and were greeted by John. He made sure that I was comfortable and introduced me to more twinless twins who came in just for the meeting that day. I was a little shy at first talking to people I didn't know, but quickly warmed up to the conversations. It was amazing to me how many people there were who had been through the same thing I went through. We all sat down at a rectangular table and the meeting got started.

John introduced himself and made an announcement that there were several new members at the meeting. He introduced me to a young woman a little younger than I, and a young man about the same age. I took notice really quickly of that man because he wore a hood and didn't make eye contact with anyone. He was also there with his mother who was very nervous. I wasn't sure why she was nervous but nonetheless it was written all over her face.

All had the opportunity to introduce themselves one by one. We were to stand up, say our name, say our twin's name, and state how long it's been since we had lost our twin. As people stood up, the date ranges varied greatly. I heard just about everything from one year ago to 35 years ago, and one that lost her twin at birth. I found this particular case to be interesting because there was no time other than in the womb to create a bond with her twin, yet she knew that there was a piece of herself missing as far back as she could remember. Once we had all been introduced, John spoke a little about twin loss and how it affects so many people. Then he asked each twinless twin to tell his or her story, if able of course.

He started just to the right of me, knowing that I might not speak considering how it wasn't that long ago that I lost Randy. The stories were so moving. One person stood up and told the group how he had lost his twin in a car accident and that his emotions were still very strong even though it had happened over eight years ago. One thing I picked up from his story was that he never had an opportunity to say goodbye to his twin. I heard that and quickly appreciated that I did get the opportunity to say goodbye to my brother. Another twin stood up and said how her twin committed suicide. This was extremely difficult for her because it was almost a rejection by her twin of herself. She asked, "I thought to myself, how could you be so selfish to take your life away from me?" This hit me hard, because I had always feared losing my brother, but never did I fear that he would take his own life. I put myself in her shoes and felt so grateful that I didn't lose Randy that way. In fact a year before Randy died, I found out that a set of twins we had grown up with were severed by suicide. I remember reaching out to him and just feeling for his situation, thinking to myself how much I would hurt if I had lost Randy. Suicide is one of the hardest losses because it feels like it is so preventable compared to most other deaths.

The twinless twin continued to explain that her healing process included having to forgive her twin for taking her own life. This was grief on two fronts, anger and depression, and to deal with both at the same time had to have been extremely difficult. There was another twin whose sister was murdered by her husband at the time. All of these stories brought into perspective how lucky I was not to have had such a dramatic event associated with the loss of Randy as these twins had.

As the next twin was about to stand up and speak, the boy with the hood got up and raced out of the room. His mom ran after him and shortly afterwards she returned. She apologized to the whole group for this and told us, "Patrick is having a hard time; I am so worried about him. His father and twin brother were in a plane accident which killed them both. He won't eat, he is having trouble sleeping, and I just don't know what else to do for him. I am so worried about him. I need help, John please help me get through to my son." John got up and went outside to talk to him. Shortly after, he came back and we all sat there quietly. I looked around at everyone and could tell that they were saying to themselves, "Well, each of our stories are bad, but I really feel for that boy." I know that is what I thought. I could tell how helpless his mom was, and how worried she was that he would hurt himself. It was evident that hearing the twin talk about suicide made him uncomfortable. John reassured everyone that he was going to keep track of Patrick and make sure that he had the right people around him to keep him safe. We continued with the stories; one by one they all were the same but different. Jessie had her turn to speak, and she gave me the courage to want to speak about Randy.

When it became my turn, Cristy looked at me along with John. John said, "Rusty, you don't have to speak, but if you do, we are all here for you to help you." I gathered my courage and started to speak. I felt the need to let everyone know about my ordeal. I started to explain everything from when Randy told me he had a tumor to the point we had to say goodbye. Cristy had her arm around me the whole time, rubbing my back, telling me it would be okay if I had to take a break from the story. Everyone was in tears hearing the story. People who were able to tell their story without crying had napkins to their eyes. It was raw emotion that each of them was able to sense with compassion. It was as though my story, as fresh as it was, hit home with all of them, opening up their wounds as though they were fresh and had just happened.

I realized when I finished that this was so important not only to me but to everyone there. We were all there to help one another, be there for each other, and share our advice and our coping tools with each other. Once I was finished there were some more words from John, and we had a closing prayer. Then we played a couple of songs and I asked if it was okay if I played one of Randy's songs. They all were very encouraging, so I played "Edge of the World" for everyone and they all loved it. When we finished the songs, we all got up and took a group picture. John had invited the whole group to lunch across the highway at a Mexican restaurant. Cristy looked at me and clearly left the decision up to me. I said, "Yeah, we will go." I looked at Jessie to see if she would go and she couldn't. I was a little disappointed she wasn't going to go, but I also saw it as an opportunity to talk to other twins and try and relate to their stories.

We went to lunch with about a third of the group, which was less intimidating than the whole group. I wound up talking to a twinless twin, Ben, who lost his brother eight years ago. We started talking about the struggles he had with the twin's significant other and it to seem to me that more and more twinless twins had issues with the significant other of the deceased twin. In his situation, his twin had a life insurance policy with his ex-girlfriend, who didn't realize it, so when he passed away she received the policy. Ben knew that in his heart his deceased brother Bob didn't want the insurance policy to go to the ex-girlfriend. Fortunately for Ben, when he confronted the ex about it, she gladly gave it back to Ben to distribute as his brother would have wanted. I was happy to hear that there were still understanding people out there, because I knew of many who would have kept the money from the policy knowing there was nothing that could be done about it.

I was learning really quickly that one cannot be too careful with estate planning. It really was great being able to connect with the twinless twins at the table. We enjoyed ourselves, and at the same time gave each other much needed therapy. I didn't want the meeting to end; however, it was time to part, and we vowed to stay in touch with each other, and parted ways. On our way back to the hotel I could tell that Cristy had a good time, and had benefited from the opportunity to see others on a similar path to mine.

Cristy and I returned to the hotel to head home, and I mentioned to her that I wanted to bring her to the field at MD Anderson so I could show her where Randy and I had played Frisbee and football for the last time. She was honored that I wanted to share this moment with her. We set off to the field and as we were passing landmarks I would explain and give her the history of what had happened at each landmark. We made it to the hospital area and we parked in the parking garage. I walked with her on the same track Randy and I walked the night before his surgery. I pointed out to Cristy that this is where I was able to tell Randy how scared I was and how much I loved him. We continued to the field and I walked the same path with her that Randy and I walked. I pointed out the spot beneath the trees where he had stood. After I explained and drew a mental picture for her about the evening, she wanted to sit in the field to take it all in. I sat where Randy had been. I looked over at Cristy and noticed she had leaned back completely and was looking up in the air. I wondered to myself and still do what she was thinking while she lay there. She had a great relationship with Randy, and I know that being there meant a lot to her. Neither one of us moved for a while, but soon enough I moved closer to her. This was a different feeling being there with Cristy than I had when I was there two days prior. I was clearer in my thinking now; I had a greater sense of being, an understanding of my life and where it was heading. As we were leaving we didn't say much to each other, still taking in what we had just experienced. I had a renewed sense of self, a rejuvenated motivation to continue the fight for Randy and make sure that the actions I took would be sincere attempts to uphold his wishes and honor his legacy. Most importantly though, I felt like I was a twin again, albeit twinless.

Chapter 42

Finding Peace

When we got back from Houston, the turmoil I had left behind greeted me with a vengeance. There was a constant barrage of bad-mouthing and public humiliation by Max and all of my "friends." Even people who had no idea what was going on were chiming in and joining the group of people who chose to publicly humiliate my family. My mom was copying everything that was being written on social media sites and also fighting back when she could. For me it was just way too much to handle; the stress of losing Randy would have been enough, but the stress of complete desertion and harassment by a group who had been my support was overwhelming.

Tolerance and dignity are carefully balanced on the scales of personal justice, and it takes a great deal of work to establish and keep that balance.

Soon afterwards Cristy and I started to talk about moving in with my parents to have an opportunity to be there for my parents and to also have them there for me. It just so happened that the tenant who moved out before we moved in texted me and asked if the apartment was available to rent. I read the text to Cristy:

"Cristy, Rachael is wanting to rent the apartment from us. It is totally up to you whether or not we leave. I'm okay with going there but I need you to be okay with it because it is my family, and although I am comfortable with it, I want you to be comfortable too."

"I am perfectly fine with moving in with your parents. When would we need to move out?"

"Let me check with Rachael." I texted Rachael. "We would need to move out in three days."

"Three days?!"

"Yeah she would need it this Friday," I said to her. "You know what, that is too short of a notice. I will just tell her that we will..."

But Cristy interrupted, "Tell her we will be out by Friday."

I replied, "Okay, I am going to tell her she can have it, and I will let my parents know we are moving in with them this weekend."

I was really happy that Cristy was comfortable to move in with my parents. I was looking forward to living in the same room that Randy and I shared for so long. My parents were excited as well, for many reasons but one of the main reasons is that they were truly concerned about my wellbeing and mental state. The excitement turned into stress as we quickly realized that we had to literally pack and move in two days. Saying yes is so much easier than actually doing the deed. Nonetheless, we packed almost everything in a mobile storage unit, and packed only bare essentials in one of our delivery trucks and moved. It all happened so quickly that neither Cristy nor I really had a chance to rest, especially since we were taking care of our five-month-old at the same time.

The first night there was really hard for me mentally. Naturally Cristy had picked my sink and my shower, out of instinct I suppose. I said to her as she was putting things around my sink, "It's not a big deal, but that was my sink growing up." She chuckled and moved her things. Then shortly after she picked Randy's and my shower instead of John's. I again told her that she instinctively picked my shower instead of John's. She quickly reassigned herself to the other one, being sensitive to my emotions at the time.

When I jumped in my shower, I closed my eyes and could smell the summertime. My mind quickly transported me to a time when we so often hung outside by the pool. I started to catch myself speeding up my shower wanting to get back downstairs with Randy and all of our friends. Then I realized that I was day dreaming and in reality Randy was no longer living. I kept that to myself as I didn't want anyone to feel sorry for me. This started my tendency to hold my grief inward as opposed to expressing the pain.

That evening Cristy had mentioned that I should go see a grief counselor, and at first I wasn't really interested in doing that. She convinced me that it would help me cope with the loss of Randy and also cope with losing my friends' support. I told her that I would consider it. She found a place that was between work and the cemetery and asked if I wanted her to make the appointment, and I said yes. Saying yes to that was a relief, because I knew that I would be able to talk about my pain and my emotions to a person who had no emotional strings attached to the situation. I really was starting to withhold my feelings from my family, so I now had an opportunity to vent to someone. One of the main reasons I held back is that I didn't want people to try to compare their sorrows to mine, feel bad for me, or even make them feel bad if they were not at the time hurting as much as I was. This was my cross to bear, no one else's.

It was not surprising that I would be late to my first meeting. At this point in my life, the amount of stress and grief I was bearing had my mind completely in a state of shock. I couldn't tell which day of the week it was, or time of the day, as time was moving at alternate speeds, sometimes moving fast and sometimes moving really slowly. The counselor's office called my phone and I quickly blurted out, "Shoot, I am on my way." I rushed to my car and got there about twenty minutes late. This was not really the best first impression I wanted to give. When I saw my psychiatrist, Beatrice, I instantly was comforted by her appearance; she looked and reminded me of my brother-in-law Bo's mom, who would talk with Randy and me about life, which we absolutely loved.

She made it apparent that she had never dealt with twin loss before, but that she has dealt with a lot of grief counseling and she made me feel comfortable. She explained that if I wasn't feeling comfortable then I could find another counselor who had handled twin loss. I am not the type of person who wants to make someone feel inadequate, so I told her that I wanted to stick with her because I felt that she resembled my brother-in-law's mom, and that was comforting. She made it clear that she would do reading on the subject and would help me to the best of her ability.

The second meeting was a tough one. I was now a little more comfortable telling Beatrice more about Randy and our losing him as well as what had happened surrounding his death. I still somewhat had my guard up not wanting to let out too many tears in a full fledge cry, but there were feelings deep inside that she was prompting to surface. The main topics of conversation were the upcoming meeting with Mara and our attorneys, issues regarding Max, that will, and issues with Mara. It was comforting to learn how appalled she was to hear what had happened after Randy died. It made her even more concerned about my wellbeing such that she gave me her personal phone number in case I needed to call and talk outside of normal business hours. I was really happy that I had that lifeline; although I never used it. It was reassuring to know that I had someone there to help me in a time of need.

Shortly afterwards I notified my counselor that we would be moving Randy to a new tomb that we had built for him and our family. She gave me the encouragement I needed and talked me through it.

Moving Randy was another stressor within itself. We were cutting it close to the time limit of moving Randy which had to be within ninety days of death. If we had missed the window we couldn't move Randy until he had been deceased for a year. We had to move so quickly that the tomb didn't even have his name engraved on it yet. This was going to be a tough day for all of us, but most of all I was worried about seeing Randy in a decomposed state, especially after the funeral director had warned of a decaying casket. Since we were experiencing turmoil within my friend network and with Mara, we chose not to involve them in the reburial of Randy. To this day I don't regret that. It was a special moment for our family, not to be shared with people who had deserted and shamed us and Randy. We had all dressed in suits and dresses, the same we had worn at his funeral. It was hotter than it was the day we buried him, but our discomfort was tolerated as something we could give back to Randy.

I stood the closest to the tomb when they opened it. They had a sheet to cover the casket and they moved quickly to the hearse with several more men than when Randy was first entombed. This was because they were concerned about the casket handles being weak and they didn't want to drop him. They placed him in the hearse and we walked beside him with our hands on the hearse. I remember sweat dripping down my back and the sun was beaming on us, but we all sucked it up and stayed with the pace. The funeral home had a tent set up for us and we had a priest there to bless the new tomb. They placed Randy in the new tomb and we gathered around to have a blessing. I played one of Randy's songs on Randy's guitar for everyone and then we had a moment of silence. Then we gathered at my parents' house afterwards which is when I asked that my name be put on the engraving of the tomb. I wanted it to say, "Randall William Perrone twin to Russell Joseph Perrone." My cousin later told me that she thought it was weird that I would want my name on a tomb already, but she just didn't understand how much it meant to me that our names were together, and one day we would be together, right next to each other per my request. I wanted the world to know that we were twins and that our tombstone would show that as long as that stone stood there.

Chapter 43

A Meeting of the Minds

The day we were to have our initial court hearing, we met Mara and her attorney at his office near the courthouse. Mara and I were somewhat communicating with each other but only via texting and short phone conversations. One thing she did text me was that Max was going to be in the meeting, and she didn't want me to be blindsided by his being there. I thought that was nice of her to tip me off.

The day of the meeting was tense for me and for my parents. When we got to the building of Mara's attorney, we waited for our lawyers to arrive in the lobby. We were escorted to a small board room. When the door opened we could see that the attorney was ready to fight for his client. He introduced himself and kept the conversation to business. We told Mara's lawyer that we had no intention of contesting Mara's or anyone else's inheritance.

The meeting started off with Mara's attorney asking what we intended to do with the will. We went down line by line as he asked our position on each line. As each bequest to Mara would come up, we said that we intended to not contest. You could see as we went through the whole will that both Mara and her attorney were becoming more complimentary. Then the question was raised by Mara's attorney, "Why then are we having this discussion if you intend to give Mara everything that the will bequests?" We answered that the business shares were not properly disclosed and we didn't feel Randy intended Mara to have a share in the family business. Victor, Mara's attorney, was silent then, but we could see that Mara was happy to hear this, which gave me the feeling that she wouldn't want to go after Randy's interest in the business. Victor said that we would have to get it valued and put the value, along with a settlement proposal, together to send over to his office so they could review the matter before making their decision on how to proceed. This was because the will provided a buy-out to Mara of half of Randy's shares of the business in that the business could only be owned by blood relatives of the Perrone family, a provision we accepted.

It was getting close to the time we had to be in court, so we all adjourned the meeting and started to head over to the courthouse. I made my way next to Mara and asked her if she would want to meet over lunch after the hearing, and she was excited that I had asked her. The lawyers went to the judge before the hearing to let her know that we were working toward a resolution, but we asked to have another hearing date set.

Having agreed to meet for lunch after the hearing, we picked a restaurant right across the street from the courthouse to meet with Mara. The conversation went well. We spoke about the parts of the will we still were challenging in court, the family business and the banked sperm being two of the topics. She made it apparent that she knew in her heart that Randy didn't want her to have any part of the business, which was a big relief to me. The other big topic was the banked sperm and she was still adamant about keeping it. She even joked that she was already pregnant, after which I am sure the look on my face spoke volumes about my feelings on that subject. My heart literally sank before she popped up with, "I am joking!" It seemed insensitive to me that this issue would be fodder for a joke.

At the end of lunch, Mara had mentioned that she was going to move to Montana for the summer, and would like to have our family over to her and Randy's house for a dinner before she went. We accepted the invitation and several nights later we were at the house, in what would be an awkward dinner with Mara's family and ours. Once the dinner was over, I feared that I had to get started working on this settlement because once she left for Montana, it might be difficult for us to get in touch with her.

Starting that week we worked diligently on what we thought was a perfect compromise and settlement to this ordeal. We honored everything Randy wrote in the will; we omitted the shares of the business, and for good faith acceptance, we put in an additional cash payout. I feared she might have a problem with one thing I wanted in the settlement: not allowing her to have Randy's sperm.

Mara had texted us that she wanted to have band practice at Randy's house before she left for Montana. I told the band about this, and they were all willing to have another practice at Randy's house, just like they used to when Randy was alive. They were very excited to do this. Mara wanted my family to be there as well as her family. At this point I was practicing every week with the band and felt much more confident in my singing ability. It was an opportunity to show my family how much I wanted to continue Randy's music and how dedicated I was to keeping it alive. The practice was going well, and my nervousness about singing in front of non-band members had waned, when Mara requested that I sing a particular song. She wanted "Beautiful Riddance" which she loved because it was a song about Randy's ex-girlfriend, written out of dislike for her actions that ended that relationship. For me it was a fitting song in many ways also.

Several days later, Mara left for Montana, leaving her mom to stay in Randy's house during the time she was gone. This prevented me from going to Randy's house just to feel his spirit because I didn't want to impose on her. I was able to go there a couple of times, especially as I was starting to inventory everything for the estate. I grabbed Randy's lyric books because I didn't want someone I didn't know to walk off with them. I felt safer that I had most of Randy's most personal possessions, and no I don't mean monetary ones, just the spiritual.

Chapter 44

A Special Hike Near Knoxville, Tennessee

I was planning some time away from New Orleans to visit Sam, an old friend from high school with whom I reconnected while Randy was in surgery. Sam's mom had died two years earlier from a brain tumor. We had a lot in common dealing with negative situations following the deaths of his mother and my brother. He lives in Knoxville, Tennessee, and he told me a couple of weeks earlier that he had a dream of Randy on a hiking trail that Sam frequented after his mom passed away. He said that he had to take me to the very spot where he dreamt of Randy, which looks like a stairway to heaven. I needed a break from all of the turmoil in my life, so Cristy and I accepted his invitation and went to visit.

The drive to Knoxville was somewhat grueling with a seven-month-old baby, but we endured and made it late in the evening. At this point I hadn't seen Sam in ten years, so it felt as though we were going to a stranger's house, but as soon as we got there his jovial spirit made us feel very much at home. We didn't have much planned other than the hike, so we ate out several times and just had plain old good fun. Sam is a very funny person, who seems to never have a depressed day, and this was extremely welcoming to me. I laughed and smiled more during our visit than I had since my meeting with my old friend in Houston after Randy died.

The apex of the trip was our hike to the top of Mt. Leconte, in the Smoky Mountains. The hike is the hardest hike in the Smoky Mountains, which is seven miles to the top, starting at a base of 3,000 feet to the peak of 5,800 feet. Sam had warned me of the strenuous hike, but he wasn't privy to my work ethic and determination of achieving whatever goals I set for myself. The hike started out great, we played Randy's music, talked, and took a lot of pictures. We joked and laughed and at one point I played a great joke on him.

Sam said to me, "Hey Rusty, on our way back we can stop here and get a snack."

"Sam, we aren't coming back," I said in my most serious tone and gave the straightest face I could muster.

"Wait, what? What do you mean we aren't coming back?"

"I am just joking, Sam," I burst out laughing at his reaction, "I just wanted to see if you were listening."

"Oh, that just isn't right," he blasted back. "I thought you were talking about jumping off the mountain. Phew! I was worried."

I didn't want to stop moving toward the top of the mountain. My desire to reach the top was trumped by my thoughts that at the top I would be closer to Randy than at sea level. This made me determined to reach the top as soon as I could. Sam at one point said to me, "Rusty, you're like a raging river, you just don't stop." It was at this point I brought him up to speed on my determination to complete a goal no matter the obstacle. It was also during this hike that we would become business partners selling the same type of imported furniture in New Orleans that he was selling in Knoxville. We

chose to call it Raging River Imports after his comment on the hike.

We stopped at a little village near the top of the mountain to get some quick lunch. After lunch we finished the last leg of the hike to the top. When we crested the top, I could see the clouds moving in and out of the valleys below. We chose to play Randy's song "Edge of the World," and as Randy sang a particular verse, "The clouds will open and close behind me," there was a large cloud that surrounded us at the top of the mountain. Both Sam and I were speechless and sat there for the remainder of the song without saying a word to each other. When the song was over, we made a rock cairn in honor of Randy. I threw some rocks down the mountain as a continuation of my tradition of throwing a rock into water or over a cliff wherever I go, and then we started to make our way back down.

On our way back down, Sam and I stopped off at a cliff edge overlooking a beautiful valley. We chose to sit down and take a break. After making the climb to the top and conquering my goal, I felt I could finally let out the whole story to Sam. Randy's surgery, his death, and everything horrible that followed just flowed out like a river. Sam is such a great listener to me and I could feel that his mom and Randy orchestrated our meeting even more so then than ever.

The trip to Knoxville was such a great getaway from life, and Sam was so giving. He wanted my mom to have a painting that he had given his mother, so we strapped it to the roof of my car because it wouldn't fit inside. I wanted to wrap it in a tarp but Sam was trying to tell me not to worry about it.

Sam looked to the sky and said, "It's not going to rain, look how clear it is."

"Sam, it may not look like it's going to rain here, but we have quite a large portion of the country to drive through, I want to make sure it won't get ruined because it was your mom's."

Good thing I had wrapped it because about thirty minutes into the drive home, it started to pour down rain. I took a picture and sent it to him. It was just the last piece of laughter my stomach could take. We took a detour to my parent's camp in Mississippi on the way back to bring them the painting. Cristy absolutely loved it and we talked with my parents about the whole trip and how much Sam had us laughing and just forgetting about all the pain and stress we had endured recently. The pain of a stomachache from laughing with a friend is a welcomed pain, unlike many pains life can and had thrown our way.

Chapter 45

Differences of Opinion

When we got back to New Orleans I jumped back into the settlement to get it done and sent to Mara's attorney. The final settlement agreement was achieved with the provision that deciding what to do with Randy's sperm would not be included.

The day of the hearing we were to go in front of the judge and read into the record the settlement. We were sworn in by raising our right hands and then the judge asked Mara if she was okay with the agreement and asked us if we were okay. Both of us nodded and she requested that the settlement be read into the record. She made both of us aware that once it is read in, it is binding. The proceedings were over quickly and we headed to my office to sign the papers and be finished with this. Finally the majority of the nightmare was over. The only thing left to handle would be the sperm, and I was confident that eventually with time and after the settlement was complete, she wouldn't be as attached to the sperm issue as she had been in her earlier days of grieving and as she had portrayed before we settled.

One of my requests to Mara was to have a weekend with Riley, Randy's dog, before she would take him permanently. When I went to pick him up, he was so excited to see me. He literally jumped up in my arms and gave me a hug. He and Maximus, my dog, loved being around each other, so when they got together it was dog party time. I was so happy to have him in the house and be able to love on him just like Randy would.

Randy was such a lover of people and of dogs. One time when we were in college, we were heading to visit with my Uncle Billy's son, William, when we spotted a dog lying in the middle of the road. I stopped the car so Randy and

I could get out and see what was wrong with the dog. It became apparent to us that he was hit and had died. Randy couldn't leave him in the middle of the road so he suggested to me that we move him. I was too afraid to pick him up, so Randy picked up the dog and moved him to the side of the road. We looked at the dog tag and made a phone call to the owners. As we got back inside the car Randy started crying, saying, "He was just so lifeless. He had no life in him at all. That is the saddest thing I have ever had to do."

It wouldn't be the only time we cried from the death of a dog. When one of our childhood dogs had to be put to sleep, Randy couldn't stand to see it happen, so he went home to dig a grave for him in the back yard, crying the whole time he had to dig and also when we laid him to rest in the hole. The other time was when our other childhood dog had to be put to sleep, however this time he would be with me as the vet gave him the medicine to euthanize our dog, Jack. It was extremely difficult for both of us to watch him take his last breath. We then took him to Randy's house and buried him in the back yard, leaving a piece of granite as his tombstone.

Our love for animals was strong, and I could tell when Riley looked at me he knew my pain for losing my best friend was just like the pain he was having for losing his best friend. It was our little bond and connection to the person we both longed for. The weekend was not long enough and unfortunately that was the last time I would see Riley.

Resolving conflicts with Mara and experiencing the reactions of mutual friends who were supportive of Mara but not of me presented a dilemma: who had been my friends, and who were my friends now. I found myself using the word "enemies." But an equally fair question was "who are my enemies and what makes them so?" One thing for certain is that the process was an education which I never wanted and for which I paid dearly. Teachers are not our enemies, but our enemies can be our teachers. If I perceived that a mutual acquaintance had moved from friend to enemy, such may well have been just my perception. One might say unfriendly behavior speaks for itself, but it speaks in sound bites and rarely tells the whole story. Perhaps some hurtful behavior and words directed my way were aspects of others' grieving. I cannot know. Perhaps the lesson being taught, if I am able to receive it, is that those I label, people who were significant to our lives before Randy died, may actually be just grieving friends or indeed may be my exposed enemies. The larger truth is that labels are not really helpful. Doing my best to honestly maintain a healthy balance between tolerance and dignity and keeping my ego out of the middle of that work was likely to best serve my brother's memory, my family, and myself. These words may capture the dilemma:

> *Life is filled with Friend and Foe,*
> *Each strutting earnestly to be seen and heard.*
> *Bringing good and bad they come and go.*
> *It can be perfect or perfectly uncanny.*
> *Credit and Blame join the fray, and for partners they hunt.*
> *So confusing! What is which and why?*
> *Credit and Blame, Friend and Foe all want*
> *To blend and blur, morph and merge, live or die.*
> *Alas! I do not know what is which or who is who.*
> *I've searched for only Friend or Foe, Credit or Blame.*
> *Truth is... I am them all. We're all the same.*
>
> "*Friend or Foe*" by *Jay Hoecker*

Chapter 46

Where You End, I Begin Absent the Second Opinion

We as a family chose to write a letter to Randy's brain surgeon letting him know that we didn't hold him responsible for Randy's death, but that we were grateful that we had him there to give us hope that he could cure Randy. Dr. McNulty was taking Randy's death hard from what we were told, and because we didn't feel it would benefit the sick community if, through Randy's death, he would second-guess his ability to handle a surgery as difficult as Randy's. We chose to give him words of encouragement and also absolve him of any guilt that he may have had for losing a patient, my twin brother. We gave him many details of the type of person Randy was, and also included Randy's CD, *Peace of Mind,* with the package of letters. We didn't get a reply from him which was a little disheartening, but at the same time I am sure he didn't want to write anything that could come back to haunt him in the future in case in his mind we weren't genuine about our absolving him of fault. It was a labor of love to perform following Randy's death that I believe we were all happy to complete.

Since Randy was Julien's Parrain, and he was no longer alive to be his godfather, we asked John to be co-parrain to Julien, and that rightful succession was based on how close the three of us were. John also wanted to show his support for me in losing Randy and wanted to move into Randy's office, which was right next to mine. I couldn't bear though looking into his office and seeing my brother John instead of Randy, so I asked John if he wouldn't mind that I take Randy's office and that John take my office. He was happy to do so and to this day we are still in that configuration. The business aspect of Randy's and my relationship was also something I had to adjust. Randy and I were true partners in crime as kids and partners in building the family business as adults. I had a comfort knowing that no matter how hard things may be, I always had someone who was just as dedicated as I was to making it work, no matter how hard the task or what type of physical or mental activity was involved. I had to learn how to change my way of thinking to adjust to his absence. It certainly was a long process to accept those changes and learn how to handle situations on my own.

Selling Randy's house was another hard task that we all had to get through. I recall going through his closet and smelling all of his clothes, wishing that I would be able to see him wearing them again. As I was exiting his closet, I noticed taped on the wall the cigar wrapper that I had given him when Julien was born. It still had written on it, "Parrain or Godfather?" I quickly took it off the wall and put it in my pocket. When I got home that day I put it in the cigar box that Dad gave Randy, and then gave to me. My brother, sisters, my parents and I managed to move everything out.

In the process of splitting things with Mara, I was fortunate enough to gain Randy's carpet that he had always used to stand on when he played at shows. I kept it knowing that when Cristy and I moved into our own home I would hang it on the wall. When we moved into our new house two days before the one-year anniversary of Randy's death, his rug was one of the first things to be hung up on the wall. My mom had an old fireplace mantle on which to mount it, which allowed us to also hang with it a picture of Randy and me when we were babies.

Life was starting to become somewhat normal again, in the business and personally. My counseling sessions were progressing smoothly and before long I was told that I had graduated that program and that I could handle life without counseling. My counselor could tell in my demeanor that I was on my way to handling the loss and its surrounding fallout on my own. It was certainly a welcomed ending to our meetings when she complimented me on my progress and my strength. As humble as I always have tried to be, it was nice to hear that someone thought of me as a strong person, especially when I felt the opposite. I guess you never know how you will react to life events such as these until you are faced with them, and then your true being is flung forward and you either fly with it or fold. I am fortunate that I accepted it.

Memory bends and morphs and gently removes rough edges so we may continue our journey otherwise impossible with too many heavy burdens to carry. Somehow we arrived at the first anniversary of Randy's death, the one-year mark of my brother no longer being physically with us. Two years earlier had been a very difficult year with business, and other challenges. We were hopeful that 2013 would be a much better year. Many of us said, "How could 2013 be any worse than 2012?" Of course we were hit quickly in 2013 with the devastating news of a brain tumor, and not just any brain tumor, but a tumor that was in the most difficult of surgical places and would wind up claiming Randy. I began this year saying, "2014 has to be better than 2013." It was better, for the reason that all the firsts without Randy were now seconds.

The most immediate first would be Randy's and my first birthday not celebrated together. I later found out that my lovely wife was planning a surprise thirtieth birthday dinner for Randy and me. The reality was that it was even more of a surprise, not knowing I would "celebrate" it without him. Being that our birthday was seven days after his death, I don't know that I truly understood the permanent reality of having a birthday on my own. For my entire life, there was always someone who shared my birthday. Now, it was just me and my brother's memory. Our first Christmas was also difficult. For the previous five years or so, we had taken a family picture in our pajamas. This was the first year one of our family members was missing. We had his picture, but pictures aren't the same. The rest of the holidays were difficult, but all those firsts had now become seconds. The notion that we were going to get used to, not so much accept, not having him for our family functions was difficult to handle, but as a close family, we were determined to endure. One can never get over, but only hope to get through such a loss.

As life continued and business and family took over my thoughts, I approached my dad and told him I wanted to come up with a private label for

Brie and Camembert cheese. I had come up with a name that was true to New Orleans' French culture, so I approached our neighbor and my dad's friend, Mr. Steve, who happened to be a patent attorney. Every time I called him he remembered our hammering nails in my dad's roof for our Christmas lights. Mr. Steve said, "In order to receive a patent for the name that name cannot have a patent on it for any other use, and unfortunately the name you chose is taken." I picked another name, made the design over for the label and sent it to him, to find out again that that name was being used. He advised that the most foolproof method is to make up a name. Mr. Steve and I asked my dad if he had any ideas for a good name: "Not a chance, you won't get any help from me, my background is Italian not French."

"I got it!" Dad said about a half hour later.

"Got what?"

"I have the name for the French Brie! It is in honor of your brother. How about Saint Randeaux Brie."

"That is perfect," I said to him, "I will send it to Mr. Steve right away and see if it is available."

Mr. Steve did his research and saw that it wasn't taken, and so just like that it was done. We proudly had a brand name that honored my brother. Just another way to keep his touch on everything we were doing in life. Business without Randy has been something that took me a while to get adjusted to. There have been many downs, but with all of those hardships, I have learned to handle them on my own, or at least with the help of a silent partner in heaven, or maybe he isn't so silent after all.

I also had a business mission in memory of Randy. Shortly after his death, I had called the small grocery store chain in Hattiesburg to let them know that Randy had passed away. It just so happened that they were about to call me and let me know that we were losing their business. I pleaded with them to give me a meeting and try to hold on to what Randy and I had cultivated. They gave me a meeting and became invigorated again with us, to which I gave a sigh and whispered, "Thank You" to Randy when I got back in my car from the meeting. Unfortunately, they weren't quite ready to continue to do business with us yet. I spent two years trying to get it back, and after hard work and perseverance, I was able to get them back. Going back to those stores so many months later without Randy was hard, but as I walked through I could see him where we used to walk, and I could feel him next to me as I walked, alone to the person observing me, but not alone to me at all.

There was a remaining order of business whose resolution would provide much relief, bringing closure to a contentious issue. Randy's sperm was the only thing that hadn't been settled when it came to Mara and the nightmare that followed Randy's death. Some time had passed, and we had waited until we felt Mara had had some time to heal and likely had spent whatever money she had gotten from our settlement. I called up my attorney and told him it was time to issue a restraining order for the sperm, especially because Mara's sister Sara had become pregnant, and I certainly didn't want Mara to get any ideas of becoming pregnant at the same time with Randy's sperm. So once the restraining order was executed, we heard news of friends being asked for money to help Mara pay for an attorney to fight the restraining order. Apparently all the supporters she had with this issue had heard my point of view and chose not to jump in and fight for her. It was obvious to everyone once they heard what I had to say that Randy wouldn't have wanted a child brought into this world without his permission, influence or presence to raise that child. It would have been different if there had been a baby already born, but in this case there had not been such. In fact, one had not even been conceived or planned. A week after we served the restraining order on the sperm bank and on Mara, we got a letter from an attorney saying that she would not contest the sperm and that she had renounced any and all rights to it.

Finally, that nightmare was over and my brother could finally be laid to rest completely. The sperm bank wanted to destroy the sperm, but I felt that it needed to be buried instead of just thrown away in the trash can. The way I looked at it, it was the last living part of Randy and I wanted it handled appropriately as such. My brother and sisters weren't really as passionate about it as I was, so I chose to handle the burial on my own. I went to the sperm bank and they gave me a paper bag with a box in it. Inside were several vials, but I didn't want to look at them. I kept the bag in Randy's office, which was now my office, in a safe place and waited for a perfect day to bury it under one of two trees we planted behind the tomb. It just so happened that I was working one Saturday, exactly one year and six months to the date of Randy's death. The weather was beautiful, similar to the day we buried Randy initially, as it also had been the day of his reburial. I left work and took the sperm with me to the cemetery. I parked Randy's car next to the tomb and started playing one of my favorite songs of his, "Edge of the World." I chose to bury it under the left tree being that the trees represented Randy and me and since Randy was older the left one was his. I dug a hole in the ground and gently placed the box in it and filled it back. His seed of life was at last home, and I could be at peace with this closure. My nightmare and Randy's nightmare were finally over. I could now focus on healing myself and learning how to move through life without my womb mate.

Time has a way of stealing away while we're not watching, and before we could imagine it the second anniversary of Randy's death was upon us. We were determined to make it a day of honoring Randy. We went to the same church that morning where Randy's services were held. To be there was very difficult, but it was comforting to know that we were still together in spirit and through God. We went to the tomb and gathered as family and friends, played some of Randy's music, planted two trees behind his resting place, and released about ten balloons. Each balloon had a message to Randy from a family member or friend, a special and symbolic way to talk to Randy and send our thoughts up to heaven: Balloons filled with messages of love, sadness, and grief. Every person has a special way to show how much Randy meant to them. Months later, our childhood friend, Zane, who swam with us from the age of 6 until the end of high school, had invited me to have a cigar with him. While we were walking in, he gave me a coin. He said, "The other person to have this same exact coin is Randy. I put it in his coat pocket at the funeral and have wanted to give it to you ever since." That was such a special gift that if I were in his shoes, I might not want to give up that special token and connection.

So as I walk through life without my twin, I leave you with his words giving him the opportunity to speak last in this book of our lives. The song is called "Edge of the World," and it has become the song that we as a family have gravitated toward representing Randy's life. I had often heard this song but didn't pay much attention to the words until Randy was on his deathbed. The irony of the song is that it was written years before his death. Many would think he wrote it when he found out he had a tumor. In fact going through Randy's lyric book, he made several references to life and how short his might be. Reading these lyrics I can only imagine that this was written asking me the questions, and I say that because he uses the term "we" as he and I had always done in life being that we were twins. It was never I, or you, it was always we, always us.

>Here I am before I walk through the door
>A new world that I've never known
>These streets they move fast as I look on past
>And imagine a life without this
>The lights are gazed up upon us
>Up here I feel as if we are free
>Ahead of myself and I might fall down
>Flat down on my face
>If these lights blind me then will you still be there
>To help me see right
>So I don't fall off the edge of the world
>Confused and lost in my ride
>The green is fine and nice sometimes
>Filling my pockets full of air
>Nice things can be so mean
>To the self-esteem and the nature of this dream
>Again my eyes could be covered up
>By the paper and gold of this world
>Weighing me down underground
>No light to see me through
>If this gold controls me then will you still be there
>To help me out of my hole
>So I don't fall off the edge of the world
>Confused and lost in my soul
>Today the sun it sees me; tomorrow it may not
>It doesn't mean it's not there
>I may be gone flying so high
>With the wings that we all try to make
>The clouds will open and close behind me
>Up through it all I will make it through
>I won't forget all of those who have helped me
>Become who it is I long to be

If I'm gone tomorrow then will you remember me
Have I done enough to leave?
Please don't forget me when I go
'cause I will always be here
Up in the trees looking down on the ground
That you all walk on, so you don't fall
Off the edge of the world confused and lost
In this ride of life when we all will, we all will die. We'll die.

"Edge of The World" by Randy Perrone

An intimate video of Randy playing this song can be seen here:
https://www.youtube.com/watch?v=fKoZy-sQeBs

EPILOGUE

I can't say thanks enough for the people who have supported me and my family. The deciding factor whether to live or not came from my beautiful wife, my adorable son, my two beautiful daughters, my loving family, and the true friends who, no matter the circumstance, were concerned about me and there for me. For this I am eternally grateful.

Many people don't understand what it is like to lose a brother or sister. Fewer truly understand what it means to lose half of one's self. That is what I feel I've had to face. One of my fellow friends from the Twinless Twins organization summed up being without a twin: "Where you end, is where I begin." This phrase means so much, and is so true. A life with a twin isn't a singular life. It is built around each other and those around us. I have had to learn how to be me all over again, and am still struggling with this. There are so many things that make life difficult without Randy. In business, Randy was the first person I would call if a challenge would arise. In life, we always shared what was making us happy, sad, and angry. We could trust in each other implicitly, and knew that there was always going to be one constant: our relationship me and him. The funny thing is we didn't have to say much to understand each other or what we needed to do to make things better. Just knowing that someone was always there, no matter what, is a comfort all in itself that most people don't get to enjoy. The joy of knowing that you can have a conversation with someone without mentioning a word takes the stress away for having to fully explain yourself. Most people learn from early childhood how to explain themselves. I never had to learn this until Randy died, and it is the hardest thing I have had to accept. This challenge of mine was also hard on my loved ones who sometimes received the brunt of my frustrations when they couldn't quite understand me as quickly, or at all, like Randy could.

My wife is my biggest support. Someone at the wake told her, "Good luck, this type of thing caused me to get a divorce." She heard this and told me. She made a point to tell me it might be the case for others, but it would not be our case because she was here for me no matter what. She has done so well at trying to understand what was going on in my life. Losing Randy was just as difficult on her life as it was for me. To see someone you love go through a transformation of mind must have been difficult to understand, but yet she has been here through it all. She is a big part of why I have come as far as I have.

It was a blessing to have had my son when we did. We questioned the timing of his birth, but now it all makes sense. Randy was able to see what it was like to be a father, feel the emotions of being a father, and make a connection with another living being that in reality shared his DNA. This is something that he never got a chance to enjoy on his own and we were able to give that gift to him. Growing up we always talked about having children at the same time, so much so I could tell when Cristy and I announced we were pregnant that he was upset that he wasn't having a child at the same time. I've often recalled the conversation a couple of days later when he apologized, and I told him that I was sorry it couldn't have happened the way we dreamed. Now I suppose things went that way for a reason. The thought of Randy having a child the age of my son and never getting to know his father is so devastating to me. I feel sorrow for the people in my life who will never get a chance to meet Randy, because he was such a great and warm person to know.

My loving mom and dad have been so great and so strong during these trying times. To bury your own child is something none of us with children want to imagine, yet they have lived this reality. There have been many crying days, many happy days, many days that I am sure they didn't want to go on, but in the end what hasn't torn them apart has made them stronger. They were there for me and my siblings more than anyone could have asked. We as siblings are so lucky to have our parents. They make me want to be a better father for my child. Life is so full when the people who brought you into it also help you through it and are as caring as my parents.

My brother and sisters are hurting as much as all of us and we have all banded together to make sure we have each other to lean on. When we sold Randy's house, we all stood behind Randy's garage for one big group hug, and said to each other, "We still have each other. Never did we think in our lives that it would be four of us instead of five, but we still have each other." This meant so much to me because for my whole life we have been a unit. We are a group of individuals who truly care for the outcome of each other's life. We have been there for each other, and I am so proud to be part of them. There has never been a moment, that when called upon, we haven't answered that call with willingness and happiness to help. I can't imagine a life other than as one with them.

Randy was such a gregarious person. He could talk to anyone and everyone, and he did. I still have people I've never met look at me and ask if I am Randy's twin. I always have a smile and say that I am. They continue to tell me how much he meant to them. Some had just met him for a short moment and were touched, and some for longer, but for both he would leave a piece of his heart. There are so many good things he did for others, such as when he and I were riding in a car and offered a man our umbrella. The sky was beginning to turn extremely dark and the wind was picking up. We noticed this man standing on a corner waiting for the bus to come. We could tell that he was concerned about the rain coming. Randy had me stop the car and he jumped out to give him our umbrella. The man looked at Randy as though God had sent him to help out right before it poured down. As soon as Randy got back in the car, the sky let out and the rain came down hard. The thought of others was his best quality, one that I try to maintain for him.

The outpouring of stories and notes that I received from others after his passing was amazing. I would love to share them all but have chosen one from Mr. Skinner, our disciplinarian who saved Randy from being expelled. He wrote:

A Tribute to Randy Perrone

I was blessed to spend eleven years of my career teaching at Randy and Rusty's school. The school's namesake always wanted to make sure that our boys knew how to make a life that they knew what was really important.

We never had to teach Randy Perrone much about that at all. He made quite a life and in the process he contributed each and every day to the lives around him; he formed us.

At school we spoke of our peers as family. And like all families we feel. We feel great pride when one of our own succeeds. We feel a deep and profound sense of emptiness when one of our own hurts. And, we constantly feel the strength and support of our community when one of our own is in need.

We feel all of these today. We are very proud of the young man Randy was. We hurt, hurt deeply, because we have lost a member of our family. And, we certainly feel the love and support of everyone Randy impacted in his life.

That love and support of family, the Perrone family and the school family, all helped to form Randy into the talented, generous, wonderful young man he was - the young man that God intended him to be.

He did so with an ever-present smile on his face and with a gentleness and goodness in his heart. We remember Randy today for his character, for his perspective, for his genuineness, and for his love of family and friends...for the difference he made in this world.

Character is a word, a concept that is talked about frequently; but how many of us really understand what it means. The word is actually derived from words meaning engraved or inscribed. Character, then, is who you are. It is written all over you; it goes right to the very heart and core of who you are. It is solid, resolute, and founded on unchanging, unwavering principles.

It is not always easy to describe; but when you see it, you know it immediately. Randy Perrone was a young man of great character and that character is something that we learn from the people around us. Randy learned that from his family, a wonderful family whom we all hold in our hearts today.

No matter what challenges, circumstances, trials, or obstacles cross their path, men of character find ways to persevere and to make an impact. Randy discovered that character must find its true home in the larger world. Randy saw that as his responsibility, his obligation, a selfless sense of duty to help others. That comes from the heart of a young man with a clear sense of his beliefs and his purpose.

Randy Perrone was a difference maker. All we need to do is look around at the members of the Class of 2002 and countless others who were loved by Randy. We are all better people today because we experienced that love. We are all also well-trained and well-equipped to help others because Randy taught us all that.

Our faith tells us that we have work to do. We have an opportunity and responsibility to make a difference. Randy taught us that also. Randy Perrone...thank you for showing us how to make a life.

We all love you and miss you dearly.

Postscript
Message to Randy

Randy, four years have passed since you left us. Four years…or 35,040 hours…any way you look at those numbers, I see a lifetime. A lifetime now without you. Still now we keep you in our minds, our actions, and our hearts. I catch myself talking to you when I say, "Hey Randy, this is Rusty talking to you," but you know that already because you talk to me, as we did with the quirky things only you and I knew, the unconscious habits identical between us, or during those instances when I knew there was no way I would have had a positive gain emotionally, spiritually, or courageously if it weren't for you. Likewise, I know it is your helping hand that has intervened when I have avoided a seemingly inevitable catastrophe. This is why I will always have you with me and why I will continue to be your voice here on Earth. The good you have done for others and your determination to ensure just treatment of others is how I strive to live.

So what has happened in four years? Well a lot has happened. Your nephew has grown, and though he will never remember you, he sure does know his "Param." He knows you played guitar because he asks me to play his "Param's matar." He enjoys hearing your songs, even though I don't play it like you, but he especially likes the one you named after him. In fact when he was an infant we would play it for him when he was crying and fussy, and every time we did, he calmed and stopped being fussy. When we do our nightly routine, Cristy and I ask for kisses, eskimos, butterflies, European kisses, and big hugs, and sometimes I ask him to give me yours. We also read books to him before bed, and we point to the animals in the book and ask him to tell us what they are, but when we are finished we point to a picture of you holding him when he was born, and I ask…"Who is that?" and he says, "Param and Juju." He knows that the picture is of his "Param," but at this age and with a beard on his daddy like his "Param," he sometimes calls you Daddy. That is when it really hurts. Our dreams as kids to play tricks on our children still happen, I just don't get to share them with you the way I would like. He certainly looks like you, and has your personality, and often times the indescribable pain and sense of unfairness overcomes my thoughts when he does something that I know you would get a kick over.

In the four years now since you left us, we have been blessed with two precious baby girls, Carmella and Sybil. Even though Julien will never remember you, just like Carmella and Sybil won't, at least he has a special gift from you that the girls won't get. I tell Cristy often that I wish they had a song written by you for them. Even without this, though, they will know you and will love you as much as you would love them. They all definitely have your happy attitude, as it isn't hard to make them smile, much like it wasn't hard to make you smile. I know that you are their guardian angel like you are to your whole family, and for that we can all say we are eternally grateful.

A whole lot has happened since you left us, and though the pain will never diminish, I think that we as a family have learned how to have you with us, even though you aren't physically with us. Your surviving sisters and brothers have become really close, when being closer than what we already were would have seemed impossible. When we sold your house and moved the last of your belongings out, Andrea called a huddle and we hugged in the driveway. She said, "Never would I think that I would say it's just the four of us now…." That was one of those moments when we had no other options other than accepting our new reality. When it was sold, I did what you would have done, I asked the new owners if I could introduce them to your home with a tour. I told them of all the work that you and I did to the house after Katrina. The entire time I spoke as if you were speaking to them. I told them that instead of making this transition a sad one, you would have wanted it to be a happy one for them. I certainly conveyed a proud sense of achievement in the house, and they left knowing that the home they were starting already had a foundation built of hard work and love before them. I suppose a way for you to speak that to me was when I found out months later that they had a baby and they named him Jack (the same name as our black lab that lived there before we had to put him to rest).

A mother's and father's devotion are so evident sometimes through a loss. Some of the hardest times for me are to see Mom and Dad hurting. There hasn't been a day since you left us that they haven't shed a tear for you. I guess that is to be expected from two people that devoted their lives to ensure we had everything we needed to become the adults we are today, with a conviction to ensure we knew right from wrong, who treated others with respect, and who had a determination to create a bond within our family that is unlike any I have seen elsewhere. That same level of conviction has turned into great sorrow and sense of loss. With as much as they love us, I know it hurts them to have lost you.

I am also happy to say that the band and I finished off the songs you recorded weeks before your death. We started a fundraiser and reached our goal just as the time limit was ending. Doing the album was hard for all of us: to hear you but not be able to work with you on the third album was certainly a difficult reality. It was unique for me to sing backup vocals to "Solai Soroi" and also sing one of your songs that you weren't able to record. You certainly made your presence felt. I hope that you would be pleased with what the band has done with your work.

So four years passed and I can say that you are no less missed than the day you departed. Since I speak to you in my mind always, I sometimes forget that you really have departed us, at least physically. I even had a moment not long ago when someone asked me, "Where is your brother today?" I said, "Which one?" Then I quickly realized what I said and felt bad for him because I know he didn't mean to create a sad moment. I guess that is just part of being a twin and having you on my mind always. As most twins know, we don't say "I or me," we say "us or we." It's a habit that I know will never leave me, just as you will never leave me.

I pray that you are enjoying yourself immensely up there, seeing our family that has gone before us. I can only imagine how great that must be. I look forward to the day that I get to see you again, but hopefully long after my children are grown, married, and have children of their own. In thirty years I will have lived longer than you were alive. Isn't that a hard statement to make? So much had taken place in our thirty years; I can only imagine what lies ahead in the next thirty years. One thing is for sure, you will be with us and will never be forgotten for the remainder of my life and our families' lives.

A Surprise: The Circle of Life

Endings always lead to new beginnings. Your life ended four years ago February 27, 2013, and on March 1, 2017, we welcomed our last child into this world. A boy who we named Randall 'Randy' Everett Perrone - to honor you. A new beginning for a legacy you left behind. It is strange to hear your name attached to this miracle, but I know every time I say it, or hear someone say it, it will remind me of how great a life I had with you in it. My heart sang watching Mom hold baby Randy and call your name. "Randy", she said, "Randy". Amazing how at that moment, I recall the same tone and voice calling your name out in our home movies when we were about the same age as little baby Randy. I could see her pain and joy trying to overcome one another, and her joy winning, because finally she shed no tears when calling your name. I know Dad had to hear it too and feel the same feelings. Oh how it makes me sad and happy at the same time.

On February 27, 2017, the fourth anniversary of your passing, we honored your life at the cemetery. On that occasion Dad told me that March 1, 2013 was the day that you came home from Houston and he and Andrea went to visit you in the funeral home. He cried when he said, "This was the day that Randy came home." This would be the day that we were blessed with a new life who was to be named Randy.

We were all hoping for baby Randy to come to us either on our birthday or on your death day. Neither happened, which is ok, because now he will have a unique day all to himself, all the while bringing joy again to this time of year.

What the future holds isn't written yet for baby Randy, Sybil, Carmella, Julien, Cristy, myself, and the rest of the family, but what I do know is that you will be with us every step of the way. Helping carve a life of happiness and joy through the gifts and miracles of God.

Your loving twin,
Rusty

dove finisci tu comincio io

A Tribute to the Author

The miracle of serendipity begs the question: which has the more profound effect on a life - chance or design. My meeting Rusty Perrone would seem to have been chance, and the two years of Monday morning conversations linked by hours of writing that followed that meeting were surely by design. However, both were so unexpected and inexplicable as to beg a second question: was a Higher Power responsible? While both questions are compelling, their answers are elusive and not essential. What is more compelling and relevant to living the uncertain existences we all travel is that being open to the rewards of chance requires a proactive design on our part. Had Rusty and I not spoken, and he not shared his rough and raw story while still grieving his losses, and had I not risked inviting myself into the midst of his journey, then one of the most rewarding and fascinating adventures of my life would have been missed. Rusty and the Perrone family define the highest principles of family life by the perseverance, patience, and empathy with which they sustain and support each other: perfection being not only impossible but also unnecessary. I have the highest respect for Rusty's willingness to adjust to the uninvited change in his life by confronting the events and memories honestly with an open heart and open mind. No less significant, no less difficult and no less admirable were the support and understanding he received from his large extended family in the telling of his story, which is also their story. I hope I do not forget the lessons taught me through my involvement in this journey, just as I hope you, the reader, were open to its messages about life and death, risk and reward, and love and forgiveness. May you be blessed by life's mysterious surprises and comforted by its uncertainties: may the ride exceed the destination wherever you may be going.

I close with advice for my young friend and able collaborator, and for you:

"Young Man, Old Man"

A story found me one day whose mystery stayed my usual rush:
It told that a man, weaker and older, met a man younger and bolder.
They had nowhere else to go really until the story reached its goal.
Time will most likely not be generous with the elder of the two.
What more might a man want than what was this old man's, the young man wondered.
Then laments dropped from aged lips like rusty dew.
Next escaped one sole tear of salty rain from deep within his soul.
Where, the old man asked, do my friends await, or have they gone?
How feels the waves or wind against one's face?
Do stars shine the same to all who stare, even as vision fails?
Your time is now the old man said.
When my trek stops, the rain will wash away my prints;
New the path will be prepared for you to walk, but not alone.
Beware: Time will not forgive the way you live;
So, I pray, it be the journey not the end you will love.
Before I go I wish your ride along the way
May exceed your destination, not just today
But every day.

By Jay Hoecker

Acknowledgements

I want to give a special thanks to Jay Hoecker, the person who chance, fate, coincidence, or more likely serendipity put sitting right next to me on a plane ride from Minneapolis to Atlanta. For without that flight and being connected to this individual, who is now my dear friend, I would have never had the courage or the drive to put into words my life experiences with Randy. A huge thank you to all who have helped me remember these events from childhood into adulthood. Also my grammar school English teacher Mrs. Maria Baisier, who writes under her pen name M. L. Davis, for her most gracious review, edit, and suggestions of the book. Also Elena Wolf for her final editing and review.

Big thanks to my good friend Sam Dalili, not only for being there for me when my life took a turn for the worst, but also for reviewing my book. And lastly for Joe R. Henry, a high school math teacher of my own age who also lost a beloved sibling and who resides at the opposite end of the Mississippi River, who graciously reviewed and helpfully provided insightful input to the book.

The inspiration for this book has come, of course, from my beloved twin brother, Randy Perrone, who best summarized our relationship in his poem,

One Is Two:
I have fallen into this world as two
Me and my twin we look the same
So we walk four feet on the ground
We're takin' our time but we will cover it all
Twenty-six now I haven't seen it all
But do know that our eyes will embrace everything
Together we make a full balance on the brain
Left and right we are different but the same
You look and never tell which one
One is two if you looked at the same time

Randy loved his music so much that he would record himself playing the guitar to post on YouTube. Those videos can be found at the link below:

https://www.youtube.com/user/rwperrone/videos

https://vimeo.com/61012943

Songs as they appear in the book

Time Moves On	*64*
Farewell	*115*
Driving Song	*133*
Beautiful Riddance	*142*
Julien	*166*
War	*198*
Destination	*268*
Tree House	*279*
Edge of The World	*311*

Also visit our website to be able to purchase Randy's CD's or download his music. Also available will be prints of his artwork.

www.rrperronepublishing.com

www.twinlessbook.com

Enjoy them as much as he enjoyed making them.

www.ingramcontent.com/pod-product-compliance
Lightning Source LLC
Chambersburg PA
CBHW021118300426
44113CB00006B/201